Professors as Academic Leaders

Also available from Bloomsbury

Academic Identities in Higher Education, edited by Linda Evans and Jon Nixon
Academic Working Lives, edited by Lynne Gornall, Caryn Cook, Lyn Daunton,
Jane Salisbury and Brychan Thomas
Cosmopolitan Perspectives on Academic Leadership in Higher Education,
Feng Su and Margaret Wood
Higher Education in Austerity Europe, edited by Jon Nixon

Professors as Academic Leaders

Expectations, Enacted Professionalism and Evolving Roles

Linda Evans

BLOOMSBURY ACADEMIC
LONDON • NEW YORK • OXFORD • NEW DELHI • SYDNEY

BLOOMSBURY ACADEMIC
Bloomsbury Publishing Plc
50 Bedford Square, London, WC1B 3DP, UK
1385 Broadway, New York, NY 10018, USA

BLOOMSBURY, BLOOMSBURY ACADEMIC and the Diana logo
are trademarks of Bloomsbury Publishing Plc

First published 2018
Paperback edition first published 2019

Copyright © Linda Evans, 2018

A catalogue record for this book is available from the British Library.

A catalog record for this book is available from the Library of Congress.

ISBN: HB: 978-1-4742-7047-2
PB: 978-1-3501-2662-6
ePDF: 978-1-4742-7049-6
ePub: 978-1-4742-7048-9

Typeset by Integra Software Services Pvt. Ltd.

To find out more about our authors and books visit
www.bloomsbury.com and sign up for our newsletters.

Contents

List of Illustrations

Figures

Tables

Acknowledgements

This book presents selected findings of four research projects, and I gratefully acknowledge the support of the three organisations that funded them: the British Educational Leadership, Management and Administration Society, the Leadership Foundation for Higher Education, and the Society for Research into Higher Education (SRHE).

In three of these projects I was fortunate to work with excellent co-investigators – Matt Homer (University of Leeds), who worked as the statistician on all three projects; Justine Mercer (University of Warwick), who was the co-investigator on the *Professorial Academic Leadership in Turbulent Times* project, and Steve Rayner (Newman University), the co-investigator on the *Leading professors* project. Their contributions were invaluable.

The fourth project, *The origins and history of university professors and professorship in the UK*, funded by the SRHE, I carried out independently, but was supported by the project mentor, David Palfreyman (New College, Oxford). I am indebted, too, to Professor Richard Rex (Queens' College, Cambridge), for generously meeting with me to fill in some of the many gaps in my knowledge of Tudor scholarship. Thanks are also due to Adrian Shindler of the British Library, whose advice on what sources to consult for information on early professors and professorship kick-started my research.

I am immensely grateful to emeritus Professor David Sugden (University of Leeds), who generously read and commented on the first draft of the manuscript in record time, allowing me to revise it before submitting it to the publishers. Finally, I must thank the anonymous research participants – questionnaire respondents and interviewees alike – who kindly gave their time, and whose voices, I hope, resound through this book.

Introduction

When I was a master's student many years ago at Lancaster University, I didn't know what a professor was. Presented with a course handbook that listed modules and those who taught them, I recall being puzzled about how a person listed as 'Professor' Somebody-or-other differed from one who went by the title 'Dr'. Chatting with fellow students, I found I was not alone. This was the pre-internet age and consulting Wikipedia was not an option, so it was not until we exposed our collective ignorance by asking a course tutor to explain, that it become clear: 'Dr' simply denoted the holder of a PhD; 'Professor' indicated a specific academic grade – the most senior one. Professors, we learned, were at the top of the academic tree – or so it appeared at the time.

Now in my third decade as an academic, I have long been aware that today's students are no less ignorant about the nomenclature of academic titles than I was all those years ago; as the *Times Higher Education* (*THE*) recently reported: 'With so many variations of lecturer, fellow, reader and professor – such as senior, associate, visiting and principal – academic job titles are sometimes seen as confusing for students' (Grove, 2015). Influenced, no doubt, by North American convention, international students typically use the term *professor* indiscriminately, as a generic label – in the same way that those brought up in the UK (like the 'lay' British public more widely) tend to refer to any university academic as a *lecturer*.[1] But it is not only international *students* who struggle; confusion within the global academic community about what the UK grades *lecturer* and *senior lecturer* denote was reported as the basis of Oxford University's recent switch to North American academic titles, in order to 'be better understood "across the globe"' by making 'the seniority of its main academic grade more easily understood' (Gibney, 2013).

On the basis of its title, then, some international readers may be expecting this book to be about *all* academics. It is not; for *professor* has quite a different meaning in the UK from in North America. In many European countries, as well as, generally, in Australasia, the term (and its derivatives: *professorial*, *professoriate* and *professorship*) imply/ies distinction, denoting 'a group of people at the apex of their discipline or profession' (Macfarlane, 2011, p. 57) – those members of the academic workforce who, if they relocated to North America, would expect, or be contenders for, *full* professorship. Whilst this book is focused narrowly on that most senior constituency of UK-based academics, it is nevertheless highly relevant to the interests of international readers, who, by reading 'full professor' for 'professor' throughout, will appreciate the discussions presented and the issues raised – both of which will undoubtedly resonate not only with researchers of higher education in any national context, but also with institutional policy-makers and senior managers. I borrow the words of one of the first educational researchers to write about professors in the UK:

> I am using the term here in the more restricted British sense, as opposed to the more open, American sense. There is a substantive American literature on professors and professing … but if it were to be re-published in the United Kingdom, it would have to be re-titled as being about lecturers and lecturing. (Tight, 2002, p. 16)

'[B]eing a professor', continues Tight (2002, p. 19) 'is a matter of "eminence" or "rank".'

Malcolm Tight's definitional clarification appears within his paper, 'What does it mean to be a professor?' (Tight, 2002) – a question that he chose as the theme of his own professorial inaugural lecture, upon which his paper is based. Evidently it was – and remains – a question worth addressing, as was revealed by my own research into professors and professorship, whose findings represent this book's predominant empirical evidence base.

Tight's rhetorical question seems to have languished for the best part of a decade, in which the issues underpinning it remained unaddressed. Of these, the overarching one was that the professorial role and purpose – if indeed professors may be considered to have a distinct role or purpose – are unclear and inexplicit. 'What is it you *do* all day, actually?' the long-term incumbent of a prestigious named chair told me he had once asked his predecessor (with wry collegial humour) when considering whether to apply for the soon-to-be-vacant professorship, whilst an education studies professor similarly recalled, on the day of his promotion, asking a professorial colleague: 'What is it to be a professor?', only to be answered, 'You won't *really* understand for a couple of years.' The subsidiary issues were that the UK-based professoriate is heterogeneous – implying, Tight (2002, p. 21) observes, that professorial status is 'contested and volatile' – and that a dearth of literature on the subject greatly limits what we know about professors or 'professordom' (to use his term). Winding up his paper with the inevitable call for more, much-needed, research on the topic, Tight, for his part – despite continuing to incorporate into his research a focus on academic working life – does not appear to have pursued examination of the professorial role and purpose beyond publication of his 2002 article.

But a handful of others have now picked up the baton that he first ran with, corroborating the perception that the role or job of being a professor is both unclearly delineated and un(der)examined, and agreeing that we really do not know very much about it. Rayner et al. (2010, p. 618), for example, observe that: '[t]he role and work of a professor remains uncertain and sketchy both as a concept and a description. … the evidence base is extremely limited: there is a limited literature available dealing with leadership and management in the university, and less still with the role of the professor'. Similarly, Bruce Macfarlane (2011, p. 57) notes that '[t]here has been surprisingly little research on the role of professors', and points out that 'while universities publish guidelines about how someone might *become* a professor, institutions pay comparatively little attention to what professors are expected to *do*' (Macfarlane, 2012a, p. 65, original emphases). And in an issue of *Times Higher Education* that gave extensive coverage to professors, the opacity and variability of the professorial role were highlighted in her leader by the then *THE* editor:

> What it means to be a professor – and more importantly what others think it means – is magnificently opaque. There's plenty of advice on how to get there, but little once you've reached your destination. There's no global job description, no template, no handbook, only the example of those who have gone before. There is no consensus: definitions vary by country, institution and mission, and it is unclear whether professors are there to improve research or teaching. (Mroz, 2011)

As Bruce Macfarlane observed in 2012, the professoriate, globally, is increasing in size: 'The university system has expanded worldwide and with it the number of those holding a full professorial title. Around a third of US academics eventually become full professors, and the title is used still more exclusively in an Australasian and UK context, representing around 10–12% of university faculty' (Macfarlane, 2012b, p. 181). Accounting for just under 10 per cent of its academic workforce, the UK university sector employed around 20,000 professors in the academic year 2015/16[2] (HESA, 2017). But how much do we know about them, and their work? Other than anecdotally: very little, it seems. The dearth of published work on the topic has been highlighted by the few educational researchers who have explored professorship and professors (e.g. Macfarlane, 2012a; Rayner et al., 2010; Tight, 2002). Their assessment is in many respects justified, for whilst higher education was described in 2008 as 'a developing field of study', which 'could be conceived of as a partially explored territory through which a variety of tribes traverse' (Tight, 2008, p. 596), it seemed back then that none of these itinerant tribes had showed much interest in forging a path from which to view professors or professorship, and which might address Malcolm Tight's (2002) question, 'What does it mean to be a professor?'

But the landscapes of research territories – particularly those that are still 'partially explored' – are seldom neatly ordered; they often appear wild and uncultivated, requiring time and patience to uncover their features. So it is with professor-related research, which falls into two main categories: studies in which professors and professorship are the main focus, and those in which they feature incidentally, and in writing this book I have drawn upon both. The first category, which places professors or professorship centre stage, is indeed in short supply – though, globally, its ranks have been swelled slightly in the last few years with the appearance of a handful of professor(ship)-focused texts (e.g. Diezmann & Grieshaber, 2010; Hoskins, 2012; Ismail & Rasdi, 2008; Macfarlane, 2011, 2012a, 2012b; Marini, 2014, 2016; Meyer, 2012; Mixon & Treviño, 2005; O'Loughlin et al., 2015; Özkanli & White, 2008; Pyke, 2013; Rayner et al., 2010; Rolfe, 2007; Sabatier et al., 2015; Sidek et al., 2015; Thompson & Watson, 2006; White, 2001), most of which relate to one or more specific national contexts; indeed, a minority of these texts are authored by UK-based researchers or relate to professorship in the UK. The second category focuses on a bigger picture or 'story', in which professors or professorship feature peripherally or fleetingly as what ranges from a mere walk-on part to the focus of a sub-plot. It is considerably more plentiful than the first category, but I have found that careful sifting is required to extract the valuable nuggets obscured within it.

This second category includes a small number of studies – among them some of the earliest ones of academics and their working lives – that are now generally recognised within the educational research community as seminal, such as Becher's (1989), and then Becher and Trowler's (2001), analyses of academic life within disciplinary communities, and Halsey's (1992) sociological study of academic life in the UK in the last quarter of the twentieth century. Several overseas-based studies also fall into the second category, including the *Changing academic profession* international research project that has yielded an impressive published output (see Teichler et al., 2013). But there is always a need to treat non-UK-based studies with caution since a great many of them adopt the

North American convention of referring to all academics as professors, making it impossible to separate out material that relates exclusively to professorship and the professoriate as understood by what Finkenstaedt (2011, p. 172) calls 'the narrow sense of the word'. '[T]he term "professor" varies considerably across national contexts and there are different traditions that determine who can call themselves one. It is a slippery term' observes Macfarlane (2012a, p. 47). For the researcher of professorship, this terminological 'slipperiness' significantly complicates and lengthens the process of seeking out informative literature. Since keyword searches throw up a large number of ineligible texts – a great many of which are American – I have found myself resorting to more labour-intensive approaches, such as painstakingly pursuing promising leads from citations and reference lists in relevant texts, in order to filter out those in which it is clear that the term *professor* and its derivatives are interpreted as in the UK. Yet the possibility – indeed, the probability – remains that some relevant texts will have slipped through my net.

In following up such leads I have not confined myself to educational research, for the largest body of professor-related literature, I have discovered, is histories and historical sources. This material includes much information that is probably too detailed – at least, in large doses – to interest and engage a general readership of educational researchers, leaders and policy-makers, so I have been selective in what I include in those chapters of this book that lend themselves to brief historical detours. But I felt it was important to incorporate a historical dimension into my discussion of certain issues, not only for the richer contextual backdrop that it provides, but also, more specifically, to help inform consideration of whether or not some of the issues and circumstances that currently reflect the nature of professorship are peculiar to modernity.

In the apparent absence of a comprehensive text dedicated to tracing the history and origins of professors and professorship, histories of the European university and its development constitute the richest source material, along with individual universities' histories – particularly those with medieval origins – and I have tapped into these. I have also gleaned valuable information from a diverse collection of historical sources whose content is largely peripheral to, but that in places touches upon, professors – such as histories of monarchs or nobles who endowed or founded professorships, or histories of science and of epistemic cultures or disciplines. The history-based literature that potentially has a bearing on the origins and nature of professorship seems vast, and unconquerable in its entirety – in any case, conquering it is unnecessary for this book. I have accordingly confined myself to having dabbled in rather than dredged it, through a relatively unsystematic scatter-gun approach to library-based research in a discipline that engages me, but in which I have no specialist academic knowledge or skills. This dabbling has afforded me a very broad historical overview, lightly peppered with some of the detail that interests me and that I anticipate may interest others.

Evident in the collective body of professor-related literature are three dominant discourses, relating to: *the nature of professorship*; *becoming a professor*; and *doing professorship*. Most of our research- and scholarship-derived knowledge about university professors and professorship falls into one or more of these broad thematic categories, and, whilst avoiding deploying them as a rigid organisational and structural framework for the book, I have nevertheless tried to ensure that they feature prominently, weaving them, as appropriate, into the chapters that follow. Much of the scant literature relating to becoming a professor, for example, is summarised in Chapter 8, while that relating to doing professorship features in several chapters. Yet this book is not confined to descriptive narrative; such content certainly features, but it is framed within what I hope will be read as in-depth analysis that offers explanations by addressing the 'why?', 'how?' and 'with what effect?' questions. In drawing together interesting narratives and original theoretical perspectives, to culminate in critical policy analysis that questions the *status quo*, my aim is both to engage readers and to challenge their thinking.

The book is organised in twelve chapters, within four parts. The first, Part One – *Contexts and Concepts* – is a scene-setting one that focuses on the policy and conceptual contextual background. Whilst the main purpose of the book is to present and discuss the findings of my recent research on professors as academic leaders, Part One represents the overture to this, but, as such, its focus is the *pre*-findings-dissemination context. Chapter 1 accordingly sets the scene by outlining what we know – mainly from research, but also from grey literature – about professors and professorship; more precisely, it outlines what was known *before* my research findings augmented the knowledge base. It is one of the book's most literature-heavy chapters, creating a backdrop against which to frame the analyses of today's evolving professoriate.

Chapters 2 and 3 constitute analyses of two concepts that feature prominently and recurrently in the book: *professionalism* and *academic leadership*. Since the first of these is recognised in the sociology of professions as a contested concept, and the second is acknowledged as an unclearly defined concept, these chapters clarify what I mean when I use the terms, and will be of particular interest to researchers and scholars who share my preoccupation with conceptual clarity and definitional precision, as well as those who value critical perspectives that deviate from mainstream thinking. For international scholars Chapter 3's conceptual analysis of academic leadership should be essential reading, for academic leadership means something quite different in the UK from what is seems to mean in North America. This book predictably applies the UK interpretation, which widens its focus to *all* professors, not just those with designated leadership roles – indeed, the book is principally concerned with what I call 'professors without portfolios'. Achieved via critical analyses, first, of the more general concept of leadership, and, second, of educational leadership, Chapter 3 outlines some of what I consider the weaknesses of educational leadership research and scholarship. The final chapter in Part One – Chapter 4 – is the research design and method chapter, augmented with narrative that outlines my motivation in undertaking the four studies described, and which provided the data that, collectively, are the book's bedrock.

These data feed into Parts Two to Four, but are particularly prominent in Parts Two and Three, whose main collective focus is the presentation and discussion of my research findings. Since my research uncovered two broad perspectives: that of professors as academic leaders, and that of those on the receiving end of professors' academic leadership – who, for simplicity, I call 'the led' (a label that I accept as contentious and problematic, and that I explain and justify at various points in the book) – Parts Two and Three each represent one of these broad perspectives. The perspective of 'the led' is presented first, in the three chapters comprising Part Two. Chapter 5 focuses on positive experientially based perceptions of professors while Chapter 6 presents considerably more negative perceptions. Pulling together these two juxtaposed perceptions, Chapter 7 considers what are the bases of such perceptions. This is an analytical chapter that examines a range of different theoretical perspectives and culminates in my proposing my own original theory – proximity theory – as a potential explanation.

Part Three, *the Professoriate's Perspectives*, represents the 'other side of the coin' to Part Two's focus on non-professorial academics. Its three chapters each convey something of being a professor and doing professorship in the twenty-first century that the book is intended to depict and analyse. Each incorporating discussion built around comments and narratives from the professorial participants in my research, Chapter 8's focus is on becoming a professor, while Chapter 9 reveals something of how professors go about enacting academic leadership. The final chapter in Part Three, Chapter 10, blends narrative and commentary with theory to examine morale and job satisfaction in the UK professoriate, and, revisiting the proximity theory introduced in Chapter 7, the bases of professors' attitudes.

Part Four, *Reshaping professorial professionalism*, comprises just two chapters. Chapter 11 problematises the notion of professorial academic leadership, highlighting issues that potentially undermine universities' effective deployment of their professoriates. These issues will resonate beyond the UK; they are relevant to institutional policy-makers and managers in all national contexts whose higher education sectors reflect neoliberal ideologies, represented by the commodification of higher education and academic workforces that are under pressure to perform. The concluding chapter – 12 – proposes ways forward that include redesigning twenty-first-century professorship in ways that aim to get the best out of professors, whilst yet pursuing goals that reflect universities' strategic priorities.

My intention in this book is to marry together engaging depictions of professorship as a form of agency that incorporates a leadership dimension, with deeply analytical perspectives that, in theorising, explain, and in conceptualising, elucidate. As a prominent critical leadership scholar, Miriam Uhl-Bien, reminds us, leadership scholarship is unbalanced in focus: 'It is accepted wisdom that there is no leadership without followers, yet followers are very often left out of the leadership research equation' (Uhl-Bien et al., 2014, p. 83). In uncovering and analysing two different perspectives – that of leaders and that of 'the led' (or, to use Uhl-Bien's term, 'followers') – as well as proposing future directions that incorporate consideration of a third perspective (that of universities' senior managers) *Professors as Academic Leaders* augments what we know not only about educational leadership generally, but also, more specifically, about academic working life in the twenty-first century.

Notes

1 Evidently, use of 'lecturer' as a generic label is not confined to the UK; New Zealand-based author, Sutherland (2017, p. 743) observes that 'many outside the university would not distinguish between a lecturer and full professor'.

2 The total number of professors employed in UK higher education institutions in 2015–16 is presented as 19,975, representing 9.9 per cent of all academic staff (excluding atypical) (HESA, 2017).

Part One

Contexts and Concepts

1

What Do We Know about Professors and Professorship? Snapshots of the Professoriate

As I observe in the Introduction, other than anecdotally we really know very little about the role or job of being a professor in the UK. The academic discourse on the nature of professorship is very much a niche one; few researchers engage with it, and even fewer have contributed to it. In its broadest sense it is concerned with what professorship and the professoriate 'look like', why they look like this, and with what consequences – for professors themselves and for the wider higher education sector and system. Within these contextual parameters, the discourse addresses issues such as: what professorship involves, what its purpose is, how its nature and purpose came about, and how and why these are still evolving.

This chapter's examination of the nature of professorship is selective. I pose questions without necessarily answering all of them, for some answers unfold through the discussions in the chapters that follow. I raise a few key issues as starting points, knowing that they are revisited later, and in some cases augmented, for the entire book is in its broadest sense about the nature of professorship. Yet, whilst my aim in this chapter is to present an overview of the evolving nature of professorship, highlighting what has changed over the years, and what remains fundamentally as it has always been, that overview depicts key features of or influences on the landscape of professor-related knowledge as it appeared *before* my research findings contributed – as do all findings – towards re-contouring it.

I begin at the beginning, by considering what we know about professorship's earliest days.

Origins and etymology: Professorship as teaching

How did professorship come about? Who were the first professors, and what did their work involve? To address these questions I followed Malcolm Tight's (2002) lead by consulting the *Oxford English Dictionary* (OED, 2007). The dictionary's entry 'professor' is within the earliest 9 per cent of its recorded entries, with its evidence source dating back to 1387. Under the category 'senses relating to academic or other professional function or status' *professor* is defined as, *inter alia*:

> A university academic of the highest rank; *spec.* (in Britain and some other English-speaking countries) the holder of a university chair in a specified faculty or subject. Also, in *N. Amer.*: any teacher at a university. Also applied to people of similar status in institutions other than universities. (OED, 2007)

According to this source (OED, 2007), professorship has its origins in the medieval European university, where the title 'professor' evolved from being a synonym of *magister* or *doctor* (denoting someone qualified to teach), to imply distinction within a gradually developing hierarchy of teachers:

> The right originally possessed by any Master or Doctor to teach publicly in the schools of a Faculty was gradually restricted to an inner circle of teachers, and the term *professor* came eventually to be confined to the holders of salaried or endowed teaching offices, or to the highest class of these, such titles as *reader, lecturer, instructor, tutor,* etc., being given to teachers of lower rank. (OED, 2007, original italics)

Verger (1992, p. 144), however, draws upon its Latin roots to argue that the origins of the word *professor* pre-date the Middle Ages: 'The function of teacher is obviously much older than the medieval universities, as the borrowing of the key terms from classical Latin would suggest: *magister* (master), *doctor* (doctor) and *professor* (professor).'

Irrespective of when the term 'professor' emerged, it seems that modern university professorship in the UK owes much to the Tudor royal dynasty,[1] for if the Tudors did not invent professorship, they certainly kick-started its momentum in England. It was Lady Margaret Beaufort, mother of the first Tudor king, who endowed the first professorships (of divinity) at the universities of Oxford and Cambridge (Brockliss, 2016; Collinson et al., 2003; Hibbert & Hibbert, 1988; Jones & Underwood, 1992; Rashdall, 1895), which persist to this day, as the Lady Margaret professorships. Brockliss (2016, p. 87) notes their innovatory significance: 'until the turn of the sixteenth century and the creation of the Lady Margaret chair in divinity in 1497 by Henry VII's mother, Lady Margaret Beaufort, Oxford had no stipendiary university professors'. (These professorships do, however, appear to have been initially called lectureships, and some references to them label them readerships. If the *Oxford English Dictionary's* summary of professorship's origins is accurate, it is likely that, during this period of terminological evolution, 'professor' had not yet emerged as a title denoting distinction, and was interchangeable with 'doctor' and 'lecturer'.)

The precise date of Lady Margaret's endowments is difficult to pin down because the endowment process seems to have been protracted. Rashdall (1895, p. 461) dates the professorships' foundation at 1497. Corroborating this, Jones and Underwood (1992, p. 207) write that in letters patent of 1497 Lady Margaret was granted a 'licence to establish her lectureships in the universities, and to endow them to the value of £20', but they add (p. 208) that '[a]nother four years were to elapse before Margaret's lectureships were officially founded, with their own regulations', and refer to 'indentures of foundation', directing the payment of the lecturers' stipends, being drawn up in 1502 – a date confirmed both by Hibbert and Hibbert (1988) and in a much more recent publication relating to the Cambridge professorship (Collinson et al., 2003).

Whilst, north of the English border, King James IV of Scotland had founded, at Aberdeen University in 1497 (Evans, R. J., 2013), what is generally accepted as the first regius chair[2] in what is now the United Kingdom, almost another half-century would elapse before regius chairs appeared in England. The practice of referring to endowed teachers as 'professor' apparently began in earnest in the 1540s when the Tudor King Henry VIII founded the first regius chairs in England, in divinity, civil law, medicine, Hebrew and Greek:

> The application of the title [of professor] to holders of endowed chairs was largely due to the creation of five *Regius* or *King's Professors* by Henry VIII (a number increased in later years) ... . The endowed teachers of some other subjects were at first called *praelectors*, but this title was gradually superseded by *professor*. (OED, 2007, original italics)

Over the centuries, as successive British monarchs created additional regius chairs, this elite cadre of senior academics has grown to number over seventy, distributed amongst over twenty British universities.

What does this excursion into British history tell us about the nature of professorship? Such posts were *endowed*, which means that effectively they came with a ring-fenced budget for remunerating teaching; Henry VIII's regius professorships at Oxford University, for example, each came with a stipend of £40 (Hibbert & Hibbert, 1988). The provision of remuneration is significant, because teaching provision had at times been unstable, prompting England's two medieval universities to seek creative solutions to what were effectively finance-related teaching staff shortages:

There had been … attempts to provide lectures with a more secure financial basis. In 1432 Oxford had pleaded with John Duke of Bedford to endow some masters to lecture in the arts and other faculties. Later in the century Cambridge arranged to give some direct support to regents lecturing for the university by a system of collection from colleges through the university bedells. In 1481–2 an attempt was made to maintain a theology lecturer out of the royal benefaction elsewhere. The bishop of Salisbury, Richard Beauchamp, had persuaded Edward IV to endow a chantry[3] in St George's chapel at Windsor and grant the nomination of the priest who would serve it to Oxford University. The university petitioned that this priest should be allowed time to lecture in theology at Oxford. (Jones & Underwood, 1992, pp. 205–6)

The essential point is that at this time professors' prime purpose – and hence a key facet of the nature of early professorship – was teaching.

From teaching to research? Shifting purposes and priorities

Comparison of sixteenth- and twenty-first-century regius professorship indicates the extent to which its nature has evolved. To mark the ninetieth birthday of Queen Elizabeth II in 2016 a competition was launched in 2015 for universities across the UK to bid for regius professorships (which were offered as marks of prestige and status only; funding them was to be the responsibility of the successful bidders). Whilst, as a key element of the competition, participating universities were to propose their disciplinary field(s), the intended nature of these professorships was made explicit in the narrative announcing the initiative: 'A Regius Professorship is a rare honour granted by the Sovereign *to recognise research excellence*', and was implicit in the clear direction given on which kinds of universities would be serious contenders: 'Applications for the new Regius Professorships are invited from all universities with *excellent records of relevant academic research*' (UK government, 2015a, emphases added). Over the course of five centuries, then, it seems that the focus of professorial purpose has shifted; the rhetoric around what in the UK is generally considered professorship of the highest order – professorship that denotes 'exceptional honour' (UK government, 2015b) – implies that, in the twenty-first century, it is all about research. The teaching element of it has been ditched.

Or has it? In fact, teaching has not consistently been sidelined in recent years. Less than three years before the launch of the 2016 regius chair initiative there had been a very similar one, to mark Elizabeth II's Golden Jubilee in 2013. But what is particularly interesting is that at this point teaching was still in the frame, evident in the accompanying narrative issued by the UK Cabinet Office (UK government, 2013): 'A Regius Professorship is a rare privilege, with only two created in the past century. It is a reflection of the exceptionally high quality of *teaching and research* at an institution.' Representing the Conservative-Liberal Democrat coalition government of that time, the then Minister for Universities and Science, David Willetts, is quoted in the post-competition Cabinet Office news item: 'Together, the successful applications demonstrated an exceptionally high level of achievement *in both teaching and research*' (emphases added).

Even more illuminating is comparison of the sets of criteria (presented, in their original wording, in Table 1.1) against which the two twenty-first-century regius professorship competitions were judged. When the 2013 and 2016 criteria are aligned in this way the distinction between them is striking. The references in the earlier (2013) set to institutions' 'work' and the 'studying' of disciplines are sufficiently ambiguous to connote teaching *or* research activity – or both. This implicit width of focus represents a sharp contrast to the 2016 criteria's narrow focus on research – specifically, research that impacts significantly upon economic and societal growth. A question-and-answer style guidance document accompanying the Cabinet Office's announcement of the 2016 regius professorship competition makes reference to this shift of focus that the Cabinet Office had clearly anticipated would be picked up on:

Why have the criteria changed from those used for the previous award of Regius Professors?
The size and quality of the UK's research base has grown dramatically during the reign of HM The Queen. The research and knowledge that has resulted underpins the UK's economic strength and has significantly improved the lives of people in the UK and beyond. These criteria recognise the excellent research from across this expanded university base that has had the greatest benefit for the UK.

What is meant by benefit?
The benefit, supported by evidence, should be improvement in the UK's economic effectiveness and productivity at a regional or national scale. Whilst this obviously includes all areas of business and the economy, it also includes activity in other areas that can demonstrate a link between excellent research and economic benefit and improved productivity; for example, health and well-being, the environment, social policy, cultural endeavour or the international standing of the UK.

Does the benefit have to occur in the UK?
The benefit does not have to be exclusive to the UK, but should include a significant UK component. (UK government, 2015b, pp. 1–2)

Table 1.1 Criteria for judging the competitions for the conferment of regius professorships to mark the Golden Jubilee and the ninetieth birthday of Queen Elizabeth II, in 2013 and 2016 respectively

2013 competition criteria	2016 competition criteria
(source: UK government 2013, emphases added)	(source: UK government 2015a, emphases added)
The excellence of the Institution's *work* in the proposed *discipline* (1–20 points)	National and international recognition of excellent *research* across any field or fields of *research* (1–15 points)
The recognition the *discipline* has gained, nationally and internationally, regardless of how long it has been *studied* (1–20 points)	The leading role of the university in translating the *research* into use in wider society as a contribution to knowledge, or to solving a problem (1–15 points)
	A direct and significant benefit to the UK's economic effectiveness and productivity at a regional or national scale (1–15 points)
Other factors, such as the chance to mark a significant event in the history of the institution or *discipline* (1–4 points)	Other factors, such as the chance to mark a significant event in history of the institution *or field of research* (1–5 points)

The set of criteria applied to the 2015–16 competition represents a tightly crafted revision – almost a retraction – of its precedent. The implication of this revision is clear: by 2015 the 2013 criteria were no longer considered fit for purpose.

Calling the shots: Influence, imposition, and instruments of state

And what *is* that purpose – more precisely: what was it considered to be in 2015–16? Evidently, it was to convey the message that universities should be aligning their research agendas with the government's economic growth policies, centred on knowledge expansion, through relevant, cutting edge, internationally excellent, impactful research – led by their most distinguished academics. The initiative to create a batch of new regius chairs had, after all, been included in the government's Productivity Plan, announced in July 2015. It was all about the nation's development and advancement. The hope and expectation seems to have been that the professoriate would be deployed as an instrument of the state. Its (the professoriate's) elite cadre – this world-leading, exclusive, brand known as *regius*, which, Malcolm Tight (2002, p. 20) suggests 'must, presumably, be near the top of the status pole' – was effectively being franchised, with those capable of safeguarding and enhancing its global reputation being invited to bid for one of the franchises.

This scenario seems entirely consistent with the nature of twenty-first-century academe – and, as such, is easy to denounce as a sign of the times: the unacceptable face of present-day professorship. Performativity has become an integral feature of academic life in many developed countries, where, to varying degrees, government-led policies have imposed marketisation upon higher education. It is often argued that much has changed since the 'golden age of academe' (Tight, 2010) – the 'time when universities were small communities of scholars, researching without state-imposed evaluation frameworks' (Bacon, 2014, p. 14), when Perkin (1969) depicted the academic profession as probably the most stable and self-confident one in the world, and when academics 'were well connected with the powers that be, and enjoyed a relatively leisured and un-pressurised existence as a kind of elite priesthood' (Tight, 2010, p. 106). At the turn of the millennium Fulton and Holland (2001, p. 301) argued that the consequences of major changes to the UK higher education sector 'are still rippling through the working life and employment conditions of the academic profession'. Halsey (1992) had given these ripple effects a name: 'proletarianization'. By the second decade of the twenty-first century, with neoliberal ideologies and the managerialism that they spawn showing few signs of relaxing their grip on the academy – prompting Kauppi (2015, p. 32) to bemoan that '[n]othing seems to stop the triumph of neoliberalism in academe' – such ripples were generally perceived to be taking on tidal wave proportions, engulfing the higher education sectors of much of the developed world.

It is therefore unremarkable that, within such a politically influenced evolving context, the UK government should expect the university sector, through its professoriate, to sign up to its policy agenda – the 2016 white paper on higher education (Department for Business, Innovation and Skills, 2016) in fact opens with a ministerial foreword that identifies universities as 'among our most valuable national assets, underpinning ... a strong economy', describing them as 'Powerhouses of intellectual and social capital [that] create the knowledge, capability and expertise that drive competitiveness' (p. 5). Indeed, using the country's university-based research and, by extension, its professoriate, to pursue government goals and aspirations is by no means peculiar to the UK; the Malaysian government has evidently created a grade of *distinguished professor* in order to support its 'systematic strategic plan to develop a culture of academic excellence', as a vehicle for building a world class knowledge-based economy (Sidek et al., 2015, p. 84).

'The Europe of the twenty-first century is not that of the fourteenth century', observes Kauppi (2015, p. 42), and one could certainly be forgiven for lamenting the passing of a 'golden age' of academic freedom, and its replacement with an era which has marketised academe, commodified academic work, and legitimised expectations that academics should support government agendas for development, and that those who do so will have the best chances of promotion and advancement. But it would be a mistake to attribute such expectations solely to *contemporary* politically derived contexts – and specifically to those that reflect neoliberal ideologies – for they are evident throughout history, including when professorship was very much in its infancy: the late Middle Ages.

Why would a medieval monarch or noble create and endow an academic post: a professorship? What would be his or her motives? In founding the first regius chair (of medicine), the Scottish King James IV had evidently hoped to promote culture and scholarship amongst his subjects:

> James was a famous patron of the arts and sciences, taking an interest in the establishment of Scotland's first printing press, hanging tapestries in his palaces, patronising poets such as William Dunbar, and giving a Royal Charter to the Edinburgh College of Surgeons in 1506. The Regius professorship was clearly part of his mission to bring Renaissance civilisation to the northern kingdom. (Evans, R. J., 2013)

The founder of the first professorships in England may have been similarly motivated. 'Both a lover of books and a true intellectual' (Weir, 2001, p. 3), Lady Margaret Beaufort was a great patron of academic learning – particularly, reflecting her celebrated piety, scholarship that was focused on religion. But she expected something back; as Jones and Underwood (1992, p. 211) observe, 'Lady Margaret's beneficence nearly always demanded a specific personal return'. In the sixteenth century, when the Margaret professorships of divinity were founded, academe was intertwined with religion; Brockliss (2016, p. 31) notes that Oxford University 'in the first centuries of its history, was an ecclesiastical institution primarily serving the needs of the Catholic Church in England'. In the case of religious or theological scholarship, the boundaries between university and church were blurred to the point of often being indistinguishable, and professors – such as Bishop John Fisher, Lady Margaret's confessor and the first appointee of her endowed professorship at Cambridge – were often ordained clergymen;[4] Verger (1992, p. 150) notes that '[i]n the fifteenth century, thirty-six of the seventy-nine English bishops (46 per cent) had taught at Oxford or

Cambridge'. The payback that Margaret typically expected – indeed, demanded, since it appeared in the small print – from her charitable endowments took the form of prayers: 'with the theology lectureships there were obligations … to pray on behalf of Margaret's husband who had died at the end of July 1504, the rest of her family, and the queen [Margaret's daughter-in-law, Elizabeth of York] who had died in February 1503' (Jones & Underwood, 1992, p. 211). Even in the dawn of the sixteenth century, it seems, she who paid the professor evidently called the tune.

Henry VIII's professorship creation was both personally- and politically-motivated. As a highly educated man (Weir, 2001) who 'prided himself on his intellectual sophistication' (Starkey, 2003, p. 258), like his brother-in-law, James IV of Scotland, he would have been keen to promote scholarship and academic learning. But, for Henry, the personal had become political. Denied papal approval to divorce his first queen, he kick-started the English Reformation by breaking from Rome and establishing the Church of England, and his regius professorships were instruments of the political fall-out from this. Just as the 2016 regius professorship initiative was included in the UK government's Productivity Plan of 2015, if Henry VIII had had such a thing as a Reformation Plan, his professorial endowments would have featured prominently in it:

> When the first English Regius chairs were founded, by Henry VIII, they were instruments of his drive to anchor the newly independent Church of England in a national academic culture, wresting major appointments away from the Church and putting them in the hands of the state. In 1540, he founded the Regius chair of civil law at Oxford to replace the teaching of Roman canon law with the teaching of, among other things, English law. (Evans, R. J., 2013)

Moreover, the king's sphere of influence on university curricula evidently extended to his dictating specific content that aligned with his own theological views: 'Henry VIII's 1535 injunctions insisted that lectures should be on the Bible "according to the true sense thereof and not after the manner of Scotus, etc." and banned lecturing on Peter Lombard's *Sentences* which had long been the staple diet of theologians' (Collinson et al., 2003, p. 5). State influence – for in the sixteenth century monarch equalled state, even though, as Elliott (1990, p. 81) observes, 'the word "State", used to describe the whole body politic, seems to have acquired a certain currency only in the closing years of the century' – on the nature of professorship is therefore as old as professorship itself. And it has evidently persisted. Evans (2013) presents 'an even more direct example of the creation of Regius professorships as an instrument of government policy, directed at educating young Englishmen – at home, through their compatriots, rather than from foreign tutors on the grand tour – in the skills needed to join the Foreign Office:

> In 1724, prompted by his ministers, George I wrote to the vice-chancellors of Oxford and Cambridge complaining of 'the prejudice that has accrued to the … University from this Defect, Persons of Foreign Nations being often employed in the Education and Tuition of Youth'. To remedy this situation, he intended to appoint 'a Person of Sober Conversation and Prudent Conduct, skilled in Modern History and in the knowledge of Modern Languages, to be Our Professor of Modern History'. The stipend was to be £400 a year, a sum 'so ample', as a grateful University of Cambridge declared in its acceptance letter, 'as wellnigh to equal the Stipends of all our other Professors put together'. (Evans, R. J., 2013)

It is, of course, relatively easy for monarchs – or, rather (increasingly, with each passing century), for governments – to call the shots in relation to regius professorship, which is, after all, in their 'gift'. But regius professors, when all is said and done, represent a very select few – less than seventy, at the time of writing (historically, their highest total complement). What of the other 19,900 or so UK-based professors? Who or what influences their professorship? And with what effect on its nature?

Universities as 'kingmakers': Role diffusion and confusion

In several European countries, who gets to be a professor is state-influenced, which, Finkenstaedt (2011, p. 171) remarks, makes for a rather 'homogenous staff structure in each country'. The professor-creating process is often underpinned by a centrally initiated one known as *habilitation*, whereby aspirant professors must write what is essentially a second thesis, whose scholarly quality is assessed by a panel of peers. While Combes et al. (2008) examine the process of recruiting economics professors in France, through a long, highly competitive process involving the *concours d'agrégation en sciences économiques* – whereby aspirant professors must deliver lectures to a panel of peers (a 'jury') – Marini (2014, p. 6) describes the recently introduced requirement of habilitation for professorial promotion in Italy as 'a new hurdle to be overcome and whose successful output does not necessarily guarantee any sort of post'. He points out that academic grading systems in Italy – as in several other European countries – are centrally determined, being enshrined in law:

The 240/2010 Law, also known as Gelmini Law … made initially entering universities with a permanent position a tougher goal. Under this new law, the levels of position were reduced from three levels, full professors, associate professors, and assistant professors and replaced with only two levels, full and associate levels. (Marini, 2014, p. 6)

In the UK, in contrast, systems of academic grading and associated nomenclature are institution-specific, with some universities, for example, having adopted North American nomenclature of *assistant* and *associate* professor, while others have retained the traditional UK academic grade titles of *lecturer, senior lecturer* and *reader* (see the Appendix for an outline of UK academic grades, listed alongside their North American equivalents). Who gets to join its professoriate is also determined by each university independently. Applying a medieval – and hence sexist – epithet, universities are thus academe's 'kingmakers'; it is they who confer the professorial title on academics – admittedly, through their peer reviewing policies they generally act on advice and recommendation from the wider (often international) academic community, but they are under no compulsion to do so. What this results in is a markedly heterogeneous professoriate, for there is no general, sector-wide, unanimity on what a professor in the UK is, should be, does, or should do, nor on what degree of experience or what level or quality of achievement the role or grade requires. As I observe elsewhere (Evans, 2017b), these issues can depend upon which sector (pre- or post-1992[5]), which university, which faculty or department, and which subject or discipline the professorship is affiliated with. The professoriate's heterogeneity is particularly apparent in the variability with which universities in the UK seem to perceive professorial purpose and role.

Of course, the UK's higher education sector is itself marked by divisions that both spawn and perpetuate disparity – indeed, Scott and Callender (2017, p. 125) refer to 'the growing complexity and heterogeneity of institutional missions'. Reputational and prestige-based pecking order reflects a status-related hierarchy of higher education institutions (HEIs), at whose pinnacle sit the universities of Oxford and Cambridge. Arguably, just below Oxbridge *in reputational terms* is the rest of the Russell Group – a self-defined group of what are considered the UK's twenty-four most research-intensive universities (including Oxford and Cambridge)[6] – along with several non-Russell Group specialist institutions (such as the London School of Hygiene & Tropical Medicine) that are considered world-leading in their fields; (yet this is a crude and over-simplistic generalisation, for Scott and Callender (2017) rightly draw attention to the achievement- and associated reputation-related diversity *within* the Russell Group). Next (again, arguably – and in relation to reputation) come the rest of the pre-1992 institutions excluded from the Russell Group, followed by the post-1992 institutions – yet the post-1992 sector itself represents a wide range of perceived quality, and, as Scott and Callender (2017) point out, the achievements of a small number of post-1992 institutions, particularly in relation to specific fields of specialism, afford them higher reputation-related status than is enjoyed by some pre-1992 institutions. Croxford and Raffe (2013) summarise this hierarchy of UK HEIs slightly differently from the above outline, by both separating Scotland from England and by grouping the elite London universities with Oxbridge, while Scott and Callender (2017, p. 128) include Manchester 'debatably' within 'a small group of UK universities that significantly outperform the others'.

Whatever the subtle distinctions between analysts' representations of the UK's institutional hierarchy, the point is that professorship is sometimes – but not consistently – perceived differently across these disparate institutional groupings. In the 1970s and 1980s when the sociologist A. H. Halsey carried out his study of UK-based academics, the binary divide was still alive and kicking. Yet, in writing up his findings as what has become the seminal text, *Decline of donnish dominion* (Halsey, 1992), he would have been aware of the major changes afoot – and that would be implemented as government reforms in the year in which his book was published – prompting his observation 'that the pattern of promotion has been diverging on the two sides of the binary divide with respect to research in recent years' (Halsey, 1992, p. 208), with university[7] professors demonstrating greater researcher prioritisation and research activity than polytechnic heads, and polytechnic professors indicating a lesser degree of research focus and activity in 1989 than in 1976.[8]

Halsey is not the only researcher to raise the issue of pre- and post-1992 sector differentiation and its implications for their respective professoriates. In the immediate aftermath of the abolition of the UK's binary divide, Kogan et al. (1994, p. 52) refer to 'the award of professorial titles in the former polytechnics and colleges of higher education who would not have been so designated in "old" universities'. This institutional hierarchy-related issue is touched upon in Tight's (2002, p. 19) consideration of 'the various distinctions currently made within the professoriate'; 'it might be assumed', he remarks:

> that gaining a professorship at a high status university is more difficult than at a lower status one. It might even be felt, and is by some, that obtaining a lectureship or fellowship at a university of the highest status is at least the equivalent, in intellectual terms, to holding a chair at a low status institution.

The dilution that Mary Henkel (2000, p. 149) identifies of research's supremacy as an indicator of, and criterion for, professorialness – 'professorships were no longer the exclusive preserve of leading researchers but may also be accorded to institutional leaders and others with senior management responsibilities in their institutions' – represented a shift in both promotion and institutional management policy and practice trends that Henkel attributes to the 1990s' spate of UK higher education reforms, and that seems to have opened the floodgates of professorial proliferation. Whilst Finkenstaedt (2011) presents figures[9] indicating a decline between the early 1960s and the 1980s in the *proportion* of academics in the UK who were professors, in 1995 *The Independent* reported a rise of almost 100 per cent over the preceding twenty years in the *number* of professors employed in UK universities, taking the figure up to 7,000 (Dobson, 1995). The next decade saw an increase of 63 per cent, to over 15,500. Summarising the reported consensual views of a range of commentators, it was observed: 'what it is to be a professor and what it takes to become one has changed significantly in recent years' (Tysome, 2007a, 2007b). Although it was by no means the post-1992 sector alone that accounted for what was presented as professorial proliferation, there was nevertheless a prevalent perception at that time (approaching the turn of the millennium) that many of the former polytechnics recognised a need to validate their new university status by creating (more) professorships. As the number of professors increased, the nature of the professorial role, it seems, was becoming more diffuse.

As I discuss in Chapters 11 and 12, what is perceived as role diffusion remains a key issue affecting contemporary professorship in the UK. Former university professor-turned-newspaper-columnist Laurie Taylor – whose amusing satire will be familiar to readers of *THE* – used his column to lampoon the proliferating professoriate and deride what is anecdotally perceived as the associated dilution of its quality. Presented as those recognised by the fictitious, post-1992, University of Poppleton, Taylor identifies six categories of professors, distinguished on the basis of justification for promotion, and perceived roles and purposes – described as 'additions to the traditional role':

> *Full and Proper Professors*: These increasingly rare professors had achieved their position by displaying continuous excellence in an academic discipline over a large number of years.
> *Sort-of Professors*: These former middle-range teachers at Poppleton Polytechnic achieved their professorial promotion only when the poly became the present university and the former Staff Room was re-designated as a 'Senior Common Room'.

Buy-in Professors: Members of this highly paid group were appointed only to bolster the university's REF submission and have never yet set foot on campus.

Pseudo-Professors: A relatively small group of managers who decided to call themselves 'professors' in the vain hope of acquiring some additional status.

Give-as-much-as-you-can Professors: These 'honorary professors' are 'honoured' only in the expectation that they will eventually cough up a few thousand quid towards the new administrative block.

At-last Professors: This group is entirely composed of academics who have simply been around too long for anyone to come up with yet another good reason for denying them the promotion they hardly deserve. (Taylor, 2012)

In similar vein, three optional modes of doing professorship are suggested by Durham University's professor of geography, Harriet Bulkeley:

One is to be Professor-of-All-Things, endlessly on the conference circuit and in the media, entertaining the first-year student crowds, holding forth in the coffee room and producing reams of publications. Or you could be Professor-of-Clever-Things, locked in a study or laboratory, beavering away at the research frontier with research grants and staff pouring in and steam pouring out. Or you could be Professor-of-Important-Things, climbing the greasy pole of university administration. (Contributors, 2016)

Despite the levity with which they are presented, these professorial categories highlight heterogeneity as a defining feature of the UK professoriate. And this heterogeneity seems destined to intensify as universities – at liberty to call the shots in relation to how they organise their academic promotions policies and procedures – continue to leap onto the bandwagon of hierarchically stratifying their professoriates through the introduction of differentiated performativity- and status-related professorial grading or banding systems. Indeed, such a policy is implicit in the recommendation of the Diamond Report of 2015 (Universities UK, 2015, p. 25) for 'a continued trend' towards 'nuanced and responsive modes of pay and reward'.[10]

A professor from one of the first universities to stratify its professoriate in this way once explained to me, with dry humour, what he called his institution's 'way of paying and ranking' professors: 'We have an A, B, C, D, E scale. E is at the bottom ("execrable", I always thought), D for dunce, C for crap, B for barely adequate, and A for acceptable (they're the Nobel prize winners!).' An A grade professor himself, he continued: 'there's probably eighteen professors [in the department]. Are they all meant to be doing the same things? Clearly not. … If you set up a system where professors are graded, the university's already basically saying, "Well, a professor isn't a professor, isn't a professor"!'

Already practised along such *very broadly* similar lines in some other European countries, such as Germany and the Netherlands (Enders, 2000), differentiation policies of this kind represent universities' attempts to separate their professorial sheep from the goats – perhaps in the wake of their finding that, as a result of proliferation, professorial quality is generally considered to have become more variable. Yet the main rationale for the policy is undoubtedly the need for UK universities, in a competitive global and inter-sectoral marketplace, to exceed remunerative norms in order to attract the world's leading researchers; as the Diamond Report of 2015 notes: 'It is important that universities are able to offer reward packages that reflect the marketplace for many staff, which involves competing with private business and international competitors' (Universities UK, 2015, p. 30).

Professorial stratification has the effect of differentiating on the basis not only of rank, status and salary, but also of professorial purpose, for what a university expects of an A grade 'star' professor must surely be different from what is expected of a B or C grade one.[11] But with this differentiation comes the risk that heterogeneity will degenerate into inequity.

Some are more equal than others: An unbalanced professoriate

Differentiated professorial grading has caught on in UK universities. Yet an important point is that it is creating a hierarchy within the professoriate that will inevitably end up being skewed in favour of those subjects and disciplines that are the most marketable: the highest grade bands are likely to be represented predominantly by top STEMM[12] professors – who can demand high salaries and status-related conditions of service – than by social scientists and arts and humanities professors. And with the former group's being more likely to comprise men than women, this situation will have gender balance implications. HESA's published data do not, at the time of writing, distinguish professors on the basis of assignment to institutional professorial grade – and since the number of grades varies from institution to institution, such data would in any case be difficult to collect and analyse. Data on academic salary ranges are published, but the highest range identified in the 2015–16 data (HESA, 2017) – £58,754 or more per annum – represents a lower salary than many professors in the lowest professorial grades or bands receive, so these data do not indicate professorial grade assignment. The proportion of women assigned to their institutions' higher or highest professorial grades is therefore unknown.

Yet what we do know is that women are significantly under-represented in the UK-based professoriate; as Morley (2013, p. 118) puts it, '[t]he data that do exist suggest that women disappear in the higher grades'. Calculating women's representation within the professoriate as well under a quarter, the 2015 Diamond Report (Universities UK, 2015, p. 25) notes: '[a]lthough levels of diversity are improving, the higher education sector has a particular challenge in attracting, promoting and retaining women at senior levels of academia'. Of the 19,970 academics who in 2015–16 were categorised by their institutions as professors, only 4,775 are recorded as female (HESA, 2017). A recent report in *THE* moreover indicates a decline at 'significant numbers of UK universities in recent years' in the proportion of professorships held by women, and presents figures that show the UK to be lagging behind many other developed countries in women's appointments to the most senior academic grade (Grove, 2017). It is unsurprising, then, that women professors and women's position and representation within the professoriate feature relatively prominently in the professor-related academic discourse. A key item on the social-justice-in-the-workplace agenda, gender issues are well-represented in the global academic literature on professors – but since there is a dearth of such literature, even such relatively good representation amounts, in real terms, to very few published texts.[13]

Three prominent themes are identifiable within this professor-related literature: women's achievements; women's experiences; and women's under-representation. The first two have received scant coverage, most of which – with the exception of Hoskins's (2012) examination of the influences on women's success in achieving promotion to the UK professoriate – appears not in professor(ship)-specific texts, but as incidental asides within texts centred on different foci, such as Blackmore's (2016) study of prestige in UK universities, which revealed that the majority of women institutional heads interviewed (and who would almost certainly have been professors) 'did not believe that they had encountered gender-related unfair treatment through their careers' (p. 22). Similarly, within Bostock's (2014) anthology of short autobiographical commentaries from a range of women employed in various capacities at Cambridge University, the small number of these commentaries that are written by them offer glimpses of what women professors present as their perspectives, attitudes, and the nature of their work – many of which defy stereotypes, such as Ottoline Leyser's refutation of the assumption of segregation that underpins the notion (one that she claims to hate) of work-life balance (p. 12), Carol Black's confession to workaholism (p. 16), and Mary Beard's comment: 'It would be a lie to say that gender has held me back in my career' (p. 38). The coverage afforded to the third identifiable theme – women's under-representation in the professoriate – though by no means extensive, is nevertheless sufficiently substantial to warrant consideration below.

Women's under-representation in the professoriate

Representing macro level analysis, the issue of the low proportion of professors who are female began to be highlighted in literature published in the 1990s (see, for example, Jonasson, 1993; Wisker, 1996), when academic working life emerged as a sub-field of sociological and/or educational research that has expanded with each passing decade. Halsey (1992) affords it coverage, drawing upon his data that were collected at a vibrant period in British social history when women's rights and opportunities were being fought for and the inequities created by their societal positions were being exposed and denounced. By the 1990s, when Halsey's findings were published, the place of women in male-dominated occupations had become a recurring theme in the sociology of work, summed up, as Bottero (1992, p. 331) observed at that time, by the argument that 'while women may have gained entry to male bastions they have not done so on the same terms as men, so their presence does not necessarily represent any breakdown in gender segregation or gender disadvantage'. Halsey's findings were consistent with this theme. Noting that 'the numbers of women in the higher ranks of teaching[14] are disproportionately low', and that, whilst 'significantly more women have entered the senior common room in recent decades … inequalities of rank persist in that men have tended to retain the more secure and more senior positions', he presented secondary data showing male professors to account for 11.4 per cent of a total of 38,098 male academics and women professors to account for 1.7 per cent of a total of 9,488 female academics employed full time in British universities in 1989–90 (Halsey, 1992, pp. 221–2). He then presented his own 1989 survey data, to show that male professors accounted for 15.3 per cent and female professors for 3.9 per cent of the distribution of women and men across three academic grading bands – 'professoriate'; 'reader/senior lecturer/ principal lecturer'; and 'lecturer'. He calculated the odds ratio or significance of this difference as 0.22, and statistically significant at the 0.05 level or less (Halsey, 1992, p. 224). His 1989 survey also revealed non-professorial women to have lower expectations of promotion than men; only 15.4 per cent of the women surveyed saw themselves 'as likely to obtain a chair', compared with 26.3 per cent of the men surveyed – a discrepancy calculated as significant at the 0.05 level or less (Halsey, 1992, p. 229). His summative analysis of the factors that account for 'the effects of sex on the probability of promotion to the professoriate' identifies women's lesser research activity and lower research output than men's as a key issue that manifests itself through women's comparatively less impressive profiles, as they are likely to be perceived by promotions panels:

> [W]omen academics generally are relatively less involved in research and lean more towards teaching. The outstanding woman researcher is therefore more visible to selection committees appointing candidates to chairs.
>
> With respect to research productivity it appears that women do have a higher proportion of non-producers and lower proportions of very high producers, and this difference also obtains for the record of publications in the last two years. (Halsey, 1992, p. 231)

As I point out in Chapter 8, Halsey's research revealed the professoriate to be dominated by Oxbridge graduates, and, given the much lower proportion of women's than men's places that would have been available at Oxbridge in the period when his female respondents were most likely to have been students, it is hardly surprising that the Oxbridge factor manifested itself indirectly through women's much lower representation in the professoriate. Yet Halsey identifies London degrees and doctorates – which, in the period in question, probably represented the most elite higher education option available to most women – as statistically significant indicators of promotion success.

Corroborating Halsey's main findings, Ward's 1995–6 postal survey of academics in five pre-1992 Scottish universities found promotion prospects to be weighted against women:

> Bivariate prohibit analysis of promotion from researcher to lecturer, lecturer to senior lecturer and senior lecturer to professor reveals evidence that female academic staff are less likely to be promoted at each rung of the job ladder. ... [T]he small representation of female professors is due to the cumulate impact of gender differences in promotion as staff move up the job hierarchy. (Ward, 2001, p. 301)

Wisker, too, in this period, highlighted women's disadvantaged position in higher education, referring to secondary data, gathered in 1996, that indicated:

- Only 7.3% of professors are women, although women make up 30% of academics.
- New universities top the league tables for women professors.

- One university (UMIST[15]) has no women professors.
- In engineering and technology the proportion of women professors is under 1%.
- There are no women professors in either agriculture or science. (Wisker, 1996, p. 75)

Over a decade later it seemed that limited progress had been made in redressing the professoriate's gender imbalance. Macfarlane's study[16] of 'mainly UK-based' professors, carried out in 2008 and 2009, 'showed that over 40 per cent of male respondents had at least eleven years' experience in the professorial role compared with only around 17 per cent of women', and men were 'slightly more likely to attribute their appointment as a professor purely on the basis of their research and scholarship compared to women' (Macfarlane, 2012a, p. 58). Moreover, in a more recent analysis, Showunmi et al. (2016) link gender imbalance with race and class disadvantage, arguing that 'women and in particular women of colour face a "glass ceiling" in higher education' (p. 917).

An emerging shape: Dots to be joined up

By flicking through a succession of selected, indicative snapshots – some in the sepia tones of bygone ages, some capturing more recently configured images – this opening chapter has presented a broad overview of the UK's evolved and evolving professoriate. While heterogeneity has emerged as a key feature, diversity is much less apparent, with privilege enduring as a discernible (albeit decreasingly so) dimension of access to and advancement within the professoriate. The chapter has conveyed something of the nature of professorship as an activity – the shifting focus from teaching to research – and touched upon its (professorship's) inextricable link, through the agency of HEIs, to government policies and agendas.

What the chapter has not done is zoom in on those snapshots of (mainly) anonymous actors – whether they be professors or those who influence professors' work and their status – to capture something of the *detail* of professorship in the UK: details such as what it means to be a professor, what the process of becoming one involves, and how professors impact upon the work and working lives of others. All it has done – all it was ever intended to do – is mark out, with a scattering of dots, the broadest of outlines of what professorship looks like. Joining up those dots to delineate more clearly the 'shape' of professors' professionalism as academic leaders is the purpose of the rest of the book, and begins in earnest with Chapter 2's analysis of the concept of professionalism.

Notes

1   The Tudor dynasty of late medieval England comprised five crowned monarchs who reigned from 1485 to 1603.

2   Regius professors – literally: the king's professors – hold professorships created by a monarch.

3   Chantries are explained by David Starkey (2003, p. 758) as 'religious foundations … which existed primarily to pray for souls in Purgatory'.

4   Not all such professors were clergymen. One of the earliest incumbents of the Lady Margaret Professorship of Divinity at Cambridge, Collinson et al. (2003) tell us, was a layman: John Cheke. Surviving accounts show him to have been in receipt of the professorial stipend between 1548 and 1550.

5   The binary divide in the UK that distinguished universities from polytechnics was abolished in 1992, when the former polytechnics were permitted to become universities. Representing two different mission groups, the 'old', pre-1992, university sector is traditionally research-focused, whilst the post-1992 sector is represented by what were for many years, post-1992, known as 'new' universities, but which now tend to be referred to as 'modern' universities, and which are traditionally more teaching-focused.

6   Croxford and Raffe (2015, p. 1632) attribute much of the UK's institutional hierarchy to the Russell Group: 'The status dimension is strongly associated with the institutional hierarchy defined by the Russell Group (a membership organisation of large "research-intensive" universities).' Blackmore (2016), too, found that, amongst his sample of twenty heads of UK HEIs, '[t]he Russell Group in particular was widely praised, sometimes ironically, for having successfully associated itself with excellence, and it was felt to be in a stronger position still with the demise of the 1994 group, which had been composed of pre-1992 institutions that were not in the Russell Group'.

7   Halsey's reference denotes those institutions that enjoyed university status before 1992.

8   Halsey gathered data in 1976 and 1989.

9   'In 1962/63 … 12% [of academics] were professors; by 1968 the percentage … had already declined to 10.1% … [and] by 1986 … the percentage of professors showed a further decline to 9.5%' (Finkenstaedt, 2011, p. 175).

10   Somewhat contrary to this recommendation, the salaries of UK universities' vice-chancellors, presidents and principals are, at the time of writing, facing scrutiny.

The Minister for Universities and Science, Jo Johnson, is reported as having called for 'greater restraint' in determining senior-level salaries, and for universities to justify salaries that exceed £150,000 per annum and to make public the details of staff earning over £100,000 per annum (Richardson, 2017).

11   Since professorial grading systems are used at the discretion of the university, they vary in nature and form across the UK's higher education sector. Some universities recognise fewer than five grades; some refer to grades by other terms – such as 'zones', 'tiers' or 'bands' – and some use numerical grade labelling.

12   Science, technology, engineering, mathematics and medicine.

13   Most texts relating to women's under-representation in senior academic roles focus predominantly on women's incumbency of designated leadership or management roles, rather than as professors without portfolios.

14   Consistent with the tradition in much twentieth-century writing on academic life, Halsey seems to use 'teaching' here as a generic term denoting all aspects of the work that university academics are paid to do.

15   The University of Manchester Institute of Science and Technology has now amalgamated with the Victoria University of Manchester.

16   Macfarlane (2012a, p. 8) describes the study as involving 'interviews with university professors from a range of disciplines' and 'a larger survey of 233 mainly UK-based professors asked to comment on how they perceived their role as professors and leaders'.

2

Professionalism: Examining the Concept

Chronicling and analysing professorial professionalism presents challenges, not least because professionalism is a very contested concept. Not only do interpretations and definitions vary amongst those who research and study it, but they are also likely to deviate considerably from those used in the vernacular. The purpose, then, of this short chapter is conceptual clarity – to clarify what I mean when, throughout this book, I refer to professors' professionalism.

Evolving conceptions of professionalism

Professionalism is not generally considered an esoteric concept; since it is a widely used term everyone has an idea of what it means, and unless they have researched it in any depth, their understanding of it is grounded in everyday usage of the term, which represents professionalism as something desirable, something commendable and praiseworthy, something worth pursuing and claiming, and whose loss or diminution is therefore regrettable. Being 'professional' carries positive connotations, whilst 'unprofessional' is uncomplimentary. Moreover – and a factor that explains why those two adjectives (professional and unprofessional) have acquired such wide general usage and application – professional status seems to have been appropriated by increasing numbers of occupational groups or workforces over the last few decades. Yet this appropriation of professional status by the many, rather than the elite few, reflects a societal shift that has reshaped academic conceptions of professionalism.

Many recent analyses redefine and/or reposition professionalism within a framework determined by the context of twenty-first-century working (and related social) life (e.g. Barnett, 2011; Noordegraaf, 2007; Scott, 2009). Precisely how this context is interpreted and depicted varies in the detail. Barnett (2011) highlights its 'networked complexity', which is defined by:

a set of infinities ... of expanding accountability demands, resource challenges, global horizons of standards and developing techniques, shifting knowledges, and changing client relationships. There is no end to these changes; rather, they accumulate and expand, entering new regions of uncertainty. (Barnett, 2011, p. 31)

He likens it to thin ice upon which the 'modern professional' must skate, trying to keep ahead of its cracking behind her. Noordegraaf (2007, p. 770) describes it as 'fuzzy' and 'loosely ordered'.

The underlying issue in these depictions is the uncertainty of the context within which modern-day professionals operate, arising out of its constantly changing form and nature, and which demand a new conception of professionalism: 'Ambiguous occupational domains call for an ambivalent understanding of present-day professionalism' (Noordegraaf, 2007, p. 771). Barnett's new conception is of the 'networked', and, more specifically, the 'ecological' professional.

In the sociology of professions the focus has shifted from issues related to professional status and who should have it;[1] in the context of twenty-first-century working life, these are no longer important (if they ever were). I am with Julia Evetts (2013, p. 780), who points out that '[t]o most researchers in the field it no longer seems important to draw a hard and fast line between professions and occupations but, instead, to regard both as similar social forms which share many common characteristics'. The consequence of this shift of priorities, she argues, is that we need 'to look again at the theories and concepts used to explain and interpret this category of occupational work' (Evetts (2013, p. 779). Accordingly, I present my own explanation and interpretation of professionalism.

Reconceptualising professionalism: An alternative interpretation

Kolsaker (2008, pp. 515–16) rightly reminds us that professionalism is 'a challenging concept to research, since the field is relatively under-researched, and such research as exists is criticised as ambiguous and lacking a solid theoretical foundation'. It is, she adds, 'inherently difficult to pinpoint' professionalism's constitution and characteristics – though, as I observe elsewhere (Evans, 2011), the implicit assumption that there is, or ought to be, a single, universally accepted delineation of these is questionable. Indeed, the shifting nature, and lack of consensus over the meaning, of professionalism is widely acknowledged, with

Gewirtz et al. (2009, p. 3) arguing for the 'need to work with plural conceptions of professionalism'.

My interpretation of professionalism is a far cry from the outmoded trait model of defining a profession and determining professional status. 'Profession' should no longer be – and, indeed, in everyday parlance often no longer is – a label applied to a few elite groups; we may now apply it fairly indiscriminately across the workforce's diverse, role-differentiated groups, making it the terminological norm, rather than the exception. Moreover, largely as a result of the reforms of the last few decades, few public sector occupations in the UK retain in full whatever autonomy they may once have enjoyed. Against classic professionalism criteria, therefore, few would technically (still) qualify for full professional status. What is often perceived as their deprofessionalisation, coupled with the trend of what may be construed as wholesale mass professionalisation (if only from a terminological perspective) has had a levelling effect that, arguably, has served to rob the label 'profession' of much of its cachet.

It is against the backdrop of this evolved and evolving context that I currently define professionalism as: *work practice that is consistent with commonly-held consensual delineations of a specific profession or occupation and that both contributes to and reflects perceptions of the profession's or occupation's purpose and status and the specific nature, range and levels of service provided by, and expertise prevalent within, the profession or occupation, as well as the general ethical code underpinning this practice.* So-defined, professionalism is quite simply a description of people's 'mode of being' in a work context, irrespective of whether that translates into practice that is praiseworthy or practice that is despicable. Involving qualitatively-neutral practice, to me it is not – as the wo/man in the street would probably have it – a merit-laden concept. A consequence of its qualitative neutrality is that the term '*un*professional' becomes both meaningless and redundant. Since it applies to *all* workers, as an overarching, comprehensive feature of them at work (I interpret 'at work' widely, to include any work-related activity, irrespective of where it occurs), professionalism does not denote status that one is likely to pursue or aspire to; it simply denotes how people 'are', at work. This interpretation probably overlaps with what is meant by 'practice', but I do not consider the two (professionalism and practice) synonymous because professionalism encompasses, yet is 'bigger' than, practice. Professionalism, as I interpret it, relates to and conveys: what practitioners do; how and why they do it; what they know and understand; where and how they acquire their knowledge and understanding; what (kinds of) attitudes they hold; what codes of behaviour they follow; what their function is – what purposes they perform; what quality of service they provide; and the level of consistency incorporated into the above. These are what I identify as the key elements or dimensions of professionalism as a concept: its 'constitution', to use Kolsaker's (2008) term.

This – my – conceptualisation essentially deconstructs professionalism into key constituent parts, labelled concisely and generically. Figure 2.1 represents my conceptualisation pictorially as a conceptual model that identifies three main constituent components of professionalism – behavioural, attitudinal and intellectual – each incorporating further elements or dimensions, explained below.

The behavioural component

The behavioural component of professionalism relates to what practitioners physically do 'at work'. Its sub-components are the *processual, procedural, productive* and *competential* dimensions of professionalism.

The processual dimension

Relating to the processes that an individual applies to her or his work, the processual dimension accounts for what is likely to be the single largest proportion

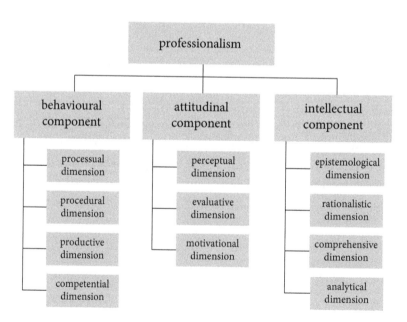

Figure 2.1 The componential structure of professionalism

of her or his work-related activity. Vast in what it covers, denoting a plethora of activities representing multiple levels of hierarchically organised categories, the processual dimension of a person's professionalism includes interpersonal interaction (which, in turn, denotes more specifically labelled activity, such as: collegial interaction; interaction with clients or students; interaction with managers; interaction with communities of practice; interaction with the public, etc.). It also includes reading, 'writing' (by hand, or through technology), speaking and listening (each of which may also – depending on its purpose and focus – represent interpersonal interaction). It includes sub-categories of each of the above list (such as chairing; debating; mediating; mentoring; public speaking). It includes occupation-specific activities, such as: driving or piloting; machine or system maintenance; demonstrating; copy editing; topiary; painting – and, of course, each of their constituent processes, for these activities may be labelled generically (e.g. researching) or specifically (e.g. data collection); each comprises multiple componential categories – layers within layers, like a Russian doll.

The procedural dimension

This relates to the procedures that an individual applies to her or his work, where a procedure is defined as an established or official way of doing something, or a series of actions carried out in a certain manner or sequence or order. In procedural activity the emphasis is thus on tradition or regulations or ritual or habit. Procedure overlaps with process; it may encompass or be encompassed within a specific process, and whilst its enactment will always involve processes, not all processes will involve procedures. It is also distinct from process insofar as it involves a set of 'rules' or 'rituals' (which may be formalised, or which may simply have been habitualised by the individual) that determine the nature of process.

The productive dimension

The productive dimension relates to an individual's output, productivity and achievement – to how much s/he 'does', and how well, and hence what s/he produces or achieves. In the example of an academic, the productive dimension of her/his professionalism is likely to be reflected in, *inter alia*, the quality and quantity of her or his: publications; research projects undertaken; conference papers presented; doctoral students supervised; courses taught; institutional citizenship undertaken; external partnerships initiated; and colleagues mentored.

The competential dimension

This dimension relates to an individual's skills and competences. It concerns what s/he is able to do or can do. It indicates skills sets and aptitude for performing key elements or aspects of the job. In relation to academics, it may, for example – depending on the discipline – reflect the extent to which, or how well, they can, *inter alia*: teach; write for publication; get on with colleagues or students; handle laboratory equipment; analyse data; make oral presentations; and explain complex ideas or processes to others.

The attitudinal component

The attitudinal component of professionalism relates to attitudes held. Its sub-components are the *perceptual, (e)valuative* and *motivational* dimensions of professionalism.

The perceptual dimension

This dimension concerns perceptions, beliefs and views held, and that (have the potential to) impact upon the individual's work. In the case of academics, the perceptual dimension may, for example, reflect their views on a multitude of wide-ranging issues, such as: the purpose of higher education; managerialism; internationalisation and globalisation; their institution's promotions policy and practice; car parking provision at work; and the gender balance in their department. This dimension also includes perceptions relating to oneself, hence *self*-perception and identity.

The (e)valuative dimension

Closely linked to the perceptual dimension, what I call the '(e)valuative' dimension relates to people's values. I interpret 'value(s)' widely, to encompass not only 'grand' values, such as social justice, democracy, or freedom of speech, but also the day-to-day minutiae of what matters to people and is important to them: what they value and what they like – such as ample car parking at work, a pleasant and attractive work environment, and efficient and effective administrative systems. In the case of academics, their values could, for example, range from relating to issues such as academic freedom, through the prestige of working at a high-ranking institution, to the flexibility of their jobs, or the pleasure of teaching a responsive group of students. Negative aspects of the work or the job – that are disliked and therefore not valued – are also encompassed in this dimension; it covers the entire positive-negative spectrum of values.

The motivational dimension

Influenced by the (e)valuative dimension, the motivational dimension – despite its abbreviated label – covers three job-related attitudes that I have demonstrated to be inter-related (Evans, 1998): motivation, job satisfaction and morale. It relates simply to the levels of one or more of these three attitudes: how high (or low) an individual's morale and/or job satisfaction are, and how motivated or demotivated s/he is.

The intellectual component

The *intellectual* component of professionalism relates to practitioners' intellectuality and cognition. Its sub-components are the *epistemological, rationalistic, comprehensive* and *analytical* dimensions of professionalism.

The epistemological dimension

As its name implies, the epistemological dimension relates to the bases of people's work-related knowledge and their knowledge structures – whether, for example, their knowledge is accepted on the basis of its having been disseminated by an expert or authority figure; whether it stems from folklore and/or superstition; whether it is derived from science or from self-discovery; as well as issues such as whether it is considered absolute or relativistic or contextual, or provisional or immutable. This dimension also covers issues related to the nature of people's knowledge structures, such as whether their knowledge represents a collection of pieces of information or integrated concepts.

The rationalistic dimension

The rationalistic dimension is about reason. It reflects people's capacity for applying reason to their practice, and the extent to and the frequency with which they underpin and justify their actions and/or decisions with a rationale.

The comprehensive dimension

The comprehensive dimension relates to the nature and extent of practitioners' work-related understanding. It is closely linked to the rationalistic dimension insofar as understanding may influence and explain rationality, while actions that have no rational basis may reflect lack of understanding of their nature and/or their consequences or implications.

The analytical dimension

This dimension relates to the nature and degree of people's analyticism and/or analytical capacity. As with the comprehensive dimension, the analytical dimension may impact upon the rationalistic dimension of people's professionalism insofar as analyticism may precede, underpin and provide the impetus for rationality.

The conceptual model: A summary

My model of the componential structure of professionalism represents my view of what professionalism *is* – what it 'looks like'. It is, as I point out above, based upon my interpretation of professionalism as a merit-independent construct – as a qualitatively neutral form of going about one's work; something that is in many respects very similar to, but is also bigger and more expansive than, practice, since it encompasses dimensions that *may* be considered the impetus for, or the bases of, practice. The model is a conceptual, not a processual, one, so it does not denote or represent how an individual or an occupational group may become professionalised, or acquire professional status – indeed, my definition and interpretation of professionalism preclude any such processual association, for I do not see professionalism as something to be gained or lost, or available for some, but not others.

Yet how professionalism is conceived is complicated by another consideration: perspectives related to its purpose, and to how 'real' it is.

Four perspectival versions of professionalism

Elsewhere (Evans, 2011) I refer to professionalism as being thought of in relation to different 'reified states' – by which I mean professionalism considered on the basis of how 'real' or authentic it is. I have distinguished between four perspectives on professionalism which reflect its substance – and which may be applied to the professionalism of any given occupational group: professionalism that is *demanded or requested*; professionalism that is *prescribed*; *deduced or assumed* professionalism; and *enacted* professionalism.

Demanded (or requested) professionalism

Demanded (or requested) professionalism denotes professionalism that one constituency – or even one individual – implicitly or explicitly demands, requests or asks of another. An employer may 'demand' a particular professionalism of her/his employees, and a government (as employer) may demand a particular professionalism of its public sector employees. Representing service level stipulations, guidelines or agreements, demanded professionalism typically manifests itself in the form of professional standards, codes of practice, or ethical guidelines, or through more explicit rules and regulations that convey the nature of how one is expected to think, behave, or feel in the context of carrying out one's work. Yet – and reflecting the form of demanded or requested professorial professionalism that is illustrated in the chapters in Part Two of this book – it can also be conveyed more subtly and implicitly through expectations that are held of a particular occupational group, and through the disappointment and dissatisfaction that is provoked by such expectations remaining unmet.

Most importantly, whilst the potency of any 'demanding' is likely to be greater if it is backed up by the kind of authority that an employer or manager may enjoy, 'demanding' in the form of expectations of a professional or occupational group may be held by anyone or any constituency impacted by, or with an interest in, how an occupational group carries out its work – including the general public, clients, work colleagues (junior or senior to the occupational group in question) and other stakeholders. Schoolteachers and parents may thus 'demand', through their expectations, a particular professionalism of a school headteacher, just as non-professorial academics may 'demand' a particular professionalism of professors.

Prescribed professionalism

This professionalism is that recommended by analysts or envisaged by them as potentially effective or beneficial for one party or another: the kind of professionalism that is not, but *ought to be*, evident. It represents, in a sense, a reflective or informed commentary on the professionalism of an occupational group. At the end of the twentieth century, for example, when government reforms in many Anglo-Saxon and European countries imposed tighter controls and standards on schoolteachers, a dominant discourse among educational researchers – as analysts or commentators on these events – urged teachers to regain control by resisting their potential deprofessionalisation through developing the kinds of internal regulation mechanisms that would make for a 'new professionalism'. In this scenario the prescribed professionalism was the 'new' professionalism recommended.

Deduced (or assumed) professionalism

Distinct from prescribed professionalism since it does not involve prescription or recommendation, this perspectival version of professionalism represents reasoned deduction and/or assumption or speculation about the nature of a specific professionalism: about what must have occurred, what must be the case, or what is likely to occur. The deduction or assumption may emanate from any party or constituency – including the occupational group whose professionalism is the focus. It is, in effect, a form of predicted or envisaged professionalism, where the prediction or envisaging are influenced by knowledge and understanding of the context within which the professionalism will develop. Characterised by analysis that goes beyond empirical data, it cannot constitute enacted professionalism since it is derived from deduction, rather than empirical observation. In a sense, deduced or assumed professionalism was the precursor to the prescribed 'new professionalism' for schoolteachers, presented as an example above, since the analysts who made it were basing their prescription on their assumption or deduction about how teacher professionalism would be impacted by the government reforms. Similarly, a French colleague and I (Evans & Cosnefroy, 2013) applied assumption or deduction, based upon our knowledge both of the policy context in France and of the outcomes of similar reform initiatives in other contexts, to our analysis of how the professionalism of academics in France was likely to change.

Enacted professionalism

The simplest and most straightforward of these four perspectival versions of professionalism, enacted professionalism – as its name implies – denotes professionalism that is enacted; that is, professional practice and its bases *as observed, perceived and interpreted* (by any observer – from outside or within the relevant occupational group, and including those doing the 'enacting').

How real? From insubstantiality to reification

The key point is that only the fourth of these versions of professionalism may be considered to represent 'reality' – albeit a phenomenologically defined reality. So, no matter what 'shape' (Evans, 2011) or nature of professionalism is 'demanded' by employers or colleagues, or 'prescribed' or 'deduced' or 'assumed' by analysts and commentators, it is 'enacted' professionalism that represents the only meaningful conception of professionalism – that which practitioners/ professionals are actually seen or believed to be 'doing'. The other three versions of professionalism remain nothing more than visions, representing insubstantiality ranging from articulated ideology to wishful thinking.

Nevertheless, as I demonstrate in this book, demanded professionalism can act as a potent force, through the expectations that it conveys, for shaping how professionalism is enacted. Demanded and enacted professionalism are thus closely linked, the one influencing the other, and it is interesting to see, through the evidence presented in chapters in Parts Two and Three of this book, how junior academics' expectations of professors appear to influence the latter's enacted professionalism. One such key expectation is that professors demonstrate – or enact – academic leadership, but this is an unclearly defined term that means different things to different people. Chapter 3 addresses that confusion and opacity by analysing the concept of academic leadership.

Note

1   For an examination of how professionalism has historically been conceptualised and defined, and how conceptualisations within the sociology of professions have evolved over recent decades, see Evans, L. (2013).

3

Academic Leadership, Leaders, and 'The Led': Clarifying Concepts and Terms

This book is about professors as academic leaders. Yet as an epithet, 'academic leader' is problematic. The term has lodged itself very firmly in the higher education lexicon, denoting, in particular, role, purpose or function associated with senior academic status, so that today it would be almost impossible to find a job advertisement and accompanying job description and person specification for a professorship in a British university that do not explicitly emphasise the need for the appointee to practise academic leadership. Yet whilst it is bandied about glibly as something of a leitmotif in university leadership-and-management-speak, what academic leadership actually *means* – what it looks like and what it involves – is far from clear. Intended to address this conceptual lacuna, this chapter presents my conceptualisations of academic leadership, leaders and 'the led', whilst also highlighting the tensions between academic language and the vernacular that problematise this terminology.

Academic leadership as a concept: What we know and don't know

Academic leadership means different things in different countries or regions. As is evident from American texts (e.g. Birnbaum, 1992; Bolman & Gallos, 2011; Gallos, 2002; Hecht et al., 1999), in North America 'academic' seems to denote the context in which the leadership is carried out, and it prefixes an unproblematised interpretation of leadership – one that equates leadership activity with appointment to a recognised middle or senior management role. This narrow interpretation is also evident in the Australasian literature (e.g. Debowski and Blake, 2004; Ramsden, 1998; Scott, Coates and Anderson, 2008; Spiller, 2010); those who seem inclined towards adopting wider interpretations of academic leadership (e.g. Juntrasook, 2014; Youngs,

2017) seem to represent the minority of Australasian-based authors to have published on the topic. Despite the narrative that frames it, distinguishing academic leadership from academic management, Bradley et al.'s (2017, p. 100) definition suggests an interpretation that, in incorporating a focus on institutional strategic vision, remains at some distance from how academic leadership tends to be interpreted in the UK:

> for the purposes of this paper, academic leadership is defined as 'the distributed practice of carrying out the institution's strategic vision while supporting the development of intellectual authority and a shared identity that fosters collegiality'.

In the UK, in contrast, academic leadership is for the most part understood as informal – often *ad hoc* – supportive development- or even empowering-focused interaction, such as mentoring or role modelling, which may occur independently of formal, designated leadership or management, and which often takes as its point of departure individuals' personal career- and work-related development needs, rather than institutional strategic vision and priorities (though, of course, the two may be closely aligned and the latter may inform the former). This conceptualisation is summarised in Bolden et al.'s (2012a) outline of the findings of their UK-based study of academic leadership:

> Findings reveal a high degree of consistency in perspectives on, and experiences of, academic leadership. In particular it was observed that *much of what could be considered as 'academic leadership' is not provided by people in formal managerial roles*. Instead, leadership arises through engagement with influential colleagues within one's own academic discipline, especially those who play a pivotal role in one's transition and acculturation into academic life. PhD supervisors, current and former colleagues and key scholars were all described as significant sources of academic leadership, exerting substantial influence throughout one's career, *whether or not they were part of the same institution.* (Bolden et al., 2012a, p. 6, emphasis added)

But with conceptual breadth comes opacity, for, so-interpreted, academic leadership has only recently begun to attract scholarly attention from what, as yet, remains a very small group of researchers (e.g. Bolden et al., 2012a; Evans et al., 2013; Juntrasook et al., 2013; Macfarlane, 2011, 2012a), and as a result, its meaning remains rather vague. Indeed, Bolden et al.'s is the only published definition of academic leadership, *so-interpreted*, that I have found:[1] [academic leadership is] 'a process through which academic values and identities are constructed, communicated and enacted' (Bolden et al., 2012a, p. 17). Most work focused on academic leadership fails to define it, or to problematise its conceptualisation.

Macfarlane (2012a, p. 7) suggests that:

> [o]ne of the problems with the phrase academic leadership (or academic management) is whether it means the leadership *of* academics or leadership *by* academics. It can, of course, refer to both, but often there is some ambiguity as to whether it implies that academics are managing or leading themselves or being led by a professional manager.

But whether academic leadership refers to leadership *of* or *by* academics is but one source of confusion; there remain others. Does it, for example, denote the leadership of *academics* or of *academic work* – or both? Or does it simply refer to leadership of and by anyone, and of any kind, *within an academic context*? An added layer of confusion perhaps arises from the ambiguity of 'academic': it may be used either as a noun or as an adjective. The problem identified by Macfarlane, above, suggests that he is interpreting 'academic' as a noun; when it prefixes 'leadership', my inclination is to interpret it as an adjective.

Applying an adjectival interpretation places academic leadership in parallel with the category of leadership (also denoted by an adjectival prefix) of which it is surely a sub-category: educational leadership. Perhaps, then, we may arrive at a clearer conceptualisation of academic leadership via a slight detour that takes in the main features that delineate the current landscape of educational leadership research and scholarship. In doing so, we cannot avoid stepping into the more expansive terrain of leadership research and scholarship.

Research into educational leadership: An evolving landscape

Educational leadership research and scholarship, Gunter (2016) reminds us, is a field, not a discipline. In fact, the qualifying adjective 'educational' denotes a *sub*-field within the wider field of leadership, whose emergence as a focus of research and scholarship Podolny et al. (2004) trace back to the 1960s. Since then, leadership seems to have seeped into every discourse about policy and practice, establishing itself as the key variable believed by many to determine (or at the very least, influence) organisational effectiveness; indeed, indicating the nature of what they call 'today's leadership obsessed culture', Alvesson and Spicer (2012, pp. 367–8) bemoan leadership's being 'seen as a catch-all solution for nearly any problem, irrespective of context'. The expansion of leadership as a field has been steady and persistent, and its rise in popularity relentless. The more context-specific *educational* leadership has followed hard on its heels, with an epistemological take-over whose impact and repercussions are outlined by Gunter (2016, p. 5):

> Leaders or those appointed to a role, leading or the activity that leaders undertake and leadership or the relational power processes, within educational services and organizations, have grown rapidly as a field of practice and study in the last thirty years. This can be evidenced through increased adoption of the labels of 'leader', 'leading' and 'leadership' for educational professional practice, whereby professional titles such as principal, headteacher and president are used interchangeably with, and increasingly subsumed by, the leadership lexicon. The acceptance that role incumbents within a division of labour hierarchy are leaders, who do leading and who exercise leadership is normal and normalizing, to the extent that much is expected of those who inhabit ... 'leaderism'.

Yet whilst educational leadership represents a spin-off of the wider field of leadership, in several respects its scholarship seems to have followed a separate development path. Educational leadership has generally been considered a sub-field not only of leadership research and scholarship but also – indeed, perhaps more so – of educational research, and so it has been the educational research community who have shaped its development (since most educational leadership researchers also affiliate themselves with this wider community). In recent years the field of leadership (as distinct from *educational* leadership) has tended to be driven mainly by academics based in business and management schools, which are amalgamations of several disciplines and disciplinary cultures, including occupational (or work) psychology, social psychology, cultural psychology, economics, law and sociology, as well as fields such as marketing and accounting.[2]

In relation to the two fields' development, divergence is evident in their respective foci. A discourse that continues to gain prominence – particularly since the turn of the millennium (though its origins go much further back) – in the business and management academic community's research into leadership[3] is a form of critical leadership study (exemplified by: Alvesson et al., 2009; Alvesson & Spicer, 2012; Collinson, 2011; Kelly, 2008; Ladkin, 2010; Tourish, 2015;[4] Uhl-Bien, 2006; Wood, 2005) that questions interpretations of leadership as a form of agency enacted by key individuals who are designated leaders, perceiving it instead as a form of relationality, and/or as a process in context. This deeply analytical discourse extends to interrogation and questioning of the very concept of leadership and even to consideration of whether it is in fact a socially constructed myth, or is otherwise ill-conceived or in need of reframing (see, for example, Gemmill & Oakley, 1992; Krantz, 2015; Meindl, 1993; Raelin, 2016).

With a few notable exceptions (e.g. Gronn, 2000, 2002, 2009; Lakomski, 1999; Lakomski & Evers, 1999; Watson & Scribner, 2005) researchers of educational leadership do not seem to have significantly contributed to this particular critical analytical discourse on leadership; indeed, as Youngs (2009) implies – highlighting the need for a broader and 'more critical' perspective, and 'to draw on the expertise within and beyond the field of school leadership' (p. 389) – educational leadership researchers seem generally reluctant to engage with the wider leadership field's research community and its output. Certainly, a vibrant critical studies discourse, that seems to straddle what Grint (1997) categorised in the late 1990s as 'modern' and 'alternative' leadership perspectives, currently enjoys a relatively, and increasingly, prominent status within the field of educational leadership, but any focus that it incorporates on the essence of leadership and its validity and appropriateness as a unit of analysis is, for the most part, more implicit than explicit. As is implied by Gunter's (2001) outline description of critical research, this discourse has tended to define itself through a dominant focus on social justice-related issues which, in recent years, has extended to exposure of the deleterious effects of neoliberalism.

Aside from this immensely valuable social justice-focused criticality, the path that much *educational* leadership research has followed, in evidently eschewing the multi-disciplinarity that Foskett et al. (2005) call for, side-steps or by-passes some of the thorny issues that preoccupy some of the most pioneering leadership researchers outside the educational research community: fundamental conceptual, existential, ontological and even paradigmatic issues that are shaking the very foundations of the field – 'challenging traditional thinking and opening up new avenues for thinking about leadership and followership' (Uhl-Bien, 2009, p. vii). Such critical perspectives interrogate the concept and question what counts as leadership.

What counts as leadership? A critical perspective

Critical leadership scholarship interprets leadership differently from how it has traditionally and conventionally been interpreted. A key point is that it represents dissatisfaction with mainstream leadership research, yet, just as there are *degrees* of dissatisfaction, there are degrees of criticality; so we may imagine a continuum, ranging from, at one (arguably, the 'moderate') end, perspectives that deviate only slightly from those dominant in the mainstream, to the paradigm-shifting perspectives located at what could be called the 'radical' end.

Whilst there are difficulties with pinpointing the defining features of a critical leadership research terrain whose contours reflect these underlying gradations, one prominent landmark is discernible across the whole landscape: an 'unblinkered' conceptualisation of leadership – one that perceives leadership as much more than the person(s) doing the leading. Though they do not apply to it the specific term *critical* leadership study or research, Denis et al. (2012, p. 254) explain how such a landmark appears to them:

> Most leadership studies … tend to equate leadership with what specific individuals identified as leaders do, starting with the existence of these distinct individuals and considering various elements such as their qualities, their behaviors, or their effectiveness. [Critical leadership[5]] … studies … differ by questioning this *a priori*: that leadership is a property of individuals (either in the singular or in the plural). This questioning leads directly to the perennial interrogation about the nature of leadership … . This interrogation opens the door to a wide variety of possibilities: philosophical inquiries, empirical studies of what, on a daily basis, leadership is about, reconceptualizations of leadership, ethical concerns, questioning of leadership discourse, etc. Yet, all the inquiries within this line of thinking share one common root: that leadership is fundamentally more about participation and collectively creating a sense of direction than it is about control and exercising authority. This assumption problematizes the individuality of leadership, which in turn *requires a reconceptualization of what leadership is and, for some, what indeed it should be.* (emphasis added)

The criticality and dissatisfaction implicit in the conceptually based critical leadership discourse are directed at researchers' prevalent tendency to default towards what I call the 'personification' of leadership – by which I mean the association of leadership with the person of the leader, prompting Krantz's (2015, p. 11) concern about 'the overriding premise that … leadership exists inside of that sack of skin we call the person'.

Peter Gronn explains his conceptualisation of leadership:

> as a status ascribed to one individual, an aggregate of separate individuals, sets of small numbers of individuals acting in concert or larger plural-member organizational units. The basis of this ascription is the influence attributed voluntarily by organization members to one or the other of these focal units. The basis of the attribution of legitimate influence by the attributing agents may be either direct experience, through first-hand engagement with the particular focal unit, or vicarious experience, and thus reputed, presumed or imagined.

The scope of attributed influence encompasses the workplace-related activities defined by the employment contracts which operate in particular contexts. (Gronn, 2002, p. 428)

He clarifies the scope of such leadership ascription:

The individuals or multiperson units to whom influence is attributed include, potentially, all organization members, not just managerial role incumbents ... the duration of the attributed influence may be short or long term. (Gronn, 2002, p. 429)

Yet, notwithstanding the precision with which it is expressed, nor the critical stance that it undoubtedly represents, there are traces of a personification perspective in Gronn's conceptualisation – not least in the choice of 'status' as the stipulative definitional noun, which connotes an ontological position and, within the definition, relationality to a person or persons to whom it (the status) is ascribed.

Personifying leadership – associating it with roles, positions and/or individuals – has a long history. It is evident in one of the earliest published definitions of leadership – as 'the preeminence of one or a few individuals in a group in the process of control of societal phenomena' (Mumford, 1906, p. 221) – and has featured recurrently in the succession of published definitions or interpretations to have followed Mumford's. Yet as a perspective on leadership it has always provoked rumblings of discomfort and disapproval – such as Hollander's (1992, p. 71) observation that 'leadership is a process, not a person', and, half a century earlier, Chester Barnard's complaint that '*leadership* was confused with *pre-eminence or extraordinary usefulness*' by participants of a conference on leadership preparation (Barnard, 1997,[6] p. 89, original emphases). Barnard then reminds us of how easy it is – today, just as in the later decades of the twentieth century – to slip into default personification mode: 'unless we are careful, I suspect that within an hour we shall be talking of leaders as if the individual were the exclusive component of leadership' (p. 91). It is clearly difficult to throw off this mode of thinking about, and 'doing', leadership – indeed, Shondrick et al. (2010) suggest that we are cognitively stymied to perpetuate familiar and habitual socially constructed perceptions of leadership hierarchies.

Nevertheless, some conceptualisations and definitions seem to avoid defaulting to hierarchical and personification mode better than others. Critical leadership study emerged in the 1970s as a recognisable discourse 'challenging prevailing assumptions in the field' (Gronn, 1999, p. 140), only to be drowned out (due to unfortunate timing) by competing discourses and key outputs. Now, having found a second wind, it seems to be gaining renewed momentum with its contribution of the kinds of conceptualisations and definitions of leadership that have implicitly been heralded (by, for example: Chrobot-Mason et al., 2016; Cullen-Lester & Yammarino, 2016; Raelin, 2016; Watson & Scribner, 2005) as a potential paradigm shift, and many of which deviate emphatically from associating leadership with leaders – however ascribed – by focusing instead on processes and/or situations, and their outcomes. Watson and Scribner (2005), for example, emphasise that leadership can 'exist independently of individuals we would refer to as leaders' and 'be conceived of as a leaderless collaborative phenomenon' (p. 8). For Denis et al. (2012) leadership is 'not … a property of individuals and their behaviors, but … a collective phenomenon that is distributed or shared among different people, potentially fluid, and constructed in interaction' (p. 212); it 'perhaps does truly lie not in the people, but in their relations or interstices' (p. 254), and to Chrobot-Mason et al. (2016), leadership is 'a collaborative, relational process' (p. 298); 'a relational property rather than an individual entity' (p. 299). To these interpretations I add my own definition of leadership, presented below as the culmination of my analysis of the concept.

What is leadership? A personal perspective

The conceptualisation of leadership presented below is very much a work in progress. Writing this book has prompted me to reach into the recesses of my consciousness, dust off some of the issues that have been languishing there for some time, and address them head-on – a protracted endeavour that cannot be rushed. Recent extended visits to France, too, have sharpened my focus on critical questions such as whether leadership is in fact a socially constructed myth that lacks a compelling empirical evidential basis, for the French have no word of their own for leader or leadership; on the rare occasions when they find a need to express themselves in such terms, they appropriate English terminology: *le leader; le leadership* (but I have yet to encounter any Franglais version of 'the led'). French culture, I have learned, has no tradition of recognising people as leaders, nor of conceiving of a form of human agency that equates to what we (the 'non-French') tend to label leadership. Participating in a recent two-year-long series of monthly seminars in Paris that was focused on the problems facing French schooling and how they might be addressed, I was struck by the absence of any consideration, on the part of French academics, practitioners and policy-makers, of school leadership as a relevant factor – one that would certainly have topped the agenda, had the seminars taken place in the UK and focused on British schooling. Are the French then missing a trick? It may be so; yet, for all its considerable imperfections (admittedly, signifying what many commentators in France call the 'crisis' of French schooling), the French education system has not yet, despite a lack of leadership rhetoric and practice, degenerated into unworkable, chaotic failure – which rather undermines the 'view expressed by some that without leaders there is chaos' (Schostak, 2016, p. 5). Or is it simply a semantic issue: is there in fact just as much leadership in France as in other countries, but it is called something different? Or is it that we in the Anglo-Saxon world, along with much of the rest of Europe, make far too much of leadership? Experiences and questions such as these have shaped my current thinking on leadership and what it is.

To convey that thinking, I begin not at the 'beginning' (wherever that may be), but at what may perhaps be considered the 'end' – the 'result' or 'product' of leadership: a person who has been 'led'. How might we recognise or identify such an individual?

Drilling down: Defining leadership, leaders and 'the led'

Leading – and being led – must be contextualised; by that, I mean that one is not, essentially, led in a *general* sense, one is always led *in relation to something*: an issue, or a matter, or a set of circumstances, or whatever. (Whilst individuals who manifest habitual followership tendencies may appear to be or have been led in a general or indiscriminate sense, in reality, reductionist analysis would reveal them to have been led repeatedly or recurrently in relation to a succession of specific issues whose separateness and distinction are at first glance imperceptible.) My interpretation of someone who has been led therefore incorporates recognition of such contextualised specificity of focus as a notional basic feature of 'led-ness'. It also incorporates recognition of what I consider a key feature of having been led: deviation from or adjustment to a 'pre-led' direction or position.

As I interpret leadership, then, an individual (A), who has been 'led' in relation to a specific issue or matter (M) chooses, without coercion, to exercise her/his agency in relation to M differently from how s/he exercised it before having been led, representing a shift or deviation (S), from the position (P) that s/he occupied or the direction that s/he was following before having been led, to a different position or direction (D), on the basis of human agentic influence (H) on A, to recognise D, at this point in time, as a potentially 'better way' than P. The shift or deviation (S) represented by position or direction D rather than P may range in magnitude from minuscule to major and must have been prompted by human agentic influence (H), in the form of direct or indirect verbal or non-verbal communication that may be recognised or unrecognised by A, but that must, in principle, be recognisable. Position or direction – whether P or D – are not restricted to visible behaviour. Occupation of a position or pursuit of a direction may therefore involve, *inter alia*: physical action, cognitive action, or attitude-formation or -adoption.

In simpler terms, what this interpretation implies is that someone who has been 'led', chooses or opts to do things (or, more precisely, at least *one* thing) differently – however slightly – (applying a wide definition of 'does', to include mental, as well as physical action[7]), as a result of her/his 'buying into' what s/he subjectively recognises, consciously or unconsciously, as a 'better' alternative that has been presented through someone else's agency. This 'doing' things differently *on this basis* is the essence of 'led-ness'. Modifying one's viewpoint or perspective is as much an indicator of having been led as is changing one's (physical, and potentially visible) way of working, or one's approach, or one's goals or strategies, or the order in which one does things – provided that the influence prompting the change may be attributable to another person or persons directly (e.g. through evidence of influential direct communication) or indirectly (e.g. through authorship of an influential text, or formulation and dissemination of an influential ideology, or through an environment – whose development is traceable to another person – that encouraged or facilitated the shift or deviation).

To illustrate this interpretation, I draw upon two examples from my research, presented as brief extracts from interviews with research participants. In the first example a junior academic, David,[8] recalls the leadership he received, as a postgraduate student, from his doctoral supervisor:

> He [the supervisor] saw immediately that I didn't understand Freud very well. ... And so he ... pointed that out to me – you know, in a very gentlemanly manner, he pointed it out to me – and made it clear that I should go off and read particular examples of ... I can't remember the articles now – probably parts of *The Interpretation of Dreams* – but, I should go off and read ... a particular text ... y'know, pointing out the, sort of, limitations of my own understanding of technical terms, and sending me off to read.

The second example features a senior professor, Elizabeth, who related the details of a 'mini crisis' that she encountered in her role as the chair of an influential university committee:

I did seriously wonder if I would *have* to resign, and I lost just about a complete night's sleep over that. I'd been briefed; we set up a formal meeting – it was unspeakably awful, and we had a de-briefing the following day with personnel, and the first thing I said at the de-briefing was, 'Do you think I have to resign?' – resign as chairman – 'I've lost a lot of emotional energy over that.' And everybody said, 'No, no, no – whatever you do, you mustn't resign!'

Table 3.1, illustrates these two examples of 'led-ness' by delineating in each case the specific actors, actions, positions and issues at stake that represent the features of being led identified in my interpretation.

This interpretation or conceptualisation of 'led-ness' seems to lead neatly onto one of a leader, who, by extension, may be defined as a person whose agency directly or indirectly prompts or facilitates an individual's shift or deviation, without coercion, from a position or direction to what s/he (the individual) perceives as a superior position or direction: a 'better way'. Similarly, a definition seems to be emerging of leadership as human agency that directly or indirectly prompts or facilitates an individual's shift or deviation, without coercion, from one position or direction to what s/he (the individual) perceives as a superior position or direction: a 'better way'. Yet this interpretive extension is not as simple and straightforward as it may appear – nor, indeed, is my interpretation of 'led-ness', presented above; both are complicated by issues relating to temporality and ascription that need elucidating if my perspective on leadership is to have any chance of contributing a path through what Krantz (2015) calls the 'quagmire' of conceptual confusion that muddies the field.

The finer detail: Temporality and ascription

My interpretation of 'led-ness' is clearly reductionist in nature and focus. It is intended to represent the 'singular unit' – if such a thing is identifiable – of what it is to be or to have been led: the constituent elements or parts that, on a theoretical level, reveal themselves when, instead of focusing on the 'big picture' that most frequently shapes our perceptions of being led, prompting us to conjure up mental images of large-scale, or repeated, or high visibility 'led-ness', we place such images under the microscope and 'zoom' in on their minute detail. Knowing generally that early career academic David was, as a doctoral student, led by his supervisor, or that senior academic Elizabeth was led by the support systems provided by her university's administrative structure and services tells us much less about the nature of such experiences of being led – and, by extension, of the nature of 'led-ness' – than does the micro-level scrutiny implied by my 'singular unit' interpretation.

Table 3.1 Examples of features of relational activity interpreted as 'led-ness'

	A (individual)	M (issue or matter)	P ('pre-led' position or direction)	H (human intervention)	D ('post-led' position or direction)	S (shift or deviation)
Example 1	David – as a doctoral student	his reading of the literature upon which to draw in his doctoral work, and understanding of specific key terms	his specific 'take' on, or understanding of, Freudian concepts; his specific approach to selecting and reading texts	doctoral supervisor's advice	deeper understanding of specific Freudian concepts and terms; wider and deeper reading	re-appraisal of his former approach to literature search and review, and of his understanding of Freudian terms and concepts
Example 2	Elizabeth – as a committee chair	her retention of the committee chairship	questioning the appropriateness of her continued status as chair	personnel department's advice	acceptance that resignation is not a good strategy	re-appraisal of the option of resigning

Through the same analytical reductionist reasoning, I argue that – again, on a theoretical level – leadership comprises basic units of activity that are temporally identifiable and, as a result, potentially, as well as inevitably, transient in occurrence. These basic units each involve the flow of influence (first- or second-hand, face-to-face or by proxy) from one person to another or others. Examples of them are: a person's reading of (and being influenced by) a text; an individual's hearing (and being influenced by) a statement made by another; or an observation of another's behaviour in a specific situation (which then influences the observer to adjust or shift her/his position or direction). Comparable to Charles Darwin's use of the term 'species' for something that 'doesn't refer to anything definitive in nature, but is nevertheless a useful way of lumping organisms together' (Menand, 2001, p. 224), the units are notional, existing in theory, since they cannot easily be discerned in practice.[9] They are similar to what I identify as theoretical basic units of activity within individuals' professional development (outlined in Evans, 2014b), and which relate to what I call 'micro-level' professional development, explaining it as: 'the individual, singular "episodes" that constitute, as far as they are discernible, the unitary components of "bigger picture", or wider scale, professional development' (Evans, 2014b, p. 186). Retaining this parallel with professional development, in the context of leadership I think of these unitary components as denoting 'micro-level' leadership activity. As a heuristic device, they serve to convey my interpretation that, within a potential leadership interaction that involves more than one basic unit of activity, the leadership activity is not *necessarily* performed and retained in a sustained way, without interruption, by a single individual; it may just as feasibly be performed first by one, and then another, and then yet another, in (sometimes rapid) succession, or alternating from one to another, like a ball being repeatedly thrown and caught randomly across a group of people, with the agency of leadership successively changing hands. Each such metaphorical change of hands is likely to constitute a basic unit, or unitary component, of the interaction 'event' or episode. Units are of variable and contestable length (i.e. duration), form and nature, since these would be subjectively determined by the identifier if the units were, or are potentially, identifiable in practice.

A practical example of an interaction constituted of such basic units of micro-level leadership influence might be a formal committee or an informal collegial meeting, in which – potentially representing one basic unit of influence – one member's articulated views[10] first take the lead, influencing others (who, by definition, then become *led* by that member, and hence assume the role of 'the led'), before a second unit of influence then occurs, as a different person's inferred viewpoint then takes over as influencing – hence, *leading* – some members' perceptions, resulting in the one who, a few seconds earlier, was leading, now potentially finding her/himself being led, before perhaps reclaiming the lead at one or more later points. It was 'leadership ... performed at the micro-level of interaction' of this kind that Choi and Schnurr (2014, p. 11) analysed within an informal collegial group of university academics. Focused on the group's discourse, the authors refer to 'examples' [that represent team members' negotiation of disagreements], which are presented as what they call 'sequences' [of transcribed conversation]. The closest the researchers come to implicitly identifying an 'example' or 'sequence' as a basic unit [of analysis] is to afford it a finiteness, with an end-point that is determined by their (the researchers') deciding that disagreements between the research participants had been reconciled, through an identifiable leadership activity:

> the disagreement in this example seems to come to an end after everyone has had a chance to disagree ... and when participants seem to be running out of steam. Bee's leadership thus emerges relatively spontaneously and is manifested in bringing the discussion to a close and making a decision. (Choi & Schnurr, 2014, p. 11)

The group's resolution of disagreement and negotiation of consensus were interpreted by the authors as an example of distributed leadership activity that occurred in a shared manner, within what they describe as a 'leaderless team', through what Gronn (2002) refers to as 'reciprocal influence'. Identifying it as one of several possible processual components of conjoint agency, Gronn explains reciprocal influence as:

> both internal and external in its effects. Reciprocity denotes the influence of two or more parties on one another and it occurs in a manner akin to a virtuous cycle or zigzagging spiral. Here, A influences B and C, and is influenced in turn by them (i.e., A ⋚ B, A ⋚ C, and also B ⋚ C) with each person subsequently bearing the accumulated effects of successive phases of influence, as they begin influencing one another once again. The internal relationship of the conjoint agents is one of reciprocal influence. And in their relations with their organizational peers, who attribute leadership to them as focal units, conjoint agents both influence colleagues and are influenced in return. (Gronn, 2002, p. 431)

As it is explained by Gronn, reciprocal influence appears in many respects very similar to my notion of variously and successively ascribed influence, which I liken to ball-throwing-and-catching across a group – certainly, both may be broadly categorised as 'shared leadership', explained by Shondrick et al. (2010): 'When leadership is shared, an individual's role may repeatedly shift from leader to follower or follower to leader' (p. 961) and 'shared leadership is characterized by dynamic, deindividualized processes within a group or organization' (p. 973)[11] – yet there is also a subtle distinction between the two: the notion I present *may* but does not *necessarily* include reciprocity, as I explain below.

The notion of micro-level leadership, with its basic units of activity denoting enacted leadership (and consequently also enactment of being 'led'), is perhaps easier to understand by imagining such a scenario (i.e. a formal committee or an informal collegial meeting) as a video-recording of the live interaction. On replaying the recording, technology makes it possible to identify and freeze the images, allowing them to be examined, frame by frame. Consideration of how a frame represents a discrete unit that conveys a fleeting moment in time – a minute fraction or proportion of activity that has been recorded – may facilitate understanding of the very broadly similar notion of micro-level leadership as basic units or unitary components; indeed, Michael Eraut (2004, p. 254) makes similar reference to film clips as an explanatory device in relation to 'implicit' learning. He, too, applies reductionist analysis to 'period[s] of performance [that] can be broken down into successive phases', which are obscured from an observer, who 'sees a fluent, unfolding sequence of events' (Eraut, 2004, pp. 256–7).

Such reductionism makes for a theoretical perspective that, in first identifying 'led-ness' (or being led) as fundamentally involving discrete units of un-coerced receptivity to the agency of another or others which influences positional or directional realignment, shift or deviation, must then identify *leadership* as fundamentally involving discrete units of direct or indirect interpersonal interaction or communicative activity. The discreteness of its fundamental units therefore precludes leadership's being, despite appearances, a continued, uninterrupted, activity – a 'fluent ... sequence', to repeat Michael Eraut's (2004) words. The ascription of leader status, within this theoretical perspective, to anyone whose direct or indirect communication with another person triggers that person's un-coerced positional or directional realignment, shift or deviation, undermines leadership's association with, and ascription of leader status, within a given context, to one person exclusively. It does not, however, *preclude* such association, for it is possible that, within a specific situation, set of circumstances, or even a single event or communicative exchange, leader status may be ascribable exclusively to a single individual. This ascription would occur through the leader-ascribed individual's agentic influencing of others' (or another's) un-coerced positional or directional realignment, shift or deviation, *without interruption by another's such agentic (and potentially reciprocal) influencing.* (Such a scenario seems quite closely aligned with Shamir's (2009, p. xviii) interpretation of leadership as only existing 'when an individual (sometimes a pair or small group) exerts disproportionate noncoercive influence on others, that is, his or her influence on the group or organization is greater than that of the other members'.)

From this – my – reductionist theoretical perspective, then, leadership (both being led and being a leader) is essentially neither enduring nor static, but in some circumstances – such as if/when it occurs through uninterrupted repeated, successive activity over a sustained period – it may *appear* to be both (enduring and static). Nevertheless – and consistent with Gronn's (2002, p. 429) stipulation (cited above) that 'the duration of the attributed influence may be short or long term' – its *fundamental* nature lends leadership more accurately to description as, *inter alia*: fleeting, transient, temporary, momentary, intermittent, or precarious.

As I conceptualise leadership, its essential feature – the key determinant of whether it is occurring or has occurred, or of whether a communicative exchange or interaction represents leadership – is influence that effects positional or directional realignment, shift or deviation, for there may be members of a group who, during the course of one or more unit(s) of (potential or attempted) leadership activity, remain unswayed – and therefore 'unled' – by expressed views or by non-verbal communication that influence(s) others. The latter (that is, those who *are* influenced), in contrast, assume – albeit perhaps temporarily or sporadically – the position of 'the led'. Enacted leadership is thus subjectively, and potentially dynamically and variably, ascribed (albeit often unconsciously or implicitly, rather than consciously and/or explicitly[12]), even within one discrete group interaction, since the extent to which people are influenced in this way is potentially very individualised, transient, and hence variable. And, of course, leadership so ascribed does not necessarily correspond with recognised leadership role incumbency.

It is important to emphasise, too, that this dynamic process of leadership enactment – the fluidity implied in the illustrative hypothetical scenario presented above, of what I liken to a ball being passed from person to person – effects 'led-ness' that does not necessarily occur contemporaneously with the interaction that is its catalyst; it may continue beyond the immediate temporal context of the interaction, as individuals reflect and mull over exchanges retrospectively, or unconsciously assimilate the ideas generated by them, before being influenced to 'led-ness'. Eraut's (2004) research-informed observations on this issue are as applicable to leadership influence as they are to their original intended focus: implicit learning:

episodes that are not recalled may nevertheless affect later performance. Hence, it is reasonable to assume that, even when episodes are recalled, information from them may have been used without the actor being aware of it. ... Thus, throughout our lives we make assumptions about people, situations and organizations based on aggregated information whose provenance we cannot easily recall and may not even be able to describe. (p. 253)

Enacted leadership, then, may be effected as 'delayed' influence just as easily as by instantaneous influence, and there is no realistic limit to the length of any such delay; influence may lie dormant for years, before being activated. By the same token, instantaneous influence may not endure. Moreover, any specific element of influence may, over time, become diluted by the continued accumulation of other elements of influence. On the basis of its time-delimited nature alone, then, leadership influence is problematic to identify, and this problem has implications for delineating the conditions that determine and hence define leadership, and therefore for analysing the concept (and its derivatives). But equally challenging to conceptual analysis of leadership is the complex issue of ascription right: that is, of who has the right to ascribe leader status to an individual, and, by extension, to identify enacted leadership.

To illustrate the problematic nature of this issue, I present an account, related by Elizabeth, the same senior professor cited above:

> I appraise somebody who publishes entirely with the same ... adequate, but not remotely distinguished, academic press, but who is a leading player in the field and ... ought to have a personal chair, but needs to tart their CV up. And I said, 'Why are you always publishing with [X Press], and why aren't you publishing with OUP [Oxford University Press]?' and the answer was: 'Because [X Press] will take my books, and I don't have to go through the peer review nonsense.' And I said, 'What about applying to OUP – or Harvard or Princeton? Wouldn't you *like* to be with a glitzier press?' And he said, 'No, it's too much trouble.'

Elizabeth concluded her account: 'I'm not very good then at when you just meet the blank wall resistance, but I have tried.'

On the basis of this account, and considered against my definition of 'led-ness', presented above, her colleague cannot be categorised as having been led in relation to the specific approach to enhancing his CV that Elizabeth suggested, since the account lacks evidence of his having shifted or deviated from the position or direction that he is represented as having held prior to Elizabeth's attempt to effect such a shift or deviation. But does the preclusion of her colleague from the status of being led automatically preclude Elizabeth from being categorised, on the basis of her action in attempting to influence her colleague, as enacting leadership, and hence as meriting leader ascription? Should ascription of leader status depend on *intention* to exercise, or *success* at having exercised, H – and *whose* attribution of either of these forms of agency should count in determining the matter: that of the agent her/himself (the putative leader – in this case, Elizabeth), that of A (the 'led' or intended 'led' – in this case, Elizabeth's colleague), or that of a third party 'observer' (such as we who read and consider the details of the related case)?

If we adhere to my interpretation of 'led-ness', presented above, the only person who seems qualified to judge whether or not Elizabeth's colleague was led is the colleague himself, and the implication of this – since leader status is dependent upon influencing 'led-ness' in another – is that he apparently is also the only person qualified to ascribe leader status to Elizabeth, in relation to this specific *potential* leadership 'episode': Elizabeth's advising him on how to enhance his CV (yet, as I outline in the list of possible scenarios below, even his qualification to make a judgement is problematic). Elizabeth's account implies that she *thinks*, based on his responses to her suggestions, that her colleague was not led, but the accuracy of her conclusion may be undermined by one or more from the following list – which I do not present as exhaustive – of possible scenarios:

- Elizabeth's colleague misrepresented his response to her suggestions.
- Her colleague accurately represented his response to Elizabeth's suggestions at the time at which they were made, but he has subsequently – unbeknown to Elizabeth – reflected on her advice and adjusted his position accordingly.
- Her colleague genuinely believed himself to have been – and perhaps to remain – uninfluenced by Elizabeth's suggestions, but, unconsciously, he has in fact been influenced to the extent of realigning or shifting, or deviating from his 'pre-led' position or direction.

'Where does leadership activity begin and end and how is it recognised?' ask Denis et al., identifying 'the issue of boundaries' as 'problematic' (2012, p. 254). As the Elizabeth-and-colleague vignette shows, that question is not always easy to answer. It cannot be answered without first defining leadership, but if it is guided by a definition that imposes rigid boundaries, demarcation risks creating an inaccessible space that remains aspirational, unattainable or notional/conceptual only. A definition that is predicated upon *objective* evidence of led-ness as an individual's un-coerced positional or directional shift or realignment that results from another person's agentic influence incorporates such rigidity and associated risk, for the requisite evidence will always remain elusive. A definition or conceptualisation that stacks up in theory may thus prove operationally shaky, collapsing under the burden of requisite objectivity. To address this problem, I propose definitions that substitute subjectivity for objectivity, and assumption, perception or belief for certainty, as bases of leader(ship) ascription. Modifying slightly (with the added text indicated by italics) the propositional definitions discussed above, I accordingly present my definition of a leader as: a person whose agency *may reasonably be considered to have* directly or indirectly prompted or facilitated an individual's shift or deviation, without coercion, from a position or direction to what s/he (the individual) perceives as a superior position or direction: a 'better way'. Similarly, I define leadership as human agency that *may reasonably be considered to* directly or indirectly prompt or have prompted or facilitate or have facilitated an individual's shift or deviation, without coercion, from one position or direction to what s/he (the individual) perceives as a superior position or direction: a 'better way'. I then define one who has been 'led' as one who *may reasonably be considered to have chosen or opted* to do things (or, more precisely, at least *one thing*) differently, without coercion, as a result of her/his 'buying into' what s/he subjectively recognises, consciously or unconsciously, as a 'better' alternative that has been presented through someone else's (facilitating or prompting) agency.

It is important to emphasise too that my conceptualisation, presented above, is focused on identifying the notional *singular units* of leadership. In practice, leadership, leaders, 'ledness' and 'the led' often appear 'bigger' or more expansive – more 'joined up' – than is implied by these singular units. In practice, we may, for example, identify as a leader someone who, quantitatively, manifests a greater capacity than do others for influencing people in the ways that constitute leadership or 'ledness' as I define them. Similarly, we may identify leaders and leadership through such *indirect* influence – such as a significant contribution to creating or fostering an institutional culture that then proves influential on people. It is important, therefore, to keep in mind the notion of singular units as just that: the basic building blocks of 'bigger' leadership, rather than as finite indicators in themselves of leadership, leaders and 'ledness'.

But if all this is leadership, what is *academic* leadership? How do we convert the definitions above into those denoting the more specific *academic* leadership and *academic* leaders?

What is academic leadership? A personal perspective

If educational leadership denotes, as seems to be consensually accepted, leadership within the context of institutions, organisations, environments or situations whose main focus or purpose is educational provision – in other words, leadership (within the context) of educational activity or endeavour – then, as a parallel notion, academic leadership may be interpreted as denoting leadership (within the context) of academic activity or endeavour. Applying a critical interpretation of leadership, as developed in the section above, and adopting the definition of leadership that I present there, academic leadership then denotes the influencing or facilitating, without coercion, of a person's positional or directional realignment, shift or deviation in relation to (the context of) academic activity or endeavour. Presented as a stipulative definition, academic leadership, as I interpret it, is: *human agency that may reasonably be considered to prompt or have prompted or to facilitate or have facilitated an individual's shift or deviation, without coercion, from a position or direction in relation to (the context of) academic activity or endeavour to what s/he (the individual) perceives as a superior position or direction: a 'better way'.*

I see academic leadership as an umbrella notion of leadership that incorporates numerous more specific sub-categories, such as intellectual leadership, research leadership – which I have conceptualised and defined as 'the influence of one or more persons on the research-related behaviour, attitudes or intellectuality of another/others' (Evans, 2014a, p. 48) – and potentially some of what Parker and Welch (2013, p. 333) identify as several different categories (or, to use their word, 'types') of leadership in STEM disciplines:

> STEM center leadership, STEM administrative leadership, and STEM discipline leadership.[13] These leadership types are not exhaustive. There are other types of leadership prevalent in the academic context. For example, it is possible to consider intellectual leadership in STEM fields in which an intellectual leader is recognized by the ideas she produces not by a formal position.

My references in this book to 'academic leadership', 'academic leaders', and 'the led' are underpinned by my umbrella definition of academic leadership, above. Yet it is not my definitions alone that feature in the chapters that follow.

Theory meets practice: Vernacularity and workability in conceptualising and defining leadership

The rationale for leadership research or study is that leadership is considered a socio-cultural device for organising and/or explaining aspects of human agency and action in certain contexts, such as the workplace – specifically, in the context of this book, the university as workplace, and academe as work environment. Compromise is therefore needed if esoteric concepts are to translate into a vernacular of labels and ideas that work for those whose agency and actions constitute leadership, for, as Meindl (1993) notes:

> A key to understanding and conceptualizing leadership must be built on the foundations of a naïve psychological perspective. *How leadership is constructed by both naïve organizational actors and by sophisticated researchers should constitute the study of leadership.* For it is those very constructions on which the effects of leadership, defined in conventional terms, are likely to depend. (p. 97, emphases added)

Since leadership is a practice-focused concept, it is important that practitioners are able to consider – to paraphrase Denis et al. (2012) – where it (leadership) begins and ends, and how it may be recognised, and that researchers are in turn able to identify and recognise such practitioner-considered interpretations and work with them. Echoing Meindl's (1993) sentiments, expressed above, pragmatist social theorists Kivinen and Piiroinen (2006) make the point that:

> [s]cientific inquiry differs from layman inquiry in that scientists participate in scientific language games in which the conventions are different from layman language games. This is not to say that non-scientific standpoints are somehow inferior as compared to scientific ones – we rather concur with P.F. Strawson's ... remark that the whole idea of settling contradictions between these points of view in a 'neutral' fashion, 'arises only if we assume the existence of some metaphysically absolute standpoint from which we can judge between the two standpoints ... But there is no such superior standpoint ...'. Moreover, both scientific knowledge and lay knowledge must ultimately be tested by acting accordingly, and both are acquired from some actor's point of view. (p. 239)

Theoretical perspectives on and conceptions of leadership and leaders – including those representing critical thinking – are of greatest value if they contribute towards elucidating, to those involved with delineating or perpetuating its practice, how leadership may potentially be done better, or indeed whether it is being or should be done at all, for, as Louis Menand observes:

> [a]n idea has no greater metaphysical stature than, say, a fork. When your fork proves inadequate to the task of eating soup, it makes little sense to argue about whether there is something inherent in the nature of forks or something inherent in the nature of soup that accounts for the failure. You just reach for a spoon. (Menand, 2001, p. 361)

So, while the analytical reductionist thinking outlined above contributes to a small, but expanding, body of critical theoretical perspectives that, collectively, have the potential to underpin an evolution of how leadership is perceived, it is important to bear in mind that this evolution has not yet been completed and it is certainly not widespread, nor has it registered on most practitioners' radars. This analytical reductionist thinking is consequently out of sync with current (and perhaps even enduring) perspectives – held not only by leadership policy-makers and practitioners but also by the general public – on leadership, and how it is and should be enacted. Conceptual and perspectival discrepancy of this kind, between researchers and 'lay' persons, is a general methodological and dissemination-related issue. As I point out elsewhere (Evans, 2002), it can threaten construct validity if researchers do not recognise the need to communicate through language and concepts that are familiar and comprehensible not only to research participants, but also to those to whom the research is disseminated.

This book represents a compromise of language and terminology use that is intended to address the discrepancy between how leadership and leaders are conceived from a critical research perspective, and how they are conceived and enacted in 'the real world'. The compromise arises from consideration that, since they were gathered from research participants (questionnaire respondents and interviewees – as explained in Chapter 4) who, for the most part, were not leadership scholars or researchers and therefore knew little or nothing of recent and current discourses that have problematised conceptions of leadership and promoted critical alternatives, the research data tended to reflect somewhat uncomplicated, conventional, laypersons' interpretations of and perspectives on leaders, leadership and 'the led'. Moreover, such interpretations and perspectives may even have been implicitly promoted by the terminology used in the data collection process, through the wording used in questionnaire items and interview conversations – for not only was my own thinking about leaders and leadership less developed at the time of data collection than it is now, insofar as I had not fully formulated and refined the critical perspectives presented above, but I was also keen to address and converse with non-leadership specialists in the kind of language, and using the constructs and terminology, that they were most likely to be familiar and comfortable with. It was certainly not a question of talking down to these constituencies of highly educated, intelligent, reflective people; it was simply that I expected them to be in most cases unlikely to want to prioritise a discussion on esoteric issues that lay outside their own spheres of research interests.

If then this book appears to deliver mixed messages, it does so in order to convey the research participants' perspectives as accurately and authentically as possible, through what I inferred from their own words to be their 'take' on professorial academic leadership. One of my purposes in writing this book is to present such perspectives to a 'lay' readership, while yet framing the research findings, the participants' terminology and associated implied concepts against a critical leadership theoretical perspective that reflects my own current thinking and that I hope may raise awareness in others that leadership is not all or only about the person of the (designated) leader.

So there is something of an irony in that, having problematised above the personification of leadership, I then – in the chapters that follow, proceed to highlight it. Indeed, I distinguish Parts Two and Three of the book on the basis that the first reflects the perspective of 'the led' and the second the perspective of the 'leaders'! This distinction represents what some critical leadership scholars denounce as 'pre-specification' of the roles of leaders and followers (see, for example, Hartley, 2009) – and, wearing my theorist's hat, I am entirely with them. But since the studies whose findings I present in this book generated data that represented just such pre-specification, I must wear a different hat in disseminating my findings.

So, whilst, here in this chapter within the context- and theoretical-focused Part One of the book, conceptual and theoretical issues are presented in what is intended as a coherent critical-focused discussion, for Parts Two and Three I switch to presenting a rather more operation-focused perspective – one that reflects the vernacular, and laypersons' ways of thinking about leadership – and pepper it with what I intend as alternative, thought-provoking observations and discussion. And since, in the vernacular, there are leaders and followers, or leaders and 'the led', and, focusing on bigger picture leadership rather than on its singular basic units, people may be considered or expected to be leaders if they manifest certain kinds of characteristics and/or hold certain roles or posts, these constituencies feature in the chapters that follow.

Such an operation-focused or pragmatic perspective is likely to ascribe leader status to Elizabeth (whose efforts to mentor a reluctant colleague are related in the vignette presented above) on the basis of her intention, willingness or attempts to lead a colleague. In the vernacular 'leader' can imply enduring or even innate characteristics or qualities on such bases, and people may be categorised, sometimes with a degree of recognition of finality or inevitability, as perpetual or 'natural' 'leaders' or 'followers' – as 'types'; as Macfarlane (2012a, p. 17) observes, 'One conventional way of thinking about leadership is in terms of traits and characteristics that make a good leader.' Such perspectives may be found within this book's analyses of professors as academic leaders because they are included amongst the manifold, wide-ranging perspectives that my[14] research uncovered. The details of that research are presented in the next chapter.

Notes

1   To be fair, Bradley et al.'s (2017) definition of academic leadership, presented above, together with the thrust of their argument in their paper, also implies the incorporation of a focus on promoting academic values and identities, but I exclude it as an example of academic leadership as the term is interpreted in the UK, not because these authors are based in Australasia, but because their discussion suggests an interpretation that associates academic leadership with formal role incumbency and the pursuit of institutional strategic goals.

2   Leadership study seems to have its origins in specific mainstream disciplinary fields, where it developed as 'spin-offs' to them. Writing towards the end of the last century, Meindl (1993, pp. 89–90), for example, highlighted the irony that 'social psychologists whose research agendas focus on leadership run the risk of being defined as marginal participants in the mainstream of social psychology', even though, 'leadership has had a prominent place in the history of social psychology'. Yet Mayo and Pastor (2007, p. 97) identify, since the 1970s, a 'steady decline among social psychologists interested in leadership'.

3   Whilst this critical discourse appears to be particularly prominent in the business and management research community, it is evident within other fields. Political scientist Archie Brown, for example, has published a critique of the notion of heroic leadership in politics (Brown, 2014).

4   This refers to an editorial, in which Dennis Tourish promotes the journal *Leadership* as a forum for critical leadership study, railing against mainstream journals that: 'simply ignore critical work, thereby curtailing academic debate. The same sterile preoccupations dominate the literature, in which the identification of ever more mediating processes and moderating factors takes precedence over interrogating fundamental assumptions … . Researchers seem content to ask smaller and smaller questions about fewer and fewer issues of genuine significance, producing statements of the blindingly obvious, the completely irrelevant or the palpably absurd' (p. 137).

5   At the risk of putting words into the authors' mouths, I have inserted this term – critical leadership – as a generic label for the specific studies that Denis et al. identify and that they group on the basis of the constituent and processual features they refer to as typifying them.

6   The chapter constitutes a reprint of a 1948 publication.

7   This is comparable to Michael Eraut's (2007, p. 406) definition of 'performance' as including thoughts and actions.

8   Pseudonyms are used throughout this book in all references to my research participants.

9   Until I have empirical research findings that allow me to identify such units, they must remain theoretical concepts. Yet it is interesting to note that, in the context of examining implicit learning, Michael Eraut (2004, 2007) presents empirical research findings that are based upon his identifying similar units.

10 It is important to note that leadership activity in such contexts need not be confined to verbal communication; non-verbal communication, such as a carefully timed raising of the eyebrows or head shaking, also has the potential to influence.

11 However, neither reciprocal influence, as explained by Gronn, nor my notion of variously and successively ascribed influence, which I liken to ball-throwing-and-catching across a group, represents what are known as complexity leadership approaches, which seem to involve more enduring shifting leadership attribution, on the basis of a group's or organisation's prevalent skills- or expertise-based needs, as Shondrick et al. (2010, p. 971) explain: 'The key idea in these approaches is that different individuals assume leadership at different times, ideally when their expertise affords them a unique perspective that has the potential to make a distinctive contribution to the group or organization.'

12 As Epitropaki et al. (2013, p. 859) observe: 'Implicit processing within the leadership domain … means that individuals tend to lack impact awareness, which reflects individuals' awareness of the influence of an activated schema on action tendencies. Thus, individuals may be unaware that certain schemas have been activated and its processing has impacted their action tendencies.'

13 Parker and Welch (2013, p. 335) explain STEM discipline leadership as including: 'individuals who have positions in professional science associations and regulatory organizations. They focus primarily on developing and enforcing standards and norms for the scientific community as a whole, which subsequently results in impacting the culture of science.'

14 For clarity and consistency in retaining a singular authorial voice throughout this book I use the singular first person possessive pronoun – 'my' – in referring to research, and its specific elements, that I conducted with co-investigators (whose contributions I acknowledge on page viii).

4

Seeking Answers: Augmenting the Professor-Focused Knowledge Base

By the end of the first decade of the twenty-first century academic work was establishing itself as a field of scholarship with a steadily accumulating knowledge base. The *Changing Academic Profession* international research project had by this time yielded over ten major texts (e.g. Aarrevaara & Pekkola, 2010; Coates et al., 2009; Jacob & Teichler, 2011; Locke & Teichler, 2007), while analyses of academic working life – emanating from numerous countries – were appearing with increasing frequency in academic journals and books. Such was researchers' response to academe's neoliberal-inspired performativity culture – a response that was fuelled by a drive to examine and expose this culture's impact on the working lives and career paths of those most affected by it. But there remained a gap in this burgeoning research output: professors and professorship scarcely featured in it as a discrete constituency of academics.

Malcolm Tight's (2002) paper, 'What does it mean to be a professor?' had grabbed my attention because its topic was already on my radar, but, as an issues- and awareness-raising paper, it poses questions without answering them. I was interested in answers – not only to Tight's overarching question, but also to several more specific ones of my own. I found myself embarking on what was to develop into a mini research programme, as one professor-related project led to another, and then another, and another. This chapter outlines the details of those projects; it is essentially a research design and method chapter, and it marks the point at which the book draws upon my own research, for the findings from my professor-related studies are the main bases of the chapters that follow in Parts Two and Three, and they feed into the discussions presented in Part Four.

A professor-related research programme: Four studies

Whilst Malcolm Tight's (2002) asking what it means to be a professor seems to have marked his becoming one, my interest in professorship pre-dates my promotion. Even as a senior lecturer (see Appendix) I had identified professors and the professoriate as a potentially rich research topic. I wanted to know what – if anything – was expected of professors, whether they themselves were aware of such expectations, and how – if at all – they responded to them. Like Tight (2002, p. 17), I had realised from my own observations that 'professors – like academics in general – are not a homogenous, equitable bunch', and I was interested in probing the bases of their heterogeneity. And as the swelling literature on academic working life revealed evidence of an evolving academic workforce, the 'shape' of whose professionalism was being reconfigured in response to shifting institutional priorities, I began to consider whether the professoriate was similarly evolving, and with what consequences for its continued survival and purpose, and for its 'image' – particularly as perceived by professors' junior colleagues.

So, when opportunities for funding professor-related research presented themselves, I grabbed them. The result was the four studies described below, whose combined database, representing both the views *of* professors and views *on* professors, comprises responses from over two thousand questionnaire respondents and transcripts of almost a hundred interviews.[1]

Details of each study are presented below. Since the designs of studies 2 and 3 were modelled very closely on study 1's design, to the point of being loose replications of it – though with different sample constituencies – much less information is presented on them than on study 1. To temper the expectations of readers who have digested the theoretical and conceptual perspectives presented in the preceding chapters – particularly my conceptualisation of leadership and the notion that it fundamentally comprises basic discrete units of influence between two or more persons (see Chapter 3) – it is important to emphasise that none of the studies gathered data that reflected or represented such forms of micro-level (potential) influential agency. Leadership-in-action was not captured directly; rather, the data took the form of representations or accounts of leaders and leadership and of the experiences of being led, as recollected by research participants. There are two main reasons for this discrepancy between my conceptualisation of leadership and the nature and form of data collected and analysed. First, at the time of data collection my own thinking on leadership was less developed than is implied by my analyses in Chapter 3, and this underdeveloped perspective resulted in adoption of the default, 'conventional' research design of seeking people's views and perspectives. I entirely accept Kelly's (2014, p. 908) point that critical leadership scholarship's 'move "outwards" from individual actors, to a shared socially constructed reality comes at a cost … the method through which leadership can be researched and data collected has to be reconsidered'. Nevertheless, I succumbed to the 'challenging difficulties' referred to by Shondrick et al. (2010, p. 961):

> dynamic, distributed, and diffuse leadership activities not only complicate the use of ILTs[2] in guiding the perceptions and behavior of organizational members, they create challenging difficulties for leadership researchers who rely on retrospective questionnaires to capture leadership processes. Specifically, typical ILTs (and most current leadership measures) reflect the assumption that leadership is portrayed by a single individual operating in a stable hierarchical structure; they are not geared to assessing more micro-level leadership events or the collaboration of multiple individuals in leadership processes.

Yet – and this is the second cause of the discrepancy referred to above – even if a more 'radical' research design (such as the discourse analytical approach that applied linguists Choi and Schnurr (2014), cited in Chapter 3, used to capture 'leadership … performed at the micro-level of interaction') had been considered, the limited funding available for the studies would have precluded it, just as it precluded the kinds of anthropologically-oriented, or other more imaginatively designed, studies that Trowler (1998, p. 118) quite rightly argues are needed to reveal 'practical consciousness: that which actors know but cannot necessarily put into words about how to "go on" in the many contexts in which they operate', and for which purpose questionnaires and interviews have limited capacity. The leadership that was 'captured', and that is examined in the chapters that follow, was thus conveyed through the accounts of, and predominantly defined and identified by, participants who reflected upon their own, and others', actions and emotional and attitudinal responses to those actions. How it was 'captured' in each study – largely through prompting participants' episodic memory[3] recall – is outlined below.

Study 1: Leading professors: Professorial academic leadership as it is perceived by 'the led'

Funded by an organisation whose remit and mission are centred on developing and improving leadership in the UK's higher education sector – the Leadership Foundation for Higher Education – this study was focused on a very specific category of such leadership: *academic* leadership provided by the professoriate. In the light of the lack of conceptual clarity associated with academic leadership, discussed in Chapter 3, the research project (whose title, for simplicity, I abbreviate throughout the book to the *Leading professors* project) was prompted, in part, by a desire to explore and examine how academic leadership was both interpreted and perceived to be being enacted.

The educational leadership and management field is dominated by examination and analyses of leaders and managers and their perspectives and experiences. Leaving aside consideration of critical perspectives that undermine such pre-specification of leaders and 'followers', this leaves an entire constituency – those on the receiving end of leadership – on the sidelines, under-researched, so I was keen for the *Leading professors* project to make a contribution towards redressing this imbalance. To this end, the study focused on the perspectives of those for whom professors, as academic leaders, might reasonably be expected to provide leadership, and who therefore represent 'the led'.[4] Whilst in some cases 'the led' (in relation to professorial leadership) may include secretarial, ancillary and technical support staff, the limited resources available for this project necessitated a narrow focus – on three non-professorial constituencies: academics, researchers (those employed solely or principally to undertake research) and university teachers (those employed on teaching-only contracts, or as teaching fellows).

The research project was carried out over one year, beginning April 2011, by a research team of three,[5] led by me. The study was designed to address the following research questions:

- What is the nature and extent of professorial academic leadership received by non-professorial academics, researchers and university teachers – what might/does it look like in practice?
- To what extent, and in what ways, does this non-professorial constituency consider itself to be receiving the academic leadership that it: a) wants, b) expects, or c) needs from professors?
- To what extent, and in what ways, are professors expected to provide academic leadership to junior colleagues?
- What are the perceived strengths and weaknesses of any such academic leadership – what, if any, models of good practice emerge?
- What factors facilitate or impede the nature and extent of professorial academic leadership?
- What is the perceived impact on their junior colleagues' working lives of professors' academic leadership enactment?

Data collection

Answers to these questions were sought by two methods of data collection – questionnaires and one-to-one interviews.

The questionnaire

To encourage participation, the questionnaire was designed to be able to be completed within ten minutes (if the respondent chose not to add comments). It was piloted on five colleagues representing three different subjects, and revisions in line with the pilot sample's responses and recommendations included the rewording of several items and the inclusion of examples aimed at providing guidance to respondents. Neither the length nor the format of the questionnaire was identified by the pilot sample as problematic. On the basis of its facility for reaching large numbers of intended respondents with relative ease, and for analysing data as they are received, an online questionnaire format was used, which was accessible via a link in an email message sent to potential respondents.

The questionnaire incorporated forty items, arranged in categories relating to:

- respondents' biographical information and information on their institutions' policy and practice in relation to professorial leadership (an example of an item presented within this category is: *Does your department operate a formal system of professorial mentoring [i.e. whereby professors have formal responsibility for facilitating and supporting the academic development of non-professorial colleagues]?*);
- perspectives on professors' role and responsibilities (an example of an item presented within this category is: *Should professors be expected to sustain a steady stream of research income?*); and
- respondents' evaluations of their experiences of professors and professorial leadership (an example of an item presented within this category is: *How often [in your current post or a previous one] have you experienced professorial leadership or mentoring that you would describe as 'excellent' or 'exemplary'?*).[6]

Other than the few of them that sought factual information, most items required respondents to indicate their opinion by selecting from a set of four- or five-point Likert scale options (e.g. ranging from 'often' to 'never', or from 'definitely agree' to 'definitely disagree'), but there were also open-ended items, offering the opportunity to add relevant comments, at seven points in the questionnaire.

The sample

A significant challenge was the perennial one facing researchers who use questionnaires: how to secure a good response rate (that would provide at least a *broadly* representative sample in relation to, *inter alia*: subject/discipline, career stage, job role/title and institution type). Publicising the project and distributing the questionnaire link via two learned society email distribution lists[7] (those of the Society for Research into Higher Education and the British Educational Leadership, Management and Administration Society) generated around 300 responses, but, reflecting these societies' respective memberships, responses mainly represented the educational research community, rather than the wider range of disciplines and subjects we had hoped for. Finding that, one month after 'launching' the questionnaire our target response total of around 1,200 was still far from being met, we adopted a new respondent recruitment strategy: 'targeted personalised requests', whereby requests for participation were emailed to 'targeted' individuals who were selected from staff lists on university department web pages.

'Targeted' is perhaps the wrong term to apply, since no individual was targeted personally; rather, specific universities were first selected in a non-systematic manner, on the basis of their representing one or both of geographical location (i.e. to ensure representation of the four UK nations), or institution type (e.g. pre- or post-1992 university, or ancient university, or specialist institution). Once the university's website was accessed, one or more of its departments were selected in a similarly non-systematic manner (though as it became evident that specific subjects were under-represented in the responses, departments were then often selected on the basis of potential for redressing the imbalance). Other practical factors were influential on the selection of a specific department or centre, such as the ease with which individuals' email addresses could be accessed and copied. The relatively greater representation of pre-1992 than of post-1992 universities amongst the questionnaire sample (not only in the *Leading professors* study, but also in studies 2 and 3) was largely due to our finding post-1992 institutions' websites generally less user-friendly and informative, for our purposes, than those of pre-1992 institutions – this problem was very similar to, and had the same consequence of, that reported by Bryson and Barnes (2000, p. 154): 'As we were unable to obtain staff addresses in much fewer post 92 HEIs than we would have wished, this group is under-represented in the sample.'

Once a department had been selected, all or most of its members listed as non-professorial academics, researchers or teachers were emailed a message that addressed each recipient by name, to encourage participation. Though laborious, this fairly automatic process – which was slotted into spare moments when a diversion from other work was welcomed – was used to generate around 40–60 personalised email messages per day, targeting an estimated total of 5,000 recipients. The process yielded an estimated total response rate of around 25–35 per cent (with variations to this estimate often depending on the targeted subject or discipline), increasing the overall number of responses and allowing us to exercise a degree of control over the balance of subjects and institutions represented. By the end of the project 1,223 largely complete responses had been received, which included a small proportion (<1 per cent) of missing responses to some questionnaire items. The seven open-ended items that invited comments yielded the responses indicated in Table 4.1.

Based on responses to an optional item asking for contact details (from respondents who indicated their willingness to participate in follow-up interviews), it is evident that at least ninety-four UK institutions were represented in the responses. Over 60 per cent (66.1 per cent) of respondents affiliated themselves with pre-1992 institutions and 33.5 per cent with post-1992 universities (0.3 per cent failed to respond to the item asking respondents to indicate whether they were employed at a pre- or a post-1992 institution). All four UK nations were represented by these universities, and 48.3 per cent of respondents identified themselves as males and 51.3 per cent as females (0.7 per cent failed to indicate their gender).

Respondents were asked to select which subject they represented from a list of the sixty-seven subject categories used in the 2008 research assessment

Table 4.1 Numbers and broad foci of respondent comments generated by open-ended questionnaire items (study 1, *Leading professors* project)

Open-ended item no.	Intended broad focus of comment (as implied by the item's location in the questionnaire)	No. of comments
1	Views on what a professor is – what the title connotes or implies	237
2	Experience of or views on institutional formal mentoring systems	298
3	Experience of or views on professors as mentors	187
4	Seeking professorial advice: experience and views	313
5	Experience of help and advice sought or received from professors	253
6	The respondent's career aspirations	458
7	Views on the professionalism of departmental professorial colleagues	461

exercise (RAE[8]). Every one of these subjects is represented in the responses, with the highest number of responses inevitably coming from education, where the research team was well known (Table 4.2 identifies those subjects represented by at least ten respondents). Business and management respondents were deliberately targeted with a view to yielding enough responses to examine whether or not this constituency – one that specialises in management and leadership expertise – was distinct in its pattern of responses: effectively, whether it practises what it preaches. It is worth adding that in all cases where the respondent selected 'other' rather than one of the sixty-seven RAE-related subjects listed, her/his subject (where the respondent specified it) did in fact fall into one of the listed sixty-seven subject categories. In terms of job role, academics constituted the largest constituency (74.2 per cent of respondents), followed by researchers (14.8 per cent) and then university teachers (3.7 per cent). A further 8.3 per cent of respondents failed to indicate their job role.

The interviews

Phase 2 of the study involved follow-up interviews with fifty of the 336 questionnaire respondents who volunteered to be interviewed. This sub-sample was selected on the basis of providing representation of a range of variables, including: professional role/generic job category (i.e. academic, researcher or teacher); gender; seniority; mission group of employing institution (i.e. pre- or post-92); discipline and subject; and geographical location. Based upon indicative questionnaire responses, interviewee sample selection was also aimed at achieving representation of a range of reported attitudes, perceptions and perspectives that were relevant to the study's focus.

By uncovering people's attitudes and emotional responses to experiences and situations that they recounted, interviews were intended to delve deeper into the factors underlying the perspectives and views implied by the questionnaire responses. Most interviews were conducted face-to-face, usually in the interviewee's university office, but occasionally in a seminar room or campus coffee shop. A minority were conducted by telephone. The average interview duration was sixty-five minutes; the shortest lasted twenty-five minutes and the longest eighty minutes. Interviews were audio-recorded (with interviewees' permission) and the recordings were transcribed to facilitate analysis.

A loose schedule afforded the interviewers the flexibility of discussing issues raised by interviewees that had the potential to address one or more research questions in depth. This flexibility (which was a feature not only of study 1, but

Table 4.2 Respondent distribution by subject for subjects represented by at least ten respondents

Respondent's selected subject	Respondent selections	
	Frequency	*%*
Education	220	18.0
Business and management studies	100	8.2
Biological sciences	63	5.2
History	48	3.9
Law	42	3.4
Computer science and informatics	35	2.9
Psychology	32	2.6
English language and literature	30	2.5
Epidemiology and public health	25	2.0
Archaeology	23	1.9
Architecture and the built environment	23	1.9
Sociology	23	1.9
Politics and international studies	22	1.8
Accounting and finance	21	1.7
Economics and econometrics	21	1.7
Nursing and midwifery	21	1.7
Earth systems and environmental sciences	19	1.6
French	19	1.6
Geography and environmental studies	19	1.6
Physics	19	1.6
Health services research	18	1.5
Mechanical, aeronautical and manufacturing engineering	16	1.3
Art and design	15	1.2
Communication, cultural and media studies	15	1.2
Electrical and electronic engineering	15	1.2
Chemistry	14	1.1
Social work and social policy and administration	13	1.1
Applied mathematics	12	1.0
Linguistics	12	1.0
Allied health professionals and studies	10	0.8
Anthropology	10	0.8
Theology, divinity and religious studies	10	0.8
Other and fewer than ten respondents per subject	232	19.0
Missing	6	0.5
Total	**1,223**	**100.0**

also of studies 2 and 3), along with some interviewees' time constraints, resulted in some disparity in topic coverage. It was impossible to ensure that every interview addressed every component of every research question – this did indeed occur in some cases, but in other cases the interviewer took the decision to focus more narrowly on what emerged from the two-way conversation. This somewhat uneven coverage of issues makes it very difficult to quantify or otherwise indicate the weight of some of the evidence (incorporated into the chapters in Parts Two and Three) of perceptions or attitudes.

Whilst the interview conversations were prompted by questions posed by the interviewers, interviewees were encouraged to speak expansively, rather than to feel obliged to offer short and concise responses to questions. The data gathered represented a combination (which varied from interviewee to interviewee) of views, perspectives and opinion, factual information, and threads of what may broadly be considered narrative – applying Clark's (2010, p. 94) interpretation: 'Narrative requires four constituents to even be considered as narrative: agentivity, linearity (sequential order), sensitivity to canon and context, and a specific perspective or set of perspectives.'

Data analysis

Analysis of quantitative questionnaire data was effected by the online questionnaire system, generating mainly descriptive statistics.[9] Qualitative data – both from open-ended questionnaire responses and from interviews – were analysed manually, through an incrementally reductive process from which key themes (relevant to the research objectives and questions) emerged that illuminated people's experiences of professorial academic leadership and related issues, and their emotions and attitudes and their bases and perceived effects on people's working and personal lives. The process of interview data analysis was inductive and involved several levels of coding, each of which related to a specific research question; the research questions – each taken in turn – were the starting points for analysis. First level coding simply identified data that were relevant to the selected research question. Subsequent levels of coding were directed towards identifying and/or considering: patterns, similarities and atypical cases; the bases of commonality, disparity and atypicality; potential interpretation of and/or explanation for incongruence and correlation; theoretical perspectives that provide universally applicable and hence general, rather than specific, explanations for why or how something appears to have occurred.

Study 2: Professorial academic leadership in turbulent times: The professoriate's perspective

Like the *Leading professors* study, study 2 was of one year's duration (2012–13), and involved three researchers.[10] Also funded by the Leadership Foundation for Higher Education, it was intended to follow up, and augment the findings of, the *Leading professors* project by presenting the 'other side of the coin' perspective – that of professors – on professorial academic leadership. The study was designed to address the following research questions:

- What is the nature and extent of academic leadership currently practised by the UK-based professoriate – what are its key strengths and weaknesses?
- What factors do professors identify as facilitators of and impediments to their capacity and willingness to provide (effective) academic leadership?
- What makes a 'leading' professor?
- How do professors envisage academic leadership's evolving in response to changes to the economic and political context?
- To what extent, and in what ways, does the professoriate's perspective on the issues identified in the above research questions correlate with non-professorial perspectives, and what accounts for any discrepancies?

Study 2's design broadly replicates that of the *Leading professors* study in relation to data collection, sample selection and recruitment approaches, and approaches to data analysis. Any deviation from that broad design and method is indicated below.

The questionnaire

To encourage participation, we designed a questionnaire that – representing a reduction by three minutes of the time estimated for completing the study 1 questionnaire – we expected could be completed within seven minutes (excluding time required for leaving comments). In the case of study 2, it was individuals indicated on web pages as holding the title 'professor' who were the targeted respondents and who were emailed participation requests. Emeritus professors were generally excluded.

The questionnaire incorporated almost twenty main items, arranged in categories relating to:

- Perceptions of professors that had originally been expressed by non-professorial participants in the *Leading professors* project. (Items within this category were presented in the form of selected comments made by study 1 questionnaire respondents, such as: *Generally, professors are promoted on the basis of their research and are not interested in leadership,* and *A professor should help junior academic colleagues to develop their own careers in both teaching and research.* Study 2 respondents – all of who were believed to be professors – were asked to indicate the extent of their agreement or disagreement with each statement);

- Academic leadership – the concept and how important it was considered;
- The purpose of professors;
- Professors' behaviour;
- Hindrances to carrying out the professorial role;
- The respondent's morale level; and
- The respondent's biographical information.

Most items required respondents to select from a set of four- or five-point Likert scale options (e.g. ranging from 'often' to 'never', or from 'definitely agree' to 'definitely disagree'). As with study 1, open-ended items (which read: 'We invite you to add further relevant comments in the space below') allowed respondents to leave comments.

The questionnaire yielded 1,268 largely complete responses, amongst which was a small proportion (<1 per cent) of missing responses to some items. The five open-ended items that invited comments yielded the responses indicated in Table 4.3.

Table 4.3 Numbers and broad foci of respondent comments generated by open-ended questionnaire items (study 2, *Professorial academic leadership in turbulent times* project)

Open-ended item no.	Intended broad focus of comment (as implied by the item's location in the questionnaire)	No. of comments
1	The respondent's definition/interpretation of academic leadership	363
2	Perceptions of and perspectives on the purpose of professors	240
3	Features of 'ideal' professorial academic leadership practice and the extent to which respondents' actual professorial practice matches up to their ideals	179
4	Impediments to the respondent's capacity to provide academic leadership	332
5	The respondent's current morale level	276

From responses to an optional item asking for contact details, it is evident that at least sixty-four British higher education institutions were represented in the responses. Pre-1992 institutions were represented by 84.8 per cent of respondents and 15.2 per cent affiliated themselves with post-1992 universities. Institutions in all four UK nations were represented. 71.1 per cent of respondents identified themselves as male and 27.3 per cent as female (1.6 per cent failed to indicate their gender[11]).

From the 394 respondents who volunteered to be interviewed forty-two were selected with the aim of representing a wide range of attitudes, perceptions and perspectives relating to the study's focus, as implied by questionnaire responses. Interviews were conducted in the same manner and under the same conditions as applied to the *Leading professors* study. Except for one telephone interview, all were conducted face-to-face.

It is important to identify a methodological weakness of studies 2 and 3: both unfortunately relied upon what was undoubtedly a sample that was skewed towards relatively positive attitudes towards the notion of professorial academic leaders – that professors should demonstrate academic leadership of some form – and receptivity towards engaging in such leadership activity, however it may be defined. Since study 1 had uncovered accounts and reports of professors who were variously perceived as reluctant or inadequate academic leaders, we were keen to include amongst the study 2 and 3 interview samples professors who were so-represented. Yet the data suggest that not only did very few such professors participate as questionnaire respondents, but they also failed to volunteer as interviewees. This imbalance made for an interview sample that represented itself, albeit to varying degrees, as broadly pro-professorial academic leadership.

Study 3: Leadership preparation and development for UK-based university professors

The purpose of this study – funded by the British Educational Management, Administration and Leadership Society (BELMAS) – was to investigate an issue to emerge in the findings of study 1, the *Leading professors* study: the evident lack of preparation and development for the professorial role. Study 3's objectives were to examine the extent and nature both of a perceived need for, and any provision of, leadership preparation for university professors, with a view to identifying lacunae and shortcomings, as well as examples of good practice. The following research questions shaped the research design and method:

- What level and quality of preparation – if any – for their various leadership roles is available to university professors?
- What lacunae and shortcomings exist, and with what consequences?
- What – if any – models of good practice (of professorial leadership preparation) exist, and what are the bases of their effectiveness?

Opportunistically, data collection was able to be merged with study 2's data collection, since the timing of the two studies overlapped, so, to avoid respondent fatigue, a dual-purpose questionnaire was designed. Not only did studies 2 and 3 share a common questionnaire and questionnaire sample, the doubling-up also extended to the interview phase; study 3 used a sub-sample (20) of study 2's interviewee sample. The distinction between the two studies was maintained by the specific content of the data sought; whilst biographical data were shared by both studies 2 and 3, specific questionnaire items were designed to service each study.

The following five questionnaire items were directed at addressing study 3's research questions:

- During your career as an academic, to what extent – if at all – have you seen any change to the professorial role and to expectations placed on professors?
- Since becoming a professor, have you ever felt the need to change any aspect of your practice to meet other people's expectations?
- Do you understand what your institution requires of you as a professor (i.e. are its expectations of its professors in general – or of you specifically – clearly articulated)?
- Do you feel that, in your earliest days as a professor, you were adequately prepared for taking on the professorial role?
- Has your current institution done all that you would want or need it to do to prepare you for your professorial role in that institution?

In relation to each question a Likert scale of responses was offered, which included the response: 'not sure/difficult to answer'. These five questions were grouped to form (within the dual-study-serving questionnaire) one section, labelled *Expectations*, at the end of which was an open-ended item inviting comments.

Within the interviews that served both studies 2 and 3, the sub-sample of twenty study 3 interviewees, in addition to being asked to discuss issues relevant to study 2, were asked to discuss in more depth issues relating to the focus of study 3, expanding on their responses to the five questionnaire items listed above. Thus two distinct datasets were generated from the interviews with professors: one serving study 2 and one serving study 3. This was achieved quite easily because I was the sole researcher for study 3 (and therefore solely responsible for gathering all data), yet I shared the interviewing for study 2 with a co-investigator, with whom it was agreed that I would supplement the study 2 interview schedule with coverage of study 3's focus, in the interviews that I undertook. The information provided for questionnaire respondents and interviewees acknowledged the funders both of study 2 and study 3, and made reference to the studies' combined foci.

In this book I refer to this study by the abbreviated title: the *Professorial leadership preparation and development study.*

Study 4: A scoping study of the origins and history of university professors and professorship in the UK

Funded by the Society for Research into Higher Education (SRHE), study 4 was a library-based one that addressed the following research questions:

1. What are the origins of professorship and the professoriate in the UK?
   a. When and where was the title 'professor' first used?

2. What purposes or roles were the earliest professors expected to carry out?
   a. What was the nature of their work?

3. What is the relationship between the work of early professors and scientific, epistemological, societal, and political development?
   a. To what extent (if at all) – and in what ways – have these developments (directly or indirectly) influenced, or been influenced by, professors?

4. In what ways, and with what consequences, has professorship evolved over the centuries?

During the course of carrying out studies 1–3, I had found myself pondering increasingly frequently over several of these questions. In particular, I began to realise that they – or, rather, the answers to them – were key to tracing the development and continued evolution of the professoriate, for in order to examine to what extent and in what ways professorship has changed, it is essential to understand what it looked like before any 'change' occurred. In the absence of any readily available reliable historical database on professors and professorship, study 4 was intended to allow me to explore something of how professorship used to look, by tapping into a small selection of relevant historical texts.

This was a one-year project that began in April 2016. It was small in scale: a scoping study, as its full title conveys, and for which a very limited budget was available. The review of sources followed recommendations from librarians at the British Library, and included consulting the *Oxford English Dictionary* for relevant entries, such as 'professor' and 'regius', and *State Papers Online*, whose database, I was advised, was likely to include information on the creation and appointments of regius professors from Tudor times onwards, whose names – together with those appearing in lists of professorial appointments at Oxford and Cambridge – could then be searched for in the *Dictionary of National Biography*.

This book draws to a limited extent upon study 4's findings. They feature noticeably in Chapter 1, otherwise they are peppered very lightly here and there, wherever I felt they might enhance the discussion without providing an unwelcome distraction.

Final remarks

From those interested in the kind of information presented in this chapter – along with those who consider such information essential to evaluating the research and its findings – there will undoubtedly be complaints that key information has been omitted, such as copies of the questionnaires, or of the interview schedules, and the questionnaire-generated data in its entirety, as well as more details on the samples. These would be justifiable complaints, but this book's word limit – agreed in advance with the publishers – would be exceeded if such information were included without making room for it by cutting the content of other chapters. Whilst this explanation may provoke protestations that this or that chapter is far too long in any case, I am aware, through long experience, that one cannot please everyone. So I have decided that this chapter will have to suffice as it stands: as an outline, rather than a comprehensive account, of how the research was carried out, and why. I have chosen to expend the word allowance on privileging two complementary features of this book that are essential to its contribution to augmenting the knowledge base on academic working life: giving a voice to those whose working lives are depicted here, and developing theoretical perspectives that help explain their articulations.

Notes

1   Where required (i.e. for studies 1–3, which involved human research subjects) ethical approval was granted by the research ethics committee of the University of Leeds's Faculty of Education, Social Sciences and Law (within which I was employed at the time of carrying out these studies).

2   Implicit leadership theories – explained in Chapter 7.

3   I apply Shondrick et al.'s (2010, p. 967) explanation: 'episodic memory involves explicit knowledge about context-dependent events which are personally experienced'.

4   My reference to 'the led' – which I accept runs counter to the criticism I present in Chapter 3 of pre-specification of leaders and followers – must be considered in the light of the discussion I present at the end of that chapter, in which I make the case for a dual-language and -terminology approach to analysing leadership, in order to engage 'lay' readers and report faithfully research findings that do not reflect a critical leadership perspective. Within analyses and examinations of leaders and/ or leadership roles I use the term 'the led' as a concise, generic label for those who do not hold the officially recognised leadership role being analysed/examined and are subject to the effects and impact of its enactment. I select it in preference to the more commonly used 'follower' because it implies a lesser degree of choice and agency in the relationality of leadership. As is evident in the presentation of my own definitions of leadership and leaders in Chapter 3, I fully accept Shamir's (2009, p. xvii) point that 'Everyone should be regarded as both a leader and a follower' – though my conceptualisation is based upon recognition that, at the micro-level, leader and 'led' actions are potentially transient and that status of leader and led potentially changes hands repeatedly and frequently within any one interactional event. Nevertheless, the concept of leadership is predicated on acceptance that it is a relational position – without someone to lead, the term would be redundant – and so, without undermining my conceptualisation of basic units of leadership activity, I also use the label 'the led' in the context of discussion or analyses of leadership *through designated, recognised or ascribed roles*, including professorship, principally to make a distinction on the basis of leadership relationality between one (or more) holding a specific leadership role (in the context of this book, arguably, professors) and those (non-professorial academics) who are not the holders of this *very same*, *specific* recognised leadership role.

5   Working with me were Matt Homer and Steven Rayner, whose contributions to the research as co-investigators are acknowledged on page viii.

6   All examples of items are presented verbatim as they appeared in the questionnaire.

7   Indirect access was granted to these email distribution lists; the societies distributed participation requests on our behalf.

8   The Research Assessment Exercise (RAE) was the precursor to what is, at the time of writing, known as the Research Excellence Framework (REF): the mechanism used in the UK for assessing the quality of research carried out by academics in each university that chooses to be entered into the mechanism, in order to be assessed for an allocation of government funding.

9   Bristol Online Surveys, which was used in all of the studies that gathered data by questionnaire, also offers the facility to generate inferential statistics.

10 Working with me were Matt Homer and Justine Mercer, whose contributions to the research as co-investigators are acknowledged on page viii.

11 Regrettably, we neglected – as one anonymous questionnaire respondent politely pointed out – to offer a third option, 'other', in the range of available responses to the item relating to respondents' gender.

Part Two

The Perspectives of 'The Led'

5

'Leading' Professors: Positive Perceptions of Professorial Academic Leadership

What makes a 'leading' professor? The answer, of course, depends on several considerations, one of which is how 'leading' is interpreted. As an adjective, it can denote 'leading' in the sense of distinction or exceptionality in relation to achievement: being prominent in the field. As a present participle it denotes engagement in the 'act' of leading – but this interpretation poses its own problems, for, as I discuss in Chapter 3, 'leading' as a verb, along with its nominative derivatives (leader and leadership), are contested concepts, and academic leadership in particular is unclearly defined. In a world where yesterday's guru may be relegated to being today's dinosaur, and today's cerebrally challenged charlatan reinvented as tomorrow's great luminary, what makes for a 'leading' professor can be as much about the currency of fads, fashions and the flexibility with which these are embraced and discarded, as about enduring excellence and timeless values. Moreover, reflecting the dynamic contextual backdrop of the twenty-first-century academy, whose neoliberal-inspired policies and development are widely considered to have changed the nature – even, as some analysts argue, impoverished the quality of – academic working life over the last two decades,[1] expectations of professors and of the kinds of activities or roles that are associated with professorship vary considerably. Such variation typically reflects stakeholder constituency membership, so that, for example, what a university's senior managers and administrators expect of its professors may be misaligned with the professoriate's own expectations of its role and purpose.

This chapter examines the perspective of one particular constituency with an interest in the nature and quality of professorial academic leadership: those on the receiving end of it. This constituency – 'the led' (as I explain the label in Chapter 3) – represents a wide range of academic experience, seniority and status, and the *Leading professors* interviewee sample was selected to include such a broad spread of non-professorial academics, from post-doctoral fellows and research assistants, to principal research fellows and readers. Some of these were explicitly asked: What makes for a leading professor?, while others addressed the question implicitly, or skirted around it in the accounts they gave. The overall picture to emerge was of a heterogeneous professoriate, summed up by a remark from one interviewee: 'I've seen the gamut of academic behaviour expressed by professorial colleagues, from the ... y'know, behaviour which I think has been impeccable, to behaviour which I think has been extremely bad.' Some interviewees highlighted their positive perceptions, while others focused predominantly on their negative experiences, and many conveyed varied experiences that made for a more balanced perspective.

Leaving the negativity for the next chapter (6), this chapter focuses on the positive perceptions, revealing the beneficial influence or impact that professors can have on the working lives and careers of their junior colleagues – whose voices take centre stage here.

Delineating the features of 'leading' professorship

At the request of a book editor, elsewhere (Evans, 2015b) I have synthesised the findings from the *Leading professors* study (whose design and methods are outlined in Chapter 4) into the compilation of the characteristics of what, from the perspective of 'the led', is an 'ideal' professor. Such a person typically:

- is distinguished in terms of scholarship, research output and intellectuality;
- is manifestly hardworking and productive;
- is internationally recognised on the basis of her/his outstanding research output;
- is agreeable, affable and relates well to others;
- is approachable and readily available to junior colleagues and students;
- is generous with her/his time and willingly supports others by offering advice, guidance and mentoring;
- is altruistically collegial;
- has a facilitative approach to leading and guiding others;
- behaves as if s/he considers it as much her/his responsibility to contribute to the professional and career development of others as to focus on her/his own career development and advancement;
- is challenging, stimulating and thought-provoking;
- is inspirational as an exemplar of a leading researcher/scholar;

- does not manifest conceit or arrogance; and
- exemplifies highly professional and ethical behaviour.

The compilation of this 'ideal' profile[2] drew upon data in the form of comments expressed in interviews, such as those of a senior STEMM academic:

> I always used to say, 'If a professor has not got time to conduct an appraisal interview with a junior member of staff, then he shouldn't be a professor.' ... Having time for junior members of staff and supporting them in developing their careers, I think's extremely important. That's what I think the ideal professor would be. (*Alan, chemistry reader, pre-1992 university*)

The compilation also drew upon questionnaire data: both descriptive statistics – such as the unequivocal agreement of 93.4 per cent of questionnaire respondents that 'a professor should demonstrate outstanding expertise in her/his discipline/subject' – and respondents' written comments, such as:

> A professor should help his/her junior academic colleagues to develop their own careers in both teaching and research.

> A professor should act as a mentor for other colleagues. I would expect a professor to be less interested in developing their own career and more interested in 'giving back' to the academic community, which means providing inspiration, leadership and support to other staff and colleagues.

> One of the softer skills a professor must have is 'approachability'. There's no point in having a leading academic in your institution if younger members of the staff and student body cannot go to them and discuss research/career options.

Representing a model of desirable professorial academic leadership, the characteristics of the archetypical 'leading' professor, listed above, convey what my research revealed academics and researchers generally to want from their most senior colleagues. But ideal types reflect wishful thinking; they are neither intended nor expected to represent 'reality'. Many research participants – particularly the more senior ones – recognised this gap between 'ideal' and 'actual'; for the most part, the more junior and less experienced the academic, the more demanding appeared her/his expectations of professors, while more realistic expectations tended to be held by more senior and/or longer-serving academics. The latter had lived through what many of them identified as sustained incremental changes to academic working life, reflecting top-down imposed shifts in perspectives on the purpose of higher education and universities' missions and priorities. This awareness of a shifting policy context often underpinned understanding of how the nature of professorship had evolved, and was continuing to evolve (see Evans, 2015a), and this understanding often made for rather nuanced perspectives that reflected a degree of tolerance for professors who were manifestly struggling to adapt to demands and expectations which had not been in place when they had been appointed. Yet, with fewer experiences of working with professors – and often with much of their limited interaction (typically as doctoral students) with professors reported as positive experiences – early career academics tended to express more *overall* satisfaction with the professoriate than did veteran and senior academics, whose longer careers and greater seniority were likely to have afforded them insight into the kinds of professorial micro-politics and power games (see, for example, Lumby, 2015) that often fail to register on junior academics' radars.

Perspectives on professorial academic leadership emerged through interview conversations. Some were woven into partial storylines, as interviewees related specific circumstances or sequences of incidents that led up to this or that professor's demonstration of what was considered effective academic leadership. In other cases successive brief illustrative descriptions – snapshots – were offered, while other perspectives were articulated less colourfully, as lists of depersonalised 'leading' professorship characteristics. Cutting across their contextually- and experientially-determined diversity, anecdotes, vignettes and viewpoints converged to delineate two essential broad features of 'leading' professorship: *distinction* and *relationality*.

Distinction

Reflecting an interpretation of 'leading' as denoting prominence in the field, a 'leading' professor was perceived as someone who had earned the status associated with her or his being recognised as standing out from the 'crowd' (where 'the crowd' denotes the field's international academic community) on the basis of achievement (including performance, output and associated reputation) and expertise (including skills, knowledge and understanding) that in some way exceeds what is considered the norm. Such distinction was interpreted as essentially intellectual in nature; the principal basis of and justification for professorship was generally considered to be intellectual capacity demonstrated by intellectually based achievement. Questionnaire-generated data revealed a widely held view that 'leading' professors are demonstrably or manifestly cerebrally distinct from 'rank and file' academics, as illustrated by the following perspectives:

Professors should be appointed *solely* on the basis of their scholarly contribution, not their administrative position.

[Professors] should be concerned with scholarly activity – not herding cats.

I think the generally agreed baseline [for professorship] should be outstanding scholarship.

Professors should not be leading administrators or managers (implicit in the idea of citizenship with a community of academics); they should be leading intellectuals.

In interview conversations, too, intellectual distinction emerged as a principal indicator of professorialness. Education studies senior lecturer, William, for example, remarked:

I still see the key criterion for a professor is intellectual ability. So, the person who supervised me for my PhD – he wasn't a professor at the time, but he is *now* – you know, to put it naively, I thought he was clever! I thought that would be a good person to interact with.

A similar concern with professors' intellectual distinction was implicit in the comments of history lecturer François. His evident disappointment with a departmental professorial colleague was based on a perceived mismatch between the level of intellectuality he expected of a professor and that demonstrated by the colleague:

He came to the university as a scholar, but he just hasn't provided the kind of intellectual leadership that you'd expect from someone with a chair.

And François's explanation of his own reluctance to assess other departmental professors' right to hold the title of professor implies a perception that professorialness is tied up with intellectual or scholarly distinction, demonstrated by high quality research output:

It's very difficult for me to judge, honestly, the other professors because in most cases I simply haven't read their work. Some colleagues would actually say that they don't deserve to be professors, but, again, until I've read their stuff I couldn't say.

For some interviewees, the distinction of professors' intellectuality and intellectual achievements was interpreted and 'measured' comparatively – sometimes against the standards perceived as prevailing within the field in question, and sometimes against their (interviewees') own, self-assessed, ability and capacity. Principal lecturer in sociology, Ken, was effusive in his praise of 'one prof who I just thought was brilliant; I thought, intellectually, he was head and shoulders above the rest of them', while associate professor of linguistics,

Viktoria, used superlatives to describe a female professorial colleague with whom she remained in contact:

> Oh! She's just ... I mean, she is probably ... I mean, at least one of the three most well-published ... famous ... you know – in terms of, y'know, being 'up there' with her research. I mean her publication list is *endless* ... also, the ways in which she's brought the field forward, essentially. She's *the one*, I would say – but I'm biased. She's clearly among the top three in the field out there. ... I'll never be like her, but, you know, I'm trying hard! (laughs).

With this last sentence Viktoria highlighted a dimension of professorial intellectual distinction that many interviewees implicitly or explicitly identified: exemplariness. Some simply acknowledged the comparative aspect or potential of professors' intellectually based distinction, implying that it serves as a yardstick against which others may be measured. Other interviewees – along with several questionnaire respondents – highlighted the motivational qualities of such distinction. A research fellow in food sciences said of her professorial line manager: 'Scientifically, she's a role model. In terms of ... the science calibre, I would want to be like her. ... I think she's very, very bright.' Asked what makes a leading professor, another female research fellow (in education studies) responded: 'I think they should be good – what's that word? exemplars? – examples of ... to strive to be like ... maybe? ... like people who're ... worthy of respect ...', and an anonymous questionnaire respondent commented:

> Certain professors stand out as clear role models – initially they are the sort of professor you want to work *for*, then work *with*, and then they are the sort that you would like to *become*.

But, taken out of context, it is unclear in these last two comments precisely what it is about such professors that junior colleagues may wish to emulate – what may make them 'clear role models' or 'exemplars' or 'people who're worthy of respect'; for a professor's capacity for motivating junior colleagues may hang on much more than her or his intellectual distinction. Indeed, revealed as key to shaping junior academics' perceptions of professors was quite a different factor: relationality.

Relationality

By 'relationality' I mean people's capacity for relating, and the extent to which they relate, to others, and the nature of such relations and relationships – or, to paraphrase Cunliffe and Eriksen's (2011, p. 1430) succinct explanation of relational leadership: people's 'way of-being-in-relation-to-others', which encompasses 'the character, judgment and personal values of leaders rather than [leadership] practices or processes' (p. 1431). So interpreted, relationality appeared the paramount concern of the majority of the *Leading professors* research participants. Engineering reader Robert, for example, identified his former professorial head of department as one of a very few members of his department's professoriate who (had ever) demonstrated the kind of relationality that he (Robert) expected of professors:

> He was quite approachable; he was quite happy for me to ask him, and to chat about difficult issues which I had to deal with, and he was able to advise me about that, and I did find that effective.

Both the questionnaire- and interview-generated data revealed professors to be typically judged on the basis of their approachability and availability – both of which featured in many positive assessments of professors' relationality:

> She's got an open door policy, so whenever I've got any issues, when I've got questions, I'll just chat to her about it. … [W]ith other people you might feel you've got to write things down – with [*names the professor*] I just pop in. If she's not got a meeting I would say, 'Well, have you got a minute?' and I'd just go and discuss the issue with her. And that's the way it works. … I'm still a junior researcher, but if I'm in the middle of something and somebody walks through the door and says, 'I've got an idea', maybe they'll feel I don't want to talk about it right now. You *never* have that with her! (*Tamara, food science research fellow, pre-1992 university, speaking of her professorial line manager*)

> I have an extremely good relationship with Professor [X] … and he's been tremendous – absolutely tremendous! He's a fantastic, sort of, star at [this university] … er … and, internationally, certainly has a big name. And any time I want to, I can, sort of, pop in and chat about this and that and the other, and he's there. (*Oliver, staff development lecturer, pre-1992 university*)

As the following comments imply, professors' manifestations of professional altruism and collegiality were evidently greatly appreciated:

> A professor in another institution … took the time and trouble when I was still a relatively new academic to read my work and go through it very carefully. But that wasn't the end of it, because she went through it very carefully and said, 'Well, y'know, there's this, there's that, and there's the other; do this and that and the other', but she then said, 'and then send me the next draft'. And I think tea and cake came into it somewhere. (*Adrian, education studies senior lecturer, pre-1992 university*)

Three ... professors ... have given me exemplary support in the past. Two of these were head of department when I went through promotion and maternity leave. In the first case, my promotion to SL [senior lecturer] was initially turned down and the professor appealed the decision and won. In the second case, the professor was a model of good practice in supporting me through the various challenges maternity leave provided. Another professor ... has made it her business to mentor me through my career and has been a great source of advice and support. (*Anonymous questionnaire respondent*)

Many positive assessments of professors were expressed as gratitude for career-building- and development-focused help and support received – often in the form of *ad hoc*, unofficial or informal mentoring. Elaborating on his positive assessment of his professorial line manager, presented above, Oliver highlighted specific examples of this professor's support:

When I first arrived at [the university] it was on the sort of level of ... almost mentoring in terms of what I would like to do ... would I like to be on committees? ... what classes I would like to teach ... very hands-on; very relaxed: 'Come in, sit down – let's have a chat.' So there was no standoffishness. There was never any question – and this, I have to say, is unusual – there was never any question of a power imbalance ... I never felt like he was on a pedestal and I was a lowly, lowly academic. It was always very collegial ... very, very collegial. ... So, brilliant ... really ... and yet I know that that's probably pretty rare. (*Oliver, staff development lecturer, pre-1992 university*)

Yet, contrary to Oliver's conviction of its rarity, experiences of professorial academic leadership in the form of professional developmental- or acculturation-focused support or advice were reported by every one of the *Leading professors* interviewees. Whether such support and advice constitutes professorial mentoring is debatable. In Hill et al's (1989, p. 15) definition of mentoring as 'a communication relationship in which a senior person supports, tutors, guides and facilitates a junior person's career development', their use of the word 'relationship', with its connotation of sustained or repeated interaction, implicitly precludes the kinds of sporadic, infrequent or isolated exchanges that some interviewees included as illustrations of the nature of valued support or advice from professors. Austin (2002, p. 103) argues that 'socialization is an on-going process, not the result of occasional events'. Yet it is also a cumulative, incremental process, and whilst the *Leading professors* interviewees related many examples of mentoring – as defined above by Hill et al. – it seems too that, however fleeting or impromptu the encounter in which they were communicated, *all* isolated nuggets of professor-dispensed wisdom were generally snatched up voraciously, and assimilated into that sphere of the recipient's consciousness that drip-feeds her or his acculturation or socialisation into academic life. Disparity across the interviewee sample's related experiences reflects variation in the frequency with which such mentoring, support and advice evidently occurred, in the number of professors from whom (in each interviewee's case) it was received, and its perceived quality and nature.

A relatively small number of research participants referred to what were evidently multiple sources of professorial support or mentoring. Some of these – as implied in the following comments from anonymous questionnaire respondents – conveyed images of being nurtured within supportive, collegial environments, which in some cases were located in the wider disciplinary communities, beyond institutional boundaries:

> In relation to my research interests, all professors who I have had contact with have been very supportive and a good role model to aspire to.

> My experience in my current job has been great. I have ideal professorial leadership that I aspire to achieve if I become a professor.

> I have always considered the standard of mentoring and advice from Swansea University's economics professors to be excellent.[3]

But being nice to people does not equate to leadership. Nor does being a professor. So, whilst such manifestations of their relationality evidently endear professors to their junior colleagues, what – if any – aspects of academic leadership do they demonstrate?

Distinction and relationality with influence

Although many comments or narratives were prompted by the question, 'What makes (for) a leading professor?', the focus on leadership that it encouraged sometimes became diffused over the course of a protracted narrative, as interviewees related their experiences of professors whom, quite simply, they seemed to like or to whom they were grateful for having extended acts of kindness. Whether or not such acts constitute leadership depends not only on their nature but also on how leadership is interpreted or defined. Interviewee Clare implied a narrow interpretation that equates leadership with management through formal designated roles:

Interviewer: What makes a leading professor?
Clare: Someone who's extremely patient, and extremely responsible ... and ... y'know, very good at dealing with people. I mean, the human side of,

sort of, managing a department – a large group of people – is the most demanding side, really, because people are very difficult to deal with. So you do need, sort of, extraordinary patience and also a kind of firmness in dealing with difficult people, I think … that you can encounter.

Interviewer: And what about leading in the sense of being a key researcher in the field?

Clare: A different set of skills, really, I think. (*Clare, arts and humanities reader, pre-1992 university*)

It was evident from their written comments that several questionnaire respondents shared Clare's narrow interpretation, often using 'manager' and 'leader' interchangeably, or assuming that 'leadership' was confined to designated middle or senior management role incumbency – to some, references in the questionnaire to 'leader' seemed to denote the departmental head. Yet most comments implied an interpretation of academic leadership as multi-faceted and involving, *inter alia*, contribution to the professional development of others, and intellectual leadership through the pioneering of innovative influential research.

White et al. (2016) link leadership with formal and informal ties, or relations, between people, and the influence that these facilitate or effect. In clarifying what counts as leadership and what counts as other forms of influence, they distinguish between: 'instrumental ties (i.e. goal oriented) and expressive ties that primarily provide friendship and social support (i.e. the tie is considered to be an end in itself)'. They continue: 'We classify leadership influence ties as being instrumental in nature as they are goal oriented, however, informal relations may be instrumental or expressive in nature' (p. 283). My own interpretation (presented in Chapter 3) does not focus on goal-orientation; rather, it holds that the key determinant of whether a communicative exchange represents leadership is evidence of influence that effects a person's positional or directional realignment, shift or deviation, on the basis of its being perceived as representing a 'better way'. Whilst such evidence is elusive in some of the research participants' comments presented above, it was fairly plentiful within the research data as a whole, alluding to leadership that mainly focused on one or more of three overlapping dimensions of academic life: career development and trajectory; professional development; and acculturation within academic communities. In extended narratives many interviewees identified pivotal, career-shaping moments, and outlined the nature of the positive impact upon their lives that were attributed to one or more professors. Extracts from three such narratives – those of Nicole, Ken and David – collectively highlight the varied forms, nature and foci of effective professorial academic leadership as perceived by 'the led'.

Nicole's narrative

Nicole presented herself as having lived something of a charmed academic life, replete with support from a small pool of professors who seemed variously to have acted as sponsors, advisors and friends. She credited several of them with having been 'instrumental' in influencing some of the major decisions she had taken: 'I've been *really* lucky, and I think it's 'cos of the different work I've done, that, actually, some of the most instrumental professors I've worked with have not necessarily come from ... the university I've been at.' She spoke of a professor who had been 'instrumental in getting me into heritage ... moving me away from just looking at [names a specific field of research]', before then acknowledging the contribution of a second professor, who had taught her as an undergraduate – '[He] was amazing – he was brilliant! – he took me under his wing, so to speak' – who had first agreed to be her undergraduate dissertation supervisor, before prompting her to consider a higher degree course:

> [He said] 'I think you need to do an MA; I think this is where you should go. I think you'd be stupid not to. Here are the three places you have to apply [to]. Apply – see which places you get ... I'll write your reference, and I'll introduce you to the people beforehand, and let's see where it gets you.' And I got accepted to *all* of them, actually! (*Nicole, history and archaeology lecturer, post-1992 university*)

The shift in direction prompted by this professor's influence became evident in Nicole's appraisal of him:

> I wanted to go into [names a specific field] ... but it became very apparent that I wasn't very apt at remembering all the names for all the [relevant information]. ... I was better at the more theoretical ... sort of stuff than I was at the science. And he saw that, and instead of saying, 'Oh, you're a bit rubbish', he was very supportive and I did get a very good mark for my dissertation because of him. ... He's a good man; I like him a lot.

In total, Nicole identified five professors whom she credited with having supported her academic career and influenced its trajectory and direction, and she made passing reference to others who had been helpful in small, less significant ways. To her, it seemed, 'leading' professors were those whom she singled out as having effected a form of influence that was often interventionist in nature, involving support (both tangible and emotional) and direction; it is perhaps significant that, without prompting, she used the word 'instrumental' five times to describe the impact on her career attributed to three different professors. Her assessments of professors were based predominantly on consideration of their relationality – their personal qualities and social skills. She used summative descriptors such as: 'brilliant', 'a good man' and 'really lovely'. Peppered with phrases such as 'he took me under his wing', her narrative implies a perception of this professorial support and leadership as paternalistic or avuncular in nature (I choose the masculine forms of these adjectives since, apart from one, all the professors identified were male), and incorporating a kind of sponsorship – even an element of protectiveness – that had encouraged and galvanised her into making decisions that she admits having been unlikely to have made otherwise.

Supportiveness seems to have been a key determinant of what, to Nicole, makes for a 'leading' professor; her most enthusiastic appreciation was reserved for those whom she attributed with having pointed her in the right direction and given her a metaphorical leg-up in climbing the greasy pole that represents an academic career. Like many of the early career research participants, she seemed to define effective professorial academic leadership – or 'leading' professorship – from a rather egocentric perspective that was focused on her own career and professional development (though, to be fair, in many respects, such a narrow focus may have been prompted by the interview questions asked, and, moreover, is probably an inevitable consequence of Nicole's limited experience of working in academe and interacting with professors as colleagues). More senior and experienced academics, in contrast, tended to articulate wider perspectives on what makes for a 'leading' professor. One such perspective was offered by Ken.

Ken's narrative

Ken was a principal lecturer of sociology in a university that was one of the highest ranked within the post-1992 sector. He presented himself as an active researcher – 'though I say so myself, well published' – who complained of an excessively burdensome administrative workload that had significantly curtailed his research activity. After a long career, first as a schoolteacher, and then as an academic, at the time of his interview he was on the cusp of retirement. His narrative indicated a sound understanding of the higher education sector, the nature and bases of institutional and departmental micro-politics and power struggles, and the university as workplace; in colloquial terms, Ken was a seasoned and streetwise academic who had been around the block, and had extensive experience of interacting and working with professors as colleagues. He singled out one whose influence on his career had been pivotal:

At least one professor has had a *huge* influence on me … when I was at X [pre-1992] University. … I did my master's degree there when I was a relatively mature man – in my thirties – and it was, in many respects, a rather disappointing experience. But I had one prof who I just thought was brilliant. I thought, intellectually, he was head and shoulders above the rest of them … and in the end he persuaded me to take the direction I did in sociology. And then he employed me afterwards. And that was an astonishingly positive experience for me; I loved every minute of working there. (*Ken, principal lecturer of sociology, post-1992 university*)

Unlike Nicole, who – perhaps because she had never worked with them as institutional colleagues and been exposed to their foibles – had tended to convey relatively unqualified approbation of the professors who had helped guide her and shape her career, Ken evidently recognised flaws in his principal 'leading' professor:

I don't think he was a very good manager; he was actually a terrible manager. He was running a research programme that I was involved in – several big research grants, all running at the same time. But his policy was, effectively: leave it to you. You carry on with it; if you've got any problems you tell him. He'll do his best to support you *if* there are problems, but otherwise, you're in charge of your own destiny.

Asked to elaborate on the nature of this professor's contribution to his work and career, Ken highlighted its intellectual focus, within research leadership whose purpose was to enhance a key skill: writing for publication:

Er … partly intellectual … er … [he had] an *enormous* impact on me, intellectually. … He taught me to write. … The first thing I ever wrote for him, he came into my room when I'd finished the first draft and – I'm exaggerating when I say, 'He threw it at me'; he didn't – but he gave it me back and said, 'When are you going to learn to write about one thing?' And … I said, 'What am I doing wrong?' and he said, 'Well, there's a million ideas there. None of them are bad ideas, but you've got to write one paper, so you've got to learn the business of getting rid of all the ideas that aren't central to this paper. Pick a topic … pick what you're going to write about, you've got ten thousand words for this journal article … write ten thousand words. And all the rest of it you put into another folder – another file – and you say to yourself, "I can use that some other time". And that was great advice! And it's the same advice that I give to people that I work with now; y'know: you don't have to deal with everything right now.

Describing the nature of the professor's developmental-focused interventions, Ken admitted that the soundness of this professorial advice had failed to strike a chord until his draft article had been returned to him, rewritten: 'He took it away and re-wrote it. … And … it was *so* much better. I mean, I just had to accept this was so much better than what I did.'

The rewriting, as Ken explained, had not been an isolated gesture of support; rather, the mentoring had been sustained until it was no longer needed:

> I took it as: this is well-intentioned advice. So I wasn't resentful at all; we had a very, very good relationship – we got on very well; we shared a flat for two years. I wanted to learn. I mean, that's the short answer. I don't think I've got so much ego that I thought, he's wrong. I thought, if he's right, then I need to learn. And when he took it [the article] away and gave it back to me – rewritten – I could see why. … And I guess for, maybe six months, he slowly – I mean, I guess, basically, I improved – but he slowly did less and less in terms of redrafting my stuff, until, after a year or so, he never touched it; he just left it to me. And I found that to be a very, very positive experience. What it did for me was, when I came to this university – there, of course, as I've intimated, there was no real research culture – I had no fears about just getting on with it. Er … so I just wrote.

Yet, despite being indebted to a professor who had taken the time and trouble to help develop his skills, Ken articulated a perspective that was distinct amongst the *Leading professors* interviewee sample. He argued that mentoring should not be a *professorial* responsibility; rather, junior academics should take responsibility for their own development by pro-actively seeking out whatever information and advice they needed to know to hone their skills and carve out successful careers for themselves – they should be propelled principally by their own initiative. But whilst he clearly did not see it as predominantly or explicitly mentoring-focused, Ken's evident perspective on what makes a 'leading' professor emerged from the implications of several of his remarks. He was critical of what he saw as expectations that his institution's professoriate would undertake major management roles, and of the conflation of management with professorship. As his comment below indicates, he equated 'leading' professorship with academic distinction: the demonstration of scholarship that serves as a pointer to others, and a yardstick against which they may measure themselves and their progress:

> I see them [professors] as at the pinnacle of *academic* achievement, not *managerial* achievement. … Certainly at professorial level – no professor – at least at *our* institution – is going to be saying, 'Yes, I'll take on an admin role that's going to be the joy of my life'! … But I was actually reasonably happy to bear most of that [in order] for them [professors] to be the research figureheads that other people should aspire towards. Other people should say, 'Yeah, these guys have published these things; I now know where *I* should be going to reach that level.'

As far as Ken was concerned, the professoriate's key role within a university was professing: demonstrating prominence in relation to others on the basis of intellectual distinction, through research and scholarship. This association of intellectuality with 'leading' professorship was evident, to varying degrees, in all interviewees' narratives. For modern foreign languages lecturer David, it was central to what makes a 'leading' professor.

David's narrative

In his late thirties, David was an early career academic whose entire academic career, from undergraduate study through to employment, had been located in the UK's Russell Group. At the time of his interview he was six years into his first permanent lectureship.

David's perspective on 'leading' professorship is particularly interesting in the light of Ken's narrative. Ken evidently equated 'leading' professorship with intellectual distinction, and, mainly on this basis, challenged expectations that professors should assume not only mentoring, but also significant management, responsibilities. It is perhaps going too far to suggest that he (Ken) perceived distinction in relation to intellectual output as *incompatible* with the kinds of institutional citizenship and active collegiality that management and mentoring represent, but he did argue that it should take precedence over them in delineating professorship's key purpose. David's narrative, in contrast, implied an interpretation of 'leading' professorship as incorporating *both* intellectual distinction *and* citizenship-cum-collegiality – even if the latter involved heavy duty administrative roles.

Without stealing too much of Chapter 6's thunder, I encroach very slightly on its focus on unfavourable evaluations of professorial academic leadership by selecting some of David's negative comments. By reading of what he *dis*approves of – evident in the comment below – aspects of his perspective on 'leading' professorship begin to surface, conveying his expectation that professors should pull their weight by taking on administrative tasks, rather than resting on their intellectuality-based laurels:

> The more I've been here at [X University], the more, I suppose, that kind of happy-go-lucky, 'well-it-doesn't-really-matter' attitude has hardened a little bit into thinking, y'know, you guys [professors] are paid very, very well … . Internal reviews have formally recognised that the majority of, y'know, kind of, admin roles – often quite *big* main admin roles – are done by early to mid-career staff. There's a sentiment – I know it's shared, it isn't just me, it's the way things are –

that junior lecturers, teaching fellows, people on teaching- and admin-only contracts ... to some extent, senior lecturers ... do the majority of the work. ... And ... some professors are quite open – effectively saying, 'Well, y'know, we have earned our right to be in that position ... we're prestigious ... we need to be allowed to pump out the research.' (*David, modern foreign languages lecturer, pre-1992 university.*)

But, for David, it was not simply a readiness to take on their fair share of administrative responsibilities that marked out 'leading' professors; he associated such citizenship with the awareness and know-how that he considered integral to the kind of academic leadership that his department lacked:

You'll sometimes get some bizarre questions from the head of department – who's a professor – about the basics ... what are students doing in their first year core course? ... who runs this year 2 module in the department? ... . Y'know, *you're* the professor! Again, with the status, and the money and the responsibility – why don't you *know* this? Part of the reason you *don't* know this is because you don't have responsibility for it ... it's a self-fulfilling prophecy!

From David's perspective, as I signal above, being a 'leading' professor evidently involves much more than demonstrating the kind of altruistic collegiality and engagement that he implied was in short supply in his own department; a key indicator of a professor's quality was her/his standing as a researcher and scholar, derived from her/his output:

It's in the area of research where I, with the very *best* professors, can see the daylight I think one needs to see between where *I* am as a junior lecturer ... and the sort of work I'm producing ... and the sort of work that I think a professor should be putting out. ... The very best in the field put out work that you think: that's really something to go for; that's ... work that builds on thirty years of knowledge and expertise ... a breadth of reading that, as I say, by definition [on account of his age and limited experience], I *can't* have done.

It was demonstrable intellectual capacity, first and foremost – 'that's actually the heart of it for me' – that, to him, was most important:

It's the breadth of knowledge, there's also the incisive analysis ... er ... it's not necessarily funding capture – not necessarily having pots of cash; in some ways I'm suspicious of people who, kind of, repeatedly go for cash ... it's the *output*.

And, as many interviewees had done, he singled out as the embodiment of the core qualities of a 'leading' professor one whom he credited with having profoundly shaped his intellectual and career development: his former doctoral supervisor. Asked to try to pinpoint precisely what those qualities had been in the person of his supervisor, David responded:

> It was the elegance of his language, and it was the analytical insight, and it was making the material work ... and sheer breadth of cultural ... reference and cultural knowledge. ... I think he showed me really what poetry was for, and what it was about. ... And he was able to do absolutely convincing things with difficult material. And one of the questions that I had for myself and generally about the material, it was just rubbish! ... So he was extremely good at pointing me in the right direction, and, I think, striking a mix of letting me find things out for myself – that I think were genuine discoveries that I'd made for myself – and developing ideas that were actually his own, but that he'd sowed in my own mind, through lots of discussion. ... I suppose it all boils down to, again, the analytical insight that led me to make my own findings, and also ... pursue ideas that he himself had about the material, but which might not have occurred to him if we hadn't been working on the thesis together.

Prompted by successive requests for illustrative examples and clarification, David's eloquent account of the nature of this professor's interaction with him and his contribution to his (David's) intellectual development was extensive in its provision of rich, colourful data that convey one individual's perspective on what makes for a 'leading professor'. Too lengthy to examine in its entirety here, much of it must await analysis elsewhere as a case of research leadership and researcher development as recollected. But, as his closing contribution to this chapter, David's delineation of a 'leading' professor is worth presenting as a summation of the kinds of personal characteristics and qualities that, as a precursor to the influence they may effect, often strike a chord with those who see or experience them in action:

> *Interviewer: Looking back at the role models you say you've had ... what do they have in common? Do they share characteristics? Y'know, can you say, 'These are what I consider to be a really top prof – a leading professor'?*
> *David:* Yes. ... Leader of a field ... er ... lucidity ... they have an idiom, but use it effectively, rather than technical terminology for its own sake ... clarity – and humour, actually ... a sense of humour. I remember laughing with ... my A level teacher; with a particularly dynamic lecturer I had at [X] University, who inspired me and my colleague ... and with my thesis supervisor ... yeah ... humour. ... Er ... individuality, too – they were, kind of ... they were *present* – you could feel when they were in the room, if you went to a conference or a seminar paper ... . They had a *presence*.

The bases of approbation

In order to lead – to merit the descriptor 'leading' – a professor must be considered influential on others. But what is the secret of being so? Whilst designated leaders who hold formal roles had perhaps been at the forefront of Paul Gentle's mind when he formulated it, his observation on how influencing skills may be honed, through what effectively involves manifesting distinction and relationality, is applicable to the more informal, *ad hoc*, academic leadership that professors may practise:

> Effective leaders in higher education institutions are likely to have built a repertoire of successful influencing skills that work inside their universities and colleges. These might include the ability to present powerful rational arguments that are articulated within theoretically informed intellectual frameworks. They may also apply a capacity for building conversational bridges that enable others to express their own expectations, hopes and fears, and in doing so, increasing the chances of successful influencing outcomes. (Gentle, 2014, p. 117)

Yet by being highly personalised, capacity for influencing is often variable; people may respond very differently to a commonly experienced communication, with some remaining unconvinced by arguments that others find compelling. Pelletier (2010, p. 373) illustrates similar variability through the example of a prominent college men's basketball coach: 'During games, when players did not play to their fullest potential, the coach would become physically and mentally abusive. Some players were angered, others felt fear, yet others stated that he was the best coach they had ever had.' Bolden et al. (2012b) make the same point more generally:

> It is clear that whilst there may be some consensus around the characteristics of leaders in academic institutions, there are also substantial variations. For instance, whilst some individuals are perceived as socially adept, others (or perhaps the same people in different situations) are considered dogmatic and self-serving. In addition, the extent to which leading members are perceived positively varies a great deal. Whilst many of the characteristics are positively valenced or neutral (e.g. strategic, committed) others are negatively valenced (e.g. bureaucratic, incompetent) and indicate scepticism about academic leaders and/or managers. (Bolden et al., 2012b, p. 9)

Cutting across such variability in how specific putative or potential leaders are perceived and responded to, what, then, are the common bases of effective professorial academic leadership, as perceived by 'the led'? This is a crucial question, for it leads us not only, first, to theory, but, second, to the contextualised application of such theory to policy and practice that have the potential to underpin good academic workplace relations and, by extension, to enhance the effectiveness with which academics carry out their work. Yet the bases of *effective* professorial academic leadership are inextricably linked to the bases of professorial academic leadership *that falls short* – the focus of Chapter 6. Accordingly, the question of what underpins perceptions – both positive and negative – of how professors carry out their work is addressed in Chapter 7, which serves to explain the perspectives of 'the led' presented in both this chapter and the next.

Notes

1 Whilst a wealth of literature supports – and serves to perpetuate – it, this perspective has been contested and/or qualified (see, for example, Barker, 2017; Evans, 2015c; McLachlan, 2017; Hartung et al., 2017).

2 The compilation process was impressionistic and unsystematic. The resultant profile is intended neither to imply unanimity amongst, nor to represent the weights of different views and perspectives held by, research participants; it simply includes those characteristics that, in featuring recurrently in the research data, seemed to convey a broadly consensual perspective.

3 Since the respondent who made this comment cannot be identified, and the sentiments expressed convey an entirely favourable assessment, I have chosen to obscure neither the identity of the university referred to, nor that of the department implied.

6

Professorship That Falls Short:
Foibles, Fecklessness, and Fiefdoms

Paul Gentle (2014) relates an anecdote involving a participant on a leadership programme that he once ran. The participant – employed at a research-intensive university – challenged Gentle's advocating the benefits of feedback on leadership performance, declaring that, in her/his institution, 'feedback isn't an option'. The author continues:

> On my pursuing this, the reasons given were that the prevailing culture was one of deference to a cadre of research professors whose reputations had nourished their egos to the extent that they behaved high-handedly and did not seek feedback from departmental colleagues on their impact on others, or indeed on any other aspects of their work. Furthermore, any feedback they themselves might give to others was likely to be so intimidating that it was never asked for! (Gentle, 2014, pp. 98–9)

Bruce Macfarlane, too, devotes several pages of his book to exposing characteristics of 'bad professors' reported by his research participants – including 'an inclination to nepotism, a lack of interest in teaching or the development of students and conveying overly negative or pessimistic attitudes about working conditions', along with 'harassing or bullying junior colleagues' (Macfarlane, 2012a, p. 64). Like those referred to in Gentle's quote, above, professors so-described contrast sharply with the 'leading' professors portrayed in Chapter 5 – not least with respect to their impact upon others.

Yet that chapter's positive slant represents only a partial picture of how professors are perceived, for my research also uncovered evidence of what has been called the 'shadow side' of leadership (Bolden, 2007; Kets de Vries & Balazs, 2010) or 'negative leadership' (Schilling, 2009): leadership that is perceived more negatively than positively, and whose influence and impact are more malign than benign. With the leadership field dominated by studies highlighting 'the effective aspects of leadership', notes Pelletier (2010, p. 374), the 'destructive ones' have been sidelined, and in the context of higher education, Bryman (2007, p. 707) observes, leadership that 'undermines collegiality, autonomy and the opportunity to participate in decisions … creates a sense of unfairness [and] damages the commitment of academics' is under-researched and merits attention.

With just such a focus, this chapter, in juxtaposition to Chapter 5, is intended to present a perspective within which the high-handed and ego-nourished professoriate alluded to in Gentle's quote, above, would not be out of place. Drawing upon the same data source that informs Chapter 5 – interviews with, and the questionnaire responses of, the non-professorial academics and researchers who participated in the *Leading professors* study – this chapter examines the nature and bases of people's disapproval of and dissatisfaction with professors as academic leaders, and highlights the impact that such professorial behaviour can have upon others.

Regrets, resentment and recriminations: Reports of professors behaving badly

The *Leading professors* study yielded over 1,200 largely complete questionnaire responses, of which those to one particular item indicated that attitudes towards professors were very varied. As Figure 6.1 shows, well under 10 per cent of its respondents selected the most positive response ('definitely') to the question: *Do the professors in your department/centre exemplify professorial professionalism as you perceive it? (i.e. do they behave as you expect professors to behave?)*, and whilst 52.1 per cent of respondents in total selected one of the three most positive options, this leaves almost a half of respondents evidently reluctant to veer towards unqualified positivity – including over a quarter of the entire sample who selected negative responses ('not really', 'a minority of them do', or 'none of them do').

It would be easy to interpret such relatively vociferous (in quantitative terms) criticism of or negativity towards professors as a sign of the times: as indicative, perhaps, of unmet expectations that, within the performativity culture that defines twenty-first-century academe in much of the developed world, weight-pulling should be commensurate with seniority and status. Yet disapproval of and disappointment with professors has a much longer history.

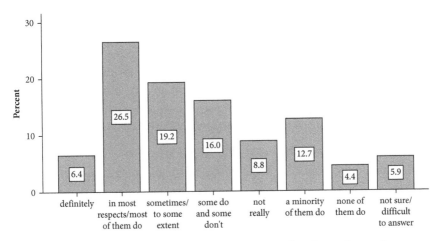

Figure 6.1 Questionnaire responses to the item asking: 'Do the professors in your department/centre exemplify professorial professionalism as you perceive it? (i.e. do they behave as you expect professors to behave?)', *Leading professors* study

A historical detour

In the days when, as I observe in Chapter 2, professors' principal purpose was lecturing, many of them disappointed by shirking their duties or performing them badly; indeed, William Chaderton, the Lady Margaret professor of divinity at Cambridge between 1567 and 1569, is reported (Collinson et al., 2003, p. 73) to have petitioned Elizabeth I's right-hand man, William Cecil, to give him the deanery of Winchester in order to 'free him from "the wearisome duty of lecturing"'. Failure to deliver evidently characterised several successive incumbents of this, England's oldest, chair, and, several centuries on, some of its incumbents are named and shamed:

> Although John Newcombe held the Chair from 1727 to 1765 ... he remained silent after giving his inaugural lecture. His successor, Zachary Brooke (1765–87), followed suit: 'in an obituary notice of him the professorship is described as a valuable sinecure which indeed it was'. In 1788 the University urged the electors to the Chair to appoint someone who would lecture regularly in accordance with the regulations. John Mainwaring, who held the Chair from 1788 to 1807, made a promising start, but as soon as the numbers attending dwindled, he too ceased to lecture. (Collinson et al., 2003, pp. 8–9)

Underperformance and rule-flouting that today would likely be denounced as fraudulent or corrupt behaviour seem to have been equally rife amongst regius professors:

The last language scholars to be nominated by the Crown [to support the work of regius professors of modern history] took up their studies in 1728. The annual reports on their progress were submitted on only two occasions. After this, the Regius professors of modern history kept the stipend for themselves rather than wasting any part of it on the appointment of language instructors. Indeed, with such a large stipend, the post quickly became a sinecure, dished out by governments as an act of political patronage. (Evans, R. J., 2013)

In an era that pre-dates the kinds of performativity regimes that are familiar in academe today, it took the intervention of King George II to try to tighten the reins on incumbents of what was, literally, the *king's* professorship. Yet the sovereign's initiative evidently had limited success in breaking a cycle of unimpressive regius professorial performance that in some cases seems to have been born of disdainful fecklessness, and in other cases, of unfettered freedom to redraft the job description. Former regius professor of history at Cambridge, Richard Evans, outlines the key details:

The monarch, wise in the ways of the world, had stipulated in the original contract that the professor would be fined if he did not deliver at least one lecture a term. Cambridge's first Regius professor of modern history, Samuel Harris, did deliver an inaugural lecture (it was in Latin), but it was also his valedictory, since he gave no more during his 11-year tenure of office, nor did he publish any history books. His successor, Shallet Turner, not only gave no lectures at all in his years in the post but never lived in Cambridge either. The third Regius, Lawrence Brockett, died before he could make any notable contribution to scholarship, breaking his head when he fell off his horse on his way to Cambridge after having dined rather too amply at his parish in the nearby village of Over. His successor, Thomas Gray, was a well-known author, but he achieved fame as a poet with his *Elegy Written in a Country Churchyard*, not as a historian.

Other Regius professors in the 18th and early 19th centuries were similarly neglectful of their duties. Robert Vansittart, Regius professor of civil law at Oxford from 1767 to 1789, spent much of his time at Sir Francis Dashwood's infamous Hellfire Club, whose pagan rituals, sexual orgies and drinking bouts became notorious. (Evans, R. J., 2013)

It was not until 1807, Evans (2013) tells us, with the appointment of William Smyth, 'that a Regius professor who took his duties seriously arrived on the scene. Smyth not only lectured regularly at Cambridge but also published a multi-volume history of the French Revolution'. Yet Smyth nevertheless provoked criticism, for by today's standards he would be considered a NSS liability;[1] his lectures 'were said to have been remarkably boring, and were even the subject of a biting caricature by James Gillray not long after he took up the post. In his later years he attracted a good deal of mockery. "Poor old Smyth," one student was reported as saying, "too old to be corrected"' (Evans, R. J., 2013).

Plus ça change: Unmet expectations and forlorn hopes

But, returning to the twenty-first century, and to consideration of those members of today's professoriate considered to be falling short, we may ask: short of *what*? – and falling short in what respects? Data yielded by another item in the *Leading professors* questionnaire may help provide answers, for, as shown in Figure 6.2, in response to being asked: *Do you feel that you receive as much help and advice as you want or need from one or more of your professorial colleagues?*, over half (53 per cent) of the respondents selected broadly negative responses ('no' or 'not really'). Perhaps, then, perceptions of inadequate or unsatisfactory mentoring are at the root of negative assessments of professors' behaviour; such an explanation is certainly consistent with the appreciation of professors' supportive relationality articulated by many academics in Chapter 5, but is it supported by the qualitative data that focused on people's dissatisfaction with or disapproval of professors?

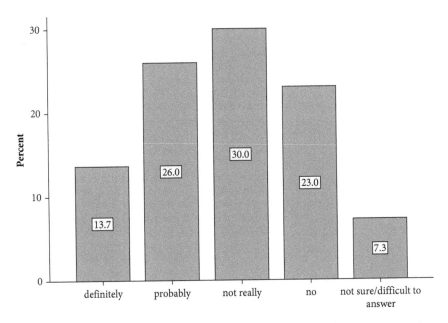

Figure 6.2 Questionnaire responses to the item asking: 'Do you feel that you receive as much help and advice as you want or need from one or more of your professorial colleagues?', *Leading professors* study

Negative reports of professors were conveyed in either or both of two forms: interview conversations and questionnaire respondents' written comments. Incorporating the facility for researcher probing, the interviews, unsurprisingly, yielded the richer and more informative set of data, including many protracted narratives, several of which were expansive in detailing interviewees' experiences and the emotional and attitudinal responses they provoked. The questionnaire-generated comments were wider-ranging in relation to, *inter alia*: length, detail, focus, intensity of sentiments expressed, and evident contributor positionality. Some were expressed briefly, using very few words, while others spanned lengthy paragraphs. Some represented vituperative diatribe; others were only mildly – sometimes even constructively – critical. Most fell somewhere between these two extremes.

Within the full data set – interview- and questionnaire-generated alike – four broad categories of negativity were discernible. These are distinguished on the bases of both the width of applicability, and the degree of subjective involvement in the substance or basis, of the 'complaint' or expressed dissatisfaction. For succinctness I label the categories: *indiscriminate-detached*; *exclusive-detached*; *exclusive-interested*; and *exclusive-self-interested* – labels that are explained below, and whose features are summarised in Table 6.1.

Indiscriminate-detached

This category – of which there were many examples – represents 'blanket' negativity: an implicit generalised perception that was applied indiscriminately.

Table 6.1 Categories of negativity towards professors: descriptors and features

Category of negativity[2]	Category descriptor	Implicit or explicit object of 'complaint' or disapproval	Complainer-identified object or recipient of professorial action/ behaviour identified	Complainer status in relation to the incident/ situation referred to
1	Indiscriminate-detached	All professors/ professors in general	None	Observer
2	Exclusive-detached	Specific professors	None	Observer
3	Exclusive-interested	Specific professors	Third party	Observer
4	Exclusive-self-interested	Specific professors	Self	Participant/ recipient

Examples of this category include the following responses to open-ended questionnaire items:

> Professors see their focus as being research and view supporting others as a distraction and not part of their role.

> Professors are self-centred and interested only in furthering their career at the expense of other members of staff.

> They [professors] expect little or no teaching, they refuse to attend important meetings for running the department, they seem always away for conferences yet their average research output does not reflect that. They do not involve non-professors in developing grant proposals (except the lucky few), they refuse to transparently use the research grant funding (normally with the help or direction of senior management). Some other characteristics which are also noticeable: they become aloof, pompous, and belittle other staff work.

> Professors are remote and unapproachable and only interested in their own research.

> [Professors are] (largely) a bunch of overpaid, over-promoted, empire-building gobshites out for little more than personal advancement.

> They [professors] are backstabbing assholes who take the credit for other people's work.

As its label implies, this category of negativity has two features: detachment and comprehensiveness. Each 'complaint' is articulated in the language of detached disapproval that incorporates no *explicit* reference to any impact on the complainer – 'I' or 'my' do not feature in it. In this sense, for the most part it (each 'complaint') conveys a disinterested perspective. The negative comments are comprehensively applied – expressed as being indiscriminately directed against the professoriate as a single entity, tarring all its members with the same brush.[3]

Exclusive-detached

The 'exclusive-detached' category is represented by the expression of detached dissatisfaction with or disapproval of one or more *specific* professors who are most commonly known to the complainer/observer as institutional or former colleagues. Distinct from category 1 by its exclusive focus, the expressed negativity is selectively applied. The predominant data source of 'exclusive-detached' negative perceptions was the *Leading professors* questionnaire, yet examples of such perspectives were also evident in the interview data. The following questionnaire-generated comments are indicative of category 2 negativity:

I have no idea what professors in my department/college are supposed to be doing, and from the looks of things, neither do they.

Many of our professors were 'bought' in for the last RAE and have done nothing to contribute to an improved research culture. Some think teaching is beneath them.

A member of staff has been made a prof so he can be head of school and he is absolutely terrible. I don't believe he is professorial material, and he is most certainly not leadership material and it is doing a great deal of damage to the department. He is not ready or suitable for the role, even if he *is* good at his research, perhaps.

The really high flyers tend not be seen in the department – they do not attend staff meetings, do little teaching and tend not to manage or engage with the department. It is extremely difficult to benefit from their experience. Two of the professors ... are so task-focussed that their conduct borders on outright bullying.

A key feature of category 2 perceptions is that – as with category 1 – they omit explicit allusion to having personally been on the receiving end, or the object, of the professorial behaviour or attitudes identified; the 'complaints' are presented as if from the perspective of a detached, 'unharmed' onlooker. Nevertheless, many – if not most – were delivered in explicitly judgemental, and sometimes emotive, language; the use of words such as 'unfortunately' 'disgraceful', 'absolutely terrible', and 'bullying' convey disapproval that cannot easily be divorced from – indeed, that is indicative of – a degree of personal involvement, whether through personal 'injury' or as a concerned onlooker with collegial sensitivities and a strong sense of fairness.

Exclusive-interested

The 'exclusive-interested' category also focuses on one or more *specific* professors, but, unlike categories 1 and 2, whose foci are on victimless 'misbehaviour', category 3 comprises cases that identify one or more 'recipients' or 'targets' – one or more specific person(s) *other than the individual relating the incident or situation* – of what are presented as examples of unsatisfactory professorial academic leadership or behaviour. The complainer or observer thus conveys an evident interest in the case, in the sense of her/his being an interested party/onlooker, but this is not conveyed as *self*-interest since there is no evidence of any *direct* impact on or repercussions for her/him. Category 3 disapproval or dissatisfaction makes *explicit* the onlooker concern that remains only *implicit* within category 2 'complaints'.

Category 3 is the least represented category of negativity. Evidence of it came mainly, but not exclusively, from the research interviews, and since these had been focused on uncovering interviewees' own experiences and their emotional and attitudinal responses to them, it is unsurprising that few accounts included reference to other people's (colleagues' or friends') experiences; any third party cases that were raised were done so at interviewees' own instigation. One such case was identified by Janice (principal lecturer in a post-1992 university), who spoke of an early career academic's apparent neglect at the hands of a professorial colleague:

> We have a young lady upstairs who's passionate about her field, and *desperate* to get a PhD – just absolutely desperate … but just can't manage to do it here. And there's a professor in that field – a very well respected professor … and she's [the professor] just down the corridor and the young lady's just up the stairs – but she [the professor] won't even meet her or help her … which is a bit shocking. … [The professor's] just not interested, because this particular professor has a field – a very specific field – and [advising the junior colleague] isn't going to help [the professor in doing her research], … But, again, shocking!

Similarly, Adrian (senior lecturer in a pre-1992 university), recalling an earlier, darker, period in his department's recent past, was scathing in his criticism of

> professors who worked all hours of the day and night themselves and actually were quite good scholars … but then expected everybody else to do the same. I've got no complaints if somebody wants to work 70 hours a week – that's fine; but it's quite inadmissible to expect other people to then go and do the same thing. And it certainly led to the departure of, I think, at least two members of staff, if not more. So there are those kinds of mishandling of people that're quite … well, I'm going to use the word 'wrong' and I actually do mean 'quite wrong', because that's putting a moral slant on it, and I think it was immoral behaviour by people who were … er … thirsty for power. And, you know, I'm very pleased if people want to make names for themselves and do all kinds of interesting, whizzy things in research … that's fine. But the knock-on effect it had on other people was … fairly dismal, and I think there are probably a few people … whose careers were probably blighted by them, in terms of … people couldn't get on and do the research they needed … because there was too much teaching to do.

And senior lecturer in education studies, William, drew upon contrasting experiences of two professors (in his pre-1992 university) to express his disapproval of the neglect shown by one of them in relation to engagement with teaching and responsibilities towards students:

I've supervised students with both [Professor X] and with [Professor Y], and
... I did feel that with [Professor X] ... we, sort of, talked about [the student],
and he [Professor X] was interested in him. Whereas the person I supervised
with [Professor Y] was a much stronger student, who I think had some really
interesting ideas, that both of us were interested in. But [Y] just wasn't interested;
I mean, he didn't read chapters and stuff like that. And, I mean ... there was no
real engagement there.

Exclusive-self-interested

The fourth category of negative perceptions represents reported first-hand
experiences of unsatisfactory interaction with specific professors. Perceiving
her/himself as having been directly on the receiving end of unacceptable
professorial behaviour, this category of complainer, rather than being a relatively
disinterested observer, is very much an interested – and in many cases an
aggrieved – party.

This category represents varied degrees both of negativity and of the extent to
which reported unsatisfactory experiences seemed to have affected interviewees.
Invited to illustrate the whole spectrum of their experiences of professors –
ranging from the best to the worst – many interviewees included reference to at
least one of what were presented as *relatively* fleeting or minor negative episodes
or situations that they had managed to put behind them and move on from.
Sometimes featuring within narratives that otherwise focused on positive relations
or interactions with senior colleagues, such negative encounters were related as
anomalies – as isolated brushes with 'rogue' professors. In contrast to her lavish
praise of an overseas-based former professorial colleague and mentor (presented
in Chapter 5), Viktoria, for example, spoke of her frustration with unimaginative
professorial decision-making closer to home, in her own department:

> So, we've had a couple of situations where I've talked to [the professor], for
> example, about research funding and about participating in a research project
> that people – colleagues of mine in other countries – were doing, and who
> wanted me to be co-investigator, and she said, 'No, you can't do that because the
> department wouldn't get any money from it.' So I was hugely disappointed. ...
> So, I think this is what I'm struggling with most, and probably also because she
> is quite new ... so she still goes very much according to the book. (*Viktoria,
> associate professor of linguistics, pre-1992 university*)

Similarly, Nicole, whose predominantly positive interaction with several
professors features within a narrative in Chapter 5, identified an isolated
experience that had upset her, but from which she seemed to have bounced back:

When I was in my very early days I gave some stuff over to a professor – this is when I was employed, who I was doing a research project with – who rehashed it and basically wrote it as his own. And that was a very tricky situation for me to deal with. I *didn't* really deal with it; I just, kind of, put it down to experience. … I haven't talked to him since. … It wasn't fun … er … but I was a bit green, you know. (*Nicole, history and archaeology lecturer, post-1992 university*)

These, and many other, incidents related during the research interviews shared the common feature of *apparently* having little lasting detrimental effect on the interviewees who experienced them. In every case, responsibility or blame for the incident was laid squarely at the feet of the professor in question, with the implication that s/he was at fault for having failed to act in a manner expected of a professor, or even that s/he was widely recognised as having a character defect. Such rationalisation was illustrated in a senior academic's account of professorial rank-pulling. Maurice – a reader in a pre-1992 university – related how, in his capacity as the director of a graduate programme, a decision he had made to reject a graduate student's travel funding application had been over-ruled by a professorial colleague: 'I was told in fairly short order that as far as [the professor] was concerned, you know, he was over-ruling my decision. It was made clear to me that if I didn't like this I could object, but that would not be in the interests of my career.' Asked to recall his emotional or attitudinal response to this incident, Maurice replied:

I think it has to be said that this was … a professorial colleague who was widely perceived as being abrasive and … er … who had a long history of … having relations with other colleagues … which, so to speak, made *my* little brush in this context, you know … put it into perspective, shall we say? So … I wasn't shocked. … So I came away feeling a little bit bruised, but not … not anything that, sort of, kept me awake night after night.

Whilst reports of aggressive behaviour (in its widest sense) on the part of professors did not feature prominently in the interview data, Maurice and Oliver were not the only interviewees claiming to have experienced it. Howard (a teaching fellow in history in a pre-1992 university) spoke of having been treated contemptuously:

One [professor] treats me with contempt – or certainly has done – and he's … well, like other people, he's been … there's been bullying by him.

He related a specific incident:

He burst into my room – knocked heavily at the door and burst into my room – started shouting at me for copying various people into an email: 'Why did you copy [so-and-so] in?' ... and he was just very ... sort of ... dismissive ... angry ... er ... telling me I shouldn't do things that I knew I *should* do. And I found that very disconcerting, because it came suddenly. There've been other occasions ... when we've had meetings or email exchanges ... and he's been very abrasive and dismissive ... about my views. And if I felt I was wrong I would, sort of, have recognised that I *was* wrong ... but I don't think I was.

Alan – who, like Maurice, was a senior academic – presented a picture of routine aggressiveness on the part of his professorial departmental colleagues:

> If you don't, kind of, conform to the successful phenotype – to use a biological word – of a professor, then you get ignored, or even sometimes bullied, perhaps. ... I mean, I've ended up *in tears* before now. ... I think in chemistry in general that there's ... er ... well, I *know* there is – and it's documented – there *is* a problem of culture, where, actually, this behaviour just becomes acceptable, so that people don't realise that they're misbehaving, because everyone else is like that. So, just, raised voices are the norm ... shouting at people's okay. (*Alan, chemistry reader, pre-1992 university*)

Whilst no blows were exchanged, the kinds of incidents and situations related by Howard and Alan represent what several analysts categorise as workplace 'violence' that is located on a 'continuum [that] allows for the examination of forms of violence ranging from covert, indirect and non-physical incidences of abuse (e.g. incivility) to extreme, overt, direct incidences of violence' (Berlingieri, 2015, p. 347). Indeed, Bourgois' references to 'daily practices and expressions of violence on a micro-interactional level' (Bourgois, 2004, p. 426, cited in Berlingieri, 2015, p. 349) seem to capture the essence of the disciplinary culture of normalised 'violence' portrayed by Alan, above. Yet the incidents and environments conveyed through these vignettes were by no means the only examples of unfortunate brushes with professors; several interviewees related experiences that seemed to have had an enduring significant negative impact on them. Three such cases, outlined briefly below, stood out on the basis of the profundity of their apparently deleterious effects on the narrator.

Janice's narrative

A principal lecturer in a post-1992 university that had declared its mission to break out of the post-1992 sector stereotype by developing its research capacity, Janice presented herself as research-active and with long-term ambitions to move to a research-intensive university. She therefore fully supported the institutional mission and tried to play her part in fulfilling it. Yet she reported being thwarted by what she described as professorial colleagues' shirking of their academic leadership responsibilities by ruthlessly protecting their own interests, focusing unwaveringly on building up their profiles and reputations, and refusing to share their knowledge and expertise. Having spoken briefly of a female professor's neglect of a junior colleague's professional development needs (presented above as an example of category 3 negativity), Janice went on to relate similar neglect of her own needs – indeed, rebuttals of her requests for help – by two male professors; 'two experiences stand out for me', she said.

The first of these experiences involved her asking (through email) a professorial colleague to sit on a doctoral student's upgrade panel[4] – one of many forms of institutional 'citizenship' for which, as Janice confirmed, it is notoriously difficult to recruit willing volunteers:

> I have the same problem every single panel: you cannot get anybody to commit to that. ... And I've even had one person [a professor] say, astonishingly, 'No, I just can't do that, because what's in it for me?' And that is a *professor* – a *nice* professor, not an awful professor ... a nice, down-to-earth professor, saying, 'What's in it for me?' And, for somebody who's at a lower level, you just tear your hair out because you just can't get anywhere.

Supporting her account, at my request Janice later forwarded me the email exchange in which this professor had declined her request. His message read:

> I can't make any meetings this year. Sorry about this but it's just not a priority for me. I'm struggling to see any 'added' for my applied research. I suggest you widen your net regarding the internal expert and find somebody else.

The second incident involved Janice's asking a second professorial colleague – someone whom she described as having a track record of research council funding success – to read and advise her on improving a draft funding proposal. She outlined what transpired:

> Now because [the professor] has experience of not only getting research council funding, but sits on panels, I approached him and said, 'I'm really interested in putting in this bid ... er ... I was wondering if you could take a look at it for me, and just generally give me some advice.' Okay? The first response I got was, 'No, not really.' I left it six months, and I approached it again in a different way and said, 'Would you mind if I just came and had a chat for five minutes, just to see what the key things I need to do are, to be fairly successful, and is there anything that I'm missing?' Didn't get a response. Er ... [I] left it about another year ... contacted him again, and he actually came back and said, 'No.' And the reason he said 'No' was ... er ... because, 'Well, quite frankly, if you're successful, that means that there's less chance of success for the people that work in my team to get it.'

Again, Janice forwarded me the very email exchange to which she referred. The professor's final response read: 'The truth is, I don't like to offer much by way of advice to prospective applicants. A success for them means a reduced pool of opportunity for my team and my research students.'

As Janice related them, both of these interactions appear to expose un-cooperative, self-absorbed and self-serving professorial practice that is the antithesis of at least three of the characteristics of the ideal professor listed in Chapter 5: altruistic collegiality; generosity (with one's time); and a willingness to contribute to the professional and career development of others as much as to focus on one's own career development and advancement. This brief narrative is not one of what could be considered workplace 'violence' (as the term is interpreted above), for Janice's experiences do not seem to have inflicted the kind or severity of damage or harm that warrants such categorisation; they left her with a nasty lingering aftertaste, certainly, but neither interaction seems to have been venomous. Yet their unfortunate legacy is summed up in Janice's articulation of the bitterness and disillusionment that they provoked: 'Maybe it's just been *my* experience, but I think those two appalling experiences are … *appalling*, and they, for me, are everything that is bad – *can* be bad – about academia, actually.'

Adrian's narrative

Whilst Janice's experiences disillusioned her, those of senior lecturer in education Adrian, had evidently provoked his despair – grinding him down to the extent of wanting to move institutions. Unlike Janice's experiences, Adrian's were not of one or two relatively isolated interactions, but of a prevailing situation that he recalled as having endured for over two years: related as the corrosive behaviour of two professors in his department who led an academic research group that delivered taught master's level courses. From Adrian's account, the repercussions of these professors' selfish pursuit of their own ambitions – which he described as 'empire-building' – impacted upon the group (of which he was a member) in ways that became increasingly detrimental to members' well-being, morale and motivation. These senior colleagues were, in Adrian's words: 'people who were completely … I think "boneheaded" is the term … just plough their own furrow regardless … professors who had no consideration about the amount of work they were expecting people to do, particularly in terms of teaching. Or if they were aware of it, couldn't care a toss! All they were interested in was building empires.'[5]

He described these professors as wanting 'to hang onto their own fiefdoms', explaining his choice of term: 'when I talk about a fiefdom I'm thinking here of somebody who tries to sustain their power, not necessarily within a subject area, but perhaps over a group of staff or over a building. But it could be over a particular subject area as well.' Asked if he could recall his emotional and attitudinal response to this prolonged situation, he replied:

> Well, one felt very stressed; I felt very tired at times. Er ... I also felt very angry. I seriously considered at one point taking my bat home. ... I actually considered the options of leaving ... I got very angry – very annoyed ... . They've [the professors] moved on now – one of them's retired – but the general consensus here was: good luck to bad rubbish! But it's left me with a very cynical view of power ... and of professors in particular.

Clare's narrative

Emerging from the *Leading professors* study as what appears the most damaging case of an academic's dealings with professors, Clare's experiences involved far-reaching repercussions that included: a nervous breakdown, extended sick leave, loss of confidence and lowered self-esteem, and formal grievance procedures invoked several years later. A reader in a pre-1992 university at the time of her interview, Clare recounted a sequence of events and circumstances that had occurred twelve years earlier, when she had been a junior academic in the same institution. By her own account, she had been suffering from depression, had felt unable to cope with her workload and the demands placed on her, and had approached two senior departmental colleagues for help and support: the female professorial head of department and another (male) professor. Her recollection of events painted a sombre picture:

> I was actually suffering from quite serious depression for most of that period ... and where my real difficulties ... have come, is in the ... er ... y'know, seeming incapacity of some, sort of, senior managers to deal with ... what, in my case, was a sort of serious health problem – *mental* health problem – and to, kind of, support anyone through that, really. How much can you expect? – I don't know, but I think you can expect an understanding of what it *is*! ... And, y'know, during the two years' difficult period that I've just alluded to, then ... er ... because I was ill enough to be having time off work, then I asked for, sort of, help from the department ... er ... and was refused! I mean, *it was refused*! Which – I mean, not only did it do me a lot of, sort of, psychological damage, I think, but it ... sort of ... became the subject of a grievance much later on and, sort of, marred

my history within the ... department, I think. It's practically all in the past now because most of the people involved in that – who refused to help – have moved on ... er ... but ... er ... yeah, the repercussions of that went on for a long time.

She elaborated on her recollection of the impact that the events had had upon her:

I did get into a *very* isolated situation for a while – *quite* a while ... where I didn't feel I had any sort of support – either just human support, or support for my research ... and that's when I, sort of, asked for it. And as far as my own, sort of, mental health was concerned, then it got quite serious because I ... y'know, I had a kind of depressive breakdown a couple of years after that and, y'know, did several years of psychotherapy in order to get myself back into a sense that I could actually ... you know, I felt completely failed by ... by society as a whole! [slight laugh] ... as a result of that period. And it took a long time – it has taken a *long* time to get the feeling back that, y'know, people aren't down on me all the time ... and that I *am* appreciated ... and valued, really. It's been going *much* better recently, but those things, y'know, stay with you for a long time.

Asked if she had contemplated direct action, such as leaving her job, she explained:

I couldn't have gone anywhere else, in a sense [brief laugh], because I wasn't in a state of mind, y'know, to impress anyone to get a job anywhere else, actually, for quite a long period, I don't think; it was more a question of sitting it out. Certainly, it got very close to me wanting to give up academia altogether, but ... not quite [brief laugh].

More than a decade after this period in Clare's life, unsavoury memories evidently remained raw, and the details that she recollected of workplace exchanges and interaction illuminate something of junior academics' vulnerability when their dependency on senior colleagues for direction and support is exposed by dysfunctional inter-generational collegial relationships. In common with the other interviewees whose accounts feature in this chapter, Clare laid responsibility squarely at the feet of her professorial colleagues for failing to deliver the kind of leadership she had both craved and expected:

I would say it was a kind of incredibly hierarchical attitude [on the part of the professors] ... and ... er ... and, sort of, poor social skills, really! [brief laugh] ... just a, sort of, jaded, cynical attitude to being a professor ... y'know, kind of, already in their mid-forties, which kind of made you think, y'know, you can't respect people who ... don't lead, and who make cynical jokes about the fact that they don't really *want* to lead and aren't regarded as leaders. So, all the sort of discourse that we get about research leadership, and having a vision about how you can develop it ... I remember the 'vision' word being a kind of joke to these people, and ... sort of, joking about not having the vision thing ... y'know – but it *was* just a joke to them! And, y'know, it's *not* a joke to a young lecturer ...'cos you do want to, sort of, have people, kind of ... you know, you think: well these people can't help me with my career at all ... because they don't take their *own* seriously!

In pinpointing the basis of what she recalled of her disappointment and disillusionment, Clare's comments highlight the emotional toll that unmet need of supportive leadership can take. Representing a degenerative sequence of what were identified as eroded resilience, undermined confidence, impaired performance and capacity, and impoverished quality of working life – to say nothing of psychological breakdown – hers may well be an atypical case: one that defines, or is located very near to, the negative extreme of a continuum representing the full range of the impact on 'the led' of professorial academic leadership perceived as falling short. Indeed, Clare's related experiences probably represent a case of toxic leadership, as Pelletier (2010, p. 377) interprets it: 'If the follower is physically or psychologically harmed by the leader's actions, and that impairment is long lasting, the leader can be considered toxic.'

Pelletier (2010, p. 374) nevertheless makes the valid point that 'one person's toxic leader may be another person's hero' – which more or less equates to van Knippenberg et al.'s (2007, p. 53) argument that 'part of what we identify as leadership – or as effective leadership – is in the eye of the beholder'. The same point may be made about the quality of professorial academic leadership – or even professorial practice more broadly. Yet, by digging deeper, below the contextual superficiality that inevitably throws up variability, it is possible to uncover what I call the 'lowest common factor' that is essential to the universal applicability that defines theory and theorising (Evans, 1998, 2002). Viewed from such depth, common bases emerge of professorship or professorial practice that is assessed as falling short. In the next chapter I examine some of these bases, in tandem with consideration of what, precisely, professors are presented as falling short *of* – and the nature of that shortfall.

Notes

1 Commissioned by the UK's Higher Education Funding Council for England (HEFCE), on behalf of, *inter alia*, all four of the UK's HE national funding councils, the National Student Survey (NSS) annually gathers the opinions on the quality of

their higher education experiences of students registered in UK HEIs. Its published results are taken very seriously by HEIs, since they are believed to influence the destination choices of applicants to UK HEIs, and hence to indirectly influence revenue and institutional reputation. Scott and Callender (2017, p. 127) in fact identify the NSS as 'one of the most important ingredients in the rankings that have proliferated in the UK since 2000'.

2 For ease of reference categories are each assigned a number, which are not intended to denote degree or intensity of negativity.

3 Some respondents may have been prompted to comment by the questionnaire item quoted above: *Do the professors in your department/centre exemplify professorial professionalism as you perceive it? (i.e. do they behave as you expect professors to behave?)*, and whose comments may therefore have been intended to apply only to the professors in their own departments or centres.

4 Refers to an internal process that, in each case of a registered research student's transition to full doctoral candidate status, involves convening a panel of academics from within the institution to assess the student's capacity to produce and defend a thesis of doctoral standard.

5 Empire-building has been identified recurrently in the modern era as an undesirable feature of specific professors' behaviour; Finkenstaedt (2011, p. 165), for example, notes that the post-war period of growth that occurred in many European countries' higher education systems and provision 'could be – and indeed was – *exploited* by a number of professors for "empire building" purposes in their own field' (emphasis added).

7

The Bases of Assessments of Professorial Academic Leadership: Drilling Down

Expectations are key to influencing attitudes. As Chapters 5 and 6 show, when professors meet or exceed people's expectations of them as academic leaders, satisfaction with and approbation of them (and the leadership they provide) are high, just as dissatisfaction and disapproval result from unmet expectations. But where do such expectations come from? To better understand what people want from professors as academic leaders, and why, we need to uncover not only the nature of expectations, but also the bases of them. This chapter aims to do that. Serving as a concluding sequel to Chapters 5 and 6, by digging below the surface of the perceptions that they present of 'leading' professorship and of professorship that falls short, it incorporates theoretical perspectives to offer *explanations for* the perspectives of 'the led'.

The bases of expectations: Implicit leadership and followership theories

There is a sub-field of leadership research and scholarship that examines *why* and *how* people ascribe leadership status and characteristics to others. This field of implicit leadership (and followership) theories is concerned much less with the processes whereby people achieve formal, designated leadership positions or roles – the decisions that lead to this or that person's being *appointed* to such a role – than with the cognitive and psychological factors that persuade or convince someone to recognise or acknowledge another as a leader, irrespective of her or his formal role; as Oc and Bashshur (2013, p. 920) point out, '[i]mplicit leadership theories … argue that leadership actually exists in the minds of followers'. Shondrick et al. (2010) explain implicit leadership theories as 'representations unconsciously held by followers that help distinguish "leaders" from "non-leaders", while the 'leadership categorization approach' or model is explained as an implicit leadership theory, whereby:

> people are … categorized as leaders though *recognition-based processes* and on the basis of the *perceived match* between their behavior or character and the attributes of a pre-existing leader category or prototype that the follower holds in memory. (Epitropaki et al., 2013, pp. 860–1, original emphases)

Essentially, what this means is that if someone is perceived, albeit unconsciously, as behaving in the manner expected, and that matches preconceptions, of a leader, then s/he is considered a leader, just as, by failing to act in ways that are congruent with the leader prototypes that people recognise, a formally designated leader risks being considered a 'non-leader'. Humphreys et al. (2015, p. 1391) explain this: 'the constructed image of the leader is of greater relevance than the leader's traits in terms of influencing follower behaviors and eliciting their attributions'.

Implicit leadership theories may incorporate more specific dimensions, such as the 'connectionist perspective', which allows for context-specific differences and fluidity in what prompts someone to recognise another as a leader, accommodating the consideration that a recognised leader in one context may, in a different context, be deemed to have little or no leadership potential or capacity. Another dimension, 'adaptive resonance theory', posits that people identify leadership prototypes, and faced with behaviour that is a contender for leadership ascription, computer-like, in an unconscious process described as 'bidirectional feedback loops' (Epitropaki et al., 2013), they compare the encountered behaviour with behaviour patterns included in their mental store of leadership prototypes. If there is a match, the encountered behaviour is unconsciously categorised as leadership, and the person performing it as a leader; if the match is weak, the behaviour is likely to be categorised as non-leadership – or a new category may be created to accommodate it (e.g. maverick leadership). Epitropaki et al. (2013, p. 861) identify this as a fluid process that involves constant adjustment:

> According to the adaptive resonance theory, not only are new categories created by unsuccessful matches, but existing categories are constantly modified and refined on the basis of inputs from the environment and interactions with target actors.

Implicit leadership theories, as Epitropaki et al. (2013) point out, are principally applied as explanations for the extent of ascription of solo, formal, leadership that is enacted through designated positions or roles:

current conceptualizations and research on ILTs and IFTs,[1] despite acknowledging group and organizational constraints, basically focus on one *single* leader or follower and in a sense adopt a traditional, individualistic and hierarchical view of leadership. (Epitropaki et al., 2013, p. 873, original emphasis)

As such, they (implicit leadership theories) do not seem geared up to explaining micro-level leadership: what I propose in Chapter 3 as the notional basic units of leadership, as I define it – and which I illustrate through the analogy of a ball being thrown from one person to another, to indicate its potential fluidity. Leadership at this basic level, and so analysed, often lies below the radar that detects leader status ascription. Theoretical perspectives, such as mine, on micro-level leadership are intended, for the most part, to address a different agenda from the one addressed by those relating to leader status ascription by participants in leader–follower exchanges or relationships. Whilst they may draw upon process for illustrative purposes, the former tend to be mainly concerned with explaining leadership as a *concept*, while the latter tend to be concerned primarily with *process*: how leadership works as a form of agency – which is also the focus of implicit leadership theories.[2]

But, putting aside micro-level leadership, and taking up consideration of what, in Chapter 3, I call more 'pragmatic' perspectives that encompass personification of leadership – specifically, academic leadership practised by professors – do implicit leadership theories offer any elucidation of the bases of its (leadership's) ascription? Do they explain the *fundamental* reasons *why* an academic may identify a professorial colleague as a 'leading' professor or as a professor whose academic leadership falls short?

Implicit leadership theories' application to professorial academic leadership ascription

As I discuss in Chapter 3, academic leadership as it is most often interpreted in the UK involves informal and sometimes *ad hoc* leadership that is not dependent on designated, formal role incumbency. Being sometimes vaguely and implicitly enacted, such leadership is often difficult to detect and discern, and may even go unrecognised by either or both of leader and 'the (putative) led'. Moreover, the focus of this book is such leadership carried out by professors, on the basis of their simply being professors, and, for the most part, independent of any administrative or management roles that they may happen to hold; it is a focus on the kinds of attitudes, intellectuality and behaviour – that is, the professionalism (as I define it in Chapter 2) – associated with and expected of this most senior grade of academics. Yet these professors without portfolios tend to be identified, and to identify themselves, first and foremost as professors, or as academics, rather than as leaders. Where they *are* recognised or recognise themselves as informal academic leaders, this is most often a subsidiary identification: an add-on. As the following selected comments from questionnaire respondents show, several of the *Leading professors* research participants admitted to having never thought of professors as leaders, or to have associated professorship with leadership:

> I don't think of professors as necessarily leaders, beyond in their research field.

> I have never thought of the two words 'professor' and 'leader' as being in any way connected.

> I have not thought of the 2 professors in the department in a 'leadership' capacity.

> I see professor as being a recognition for being a good researcher. ... I don't see that they need to be involved in 'leadership', unless that's an additional skill.

Yet, despite what, for identity and identification purposes, may be described as professors' semi-detachment from (association with) leadership, implicit leadership theories seem to have some applicability to analysis of the *Leading professors* research findings.

Illustrating implicit leadership theories: The Leading professors research findings

The kind of adjustment that constitutes adaptive resonance theory, as it is described above, was evident in comments and narratives provided by several interviewees, illustrating what seems to have been their widening of the parameters of what, for them, counted as 'leading' professorship. Senior lecturer Adrian, for example, spoke of a professor whose leadership he considered to fall short in some respects, but whom he nevertheless considered to have demonstrated satisfactory leadership of a different kind, and which effectively compensated for other deficiencies:

> He made one or two daft decisions, but actually, in terms of providing support to people, was actually quite good ... including, on one occasion with me, taking me out for a meal one evening. I didn't quite understand – I'd known him for some time before he actually arrived in our department – and he'd obviously noticed that I was clearly somewhat upset about something and wasn't saying anything. ... And he was extremely helpful, but, as I say, in terms of his, sort

of, administrative-political leadership, I think he made a few daft decisions.
(*Adrian, senior lecturer in education studies, pre-1992 university*)

Elaborating slightly on the explanations of implicit leadership theories presented in the literature citations above, Shondrick et al. (2010) argue that, with implicit leadership theories – and, specifically, leadership categorisation theory – 'information is represented abstractly in *schemas*, which are cognitive categories that people use to represent the prototypical characteristics', and 'which help guide perceptions and the active construal of others by providing a set of generic assumptions and beliefs as what to expect' (p. 961, original emphasis). Adrian's remarks (above) imply that his 'schemas of what a prototypical leader should be' (Shondrick et al., 2010, p. 961) included characteristics relating to micro-political awareness and administrative competence, and that, on this basis, the professor he refers to would ordinarily have been categorised as a 'non-leader'. Yet Adrian implies adjusting his leadership categorisation-informing schemas to encompass interpersonal relational characteristics, such as empathy and concern and consideration for others, effectively compromising on what he considered criteria for professorial academic leader status by shifting the balance of his schematic categorisation, allowing his positive assessment of the professor's relationality to outweigh his (Adrian's) negative assessment of the professor's administrative and political decision-making capacity.

A similar kind of schematic categorisation compromise was evident in the remarks of other interviewees, whose compromising seems to have been facilitated by their holding multiple schemas, rather than – as was the case with some, mainly early career, interviewees – seeming to confine themselves rigidly and uncompromisingly to one schema, of how a 'leading' professor or a professor-as-academic-leader should behave. Following up her comment that 'one or two [departmental professors] … are conspicuously absent at things like research seminars – never come to *any* research seminars … would never *give* a paper in the department', Eleanor responded to being asked if she felt these 'absent' professors were neglectful or deficient in carrying out their roles:

There are so many different aspects to the professorial role. Er … and actually, y'know, people who don't come to research seminars are very, very good in other areas, and actually often very good in research – for example, they produce a lot and it's all very good quality. So, in that respect, y'know, it's not that they're *deficient*, it's more that there's just a part of their job that they're, sort of, neglecting a little bit in order to be able to do other bits of it better, perhaps.
(*Eleanor, associate professor, modern foreign languages, pre-1992 university*)

In referring to professors whom they implicitly considered to fall short of achieving a good match with some of their schemas of prototypical professorial academic leadership, whilst yet matching up to other of their schemas, several senior non-professorial academics spoke of the multifarious and highly varied and variable nature of professorial roles and responsibilities. Chemistry reader Alan, for example, implied a willingness to compromise on his ideal (conveyed in his comments presented in Chapter 5) of a 'leading' professor as one who has time for junior colleagues and supports their development. His evident acceptance that professorship may take many shapes and forms suggests that he holds multiple schemas for categorising professorial academic leadership, one of which recognises intellectual leadership through research excellence:

> People have been appointed to chairs *exclusively* on the basis of their research. So, there can be no reasonable expectation that they have other skills. And, indeed … in some cases it may be that it's precisely *because* they haven't bothered with those things that they've succeeded with research. (*Alan, chemistry reader, pre-1992 university*)

Adaptive resonance theory was also evident as adaptations from negative to more positive leadership prototypical schemas. On arriving in the UK, Oliver found himself modifying a schema that had been formed by his earlier experiences of academe in his native North America, and that represented prototypical professorial academic leadership as heavy on scholarly distinction and administrative responsibility, and light on relationality:

> Full professors in [names a North American country] … wouldn't necessarily deign to speak to someone who's on an associate level. It's probably a bit different from here; there's quite a sense of: they're in a different head-space [in North America]. And they're often heavily involved in the administration – you wouldn't actually normally *see* them, to be perfectly honest. … So I actually found it really refreshing, and coming from [North American country], I thought, wow! you know? And [UK-based] professors would listen to you; they would respond to your questions! (*Oliver, staff development lecturer, pre-1992 university*)

The 'connectionist perspective', too – explained above as facilitating context-specific differences and fluidity in what prompts someone to recognise another as a leader – was implicit in several interviewees' comments. It was particularly evident in expressions of understanding of the difficulties experienced by, and sympathy for, professors who were struggling to meet the changing demands on them that had occurred since their promotions. Manifesting itself as recognition that what determines effective academic leadership is influenced by, *inter alia*, temporally-dependent factors such as shifting institutional agendas and priorities, the connectionist perspective is illustrated by François's implicit observation that some who used to be 'leading' professors no longer are, in the current academic environment:

> I mean, the job is changing at some pace at the moment, as we all know … but, even though I tend to be quite critical of some senior colleagues, I can also see how difficult it must be; you know, you've been promoted in the mid-80s or even in the early '90s – because you find yourself now in a very different position. If you think, for instance, about research funding – especially in the arts and humanities – the tradition of the lone scholar is … largely gone, and these guys [professors] are being asked to apply for funding, and in some cases they've never done it. … I can … see why, you know, when you come to the end of your career you might think: well, I've been working very hard for 30 or 40 years; I've made my contribution to the field, it's time for me to – I dunno – concentrate on teaching, or perhaps just concentrate on writing this final book. (*François, arts and humanities lecturer, pre-1992 university*)

Implicit leadership theories, then, do seem to have some resonance with the perspectives of 'the led' uncovered by the *Leading professors* study, and to go some way towards explaining their bases. They offer an explanation for the subtly (and sometimes not so subtly) varied standards applied to 'leading' professor status ascription that were evident in interviewees' narratives and comments. They offer a degree of elucidation, for example, on what may have influenced the somewhat different perspectives discernible in the three narratives presented in Chapter 5 – those of Nicole, Ken and David – on what makes for a 'leading' professor. They also help explain the evident greater propensity that some interviewees (compared with others) showed for tolerance or understanding of professors who were described as struggling to meet the shifting demands of a constantly evolving role, or who – as described by Eleanor, quoted above – seemed to focus more on certain selected aspects of 'leading' professorship than on others.

Yet implicit leadership theories do not *fully* explain the bases of such perspectives. As analytical frameworks for drilling down to expose why, fundamentally, academics who are not themselves professors want or expect professors to act in certain ways, they have limitations. They represent a digging tool that is not entirely fit for purpose since it not only seems capable of scratching only a little below the surface of the depths it ought to be plumbing, but its design also equips it for a limited range of use. I follow up on these observations below.

From implicit leadership theories to implicit *professorship* theories

I return first to a point raised above: that most professors – particularly those without portfolios – tend to be seen and to see themselves first and foremost as professors, rather than as academic leaders. The implications of this tendency are that, in the *Leading professors* study, despite its explicit intended focus on professors *as academic leaders*, research participants frequently defaulted to considering and addressing issues that related to the nature simply of professorship, rather than more specifically of professorial academic leadership, or they defaulted to focusing on professors as academic colleagues, rather than as academic *leaders*. In some cases the interview conversation or narrative slipped seamlessly and often imperceptibly in and out of these different foci of consideration – slippage that was facilitated by a pervasive uncertainty and lack of clarity about what is meant by academic leadership.

The recurrence of this vacillating ambiguity represented what is perhaps one of the study's methodological weaknesses: the difficulty in ascertaining, on occasions in the course of data collection and analysis, and despite interviewer probing, whether articulated perceptions of a specific professor's – or, more generally, the professoriate's – professionalism were based upon assessments of them as *professors*, or more broadly as *academics* – or even simply of their relationality as *people* (or of a combination of all three). This uncertainty is, of course, a feature of most social science research that is intended to focus on specific role incumbency or categories – including leadership research generally, for it is impossible to separate out people's personal characteristics from those associated with or denoting their leadership roles and responsibilities; indeed, Middlehurst (1993, p. 7) acknowledges 'the difficulty of disentangling "real leadership" from other social influence processes'. It (the uncertainty) does, however, dilute the validity of data collection. So, for example, an interviewee's account of an interaction with a professor depicted as aggressive begs questions such as:

- Did the interviewee seem genuinely to relate the professor's professorial status to her/his aggressiveness – that is: was the 'complaint' against someone who, *on the basis of her/his being a professor*, was unacceptably aggressive, or against an unacceptably aggressive colleague who *incidentally happened to be a professor*?
- Would the aggressiveness have been so perceived no matter whom it emanated from – professor or non-professor?
    - If so, is it reasonable to interpret or present it as indicative of, specifically, *professorship* that falls short?

The difficulty in answering such questions reflects the blurring of the boundaries between personality and role or job incumbency, and which clouds the processes involved in research that, by incorporating layers of complexity in the form of additional categories that must be considered, goes beyond simple examination of people's characteristics or behaviour and their impact on human interaction. Such was the multidimensional complexity of the *Leading professors* study: it sought consideration not simply of collegial interaction in academe, but, more specifically, of the significance on such interaction of specific role incumbency and purpose, and of seniority and status in the form of professorship as a category of academic leadership.

Used principally as explanations for the ascription of the kind of designated formal leadership that is very much in the limelight and centre stage, implicit leadership theories are not quite up to the task of explaining why people might recognise as leaders those who, like professors without portfolios, operate in the shadows of leadership's twilight zone, their leadership often obscured and difficult to discern. The features of their work that *are* on display and in full view may not necessarily be associated with any crepuscular leadership they may appear, or happen, to do incidentally, 'on the side'. The danger therefore remains that the consideration and assessment underpinning *leader* status ascription will be eclipsed by what is illuminated by the spotlight directed at these people as they carry out what is perceived as their principal role and function: professorship.

Yet implicit leadership theories can surely be easily adapted into a more multi-purpose tool that copes with such ambiguity or plurality of role ascription, for, by substituting throughout the word 'professor' – or variations of this, such as 'professorial academic leader' – for 'leader', it is a simple process to transform implicit *leadership* theories into implicit *professorship* theories. The latter would operate on the same basis and principles as do the former, yet they would be focused not on leadership broadly but on professorship or 'professorialness', intended to explain the bases of people's assessment of the extent to which they consider this or that senior academic to manifest the characteristics associated with professorship, or with professorial academic leadership. Indeed, several of the examples presented above, of implicit leadership theories' application to some of the *Leading professors* research findings, seem to represent just such adaptation, insofar as the research participants quoted are likely to have formulated their assessments by matching up professors' behaviour, as they perceived it, with their (the interviewees') schemas, not (only) of how *leaders*, but (also) of how *professors*, ought to behave.

Even with such adaptation – and quite apart from what I consider their inaccurate appropriation of the word 'theories'[3] – implicit theories (whether of leadership or professorship, or indeed of any other 'ship') nevertheless seem to have limited explicatory capacity; for, if we accept that people ascribe leadership (including professorial academic leadership) status to others by such conscious or unconscious rapid mental comparative processes – effectively using prototypes as yardsticks against which to measure observed behaviour – the question remains: where do such prototypes come from? As Epitropaki et al. (2013) point out, there has been little research into this; Keller (1999, 2003) is one of the few researchers to have addressed such questions, concluding that mirror descriptions of the traits identified in their parents influenced the formation of some people's prototypes, while others (also) based prototypical characteristics on those they recognised in themselves.

In an effort to achieve a little more elucidatory depth than has been achieved by the application of implicit learning theories, I propose a theoretical perspective – what I call 'proximity theory' – as a plausible explanation for what shapes the prototypes of 'leading' professors against which non-professorial academics assess their senior colleagues' enacted professorial professionalism.

Proximity theory and uncompromising work contexts

The perspectives that I label 'proximity theory' have their genesis in my analyses of data that I collected in the 1990s in the course of researching, first, schoolteacher, and then academics' attitudes to their work and their jobs – particularly their morale and job satisfaction.[4] Faced with data that indicated considerable disparity in my research participants' job-related attitudes, despite their exposure to common institutional environments and cultures and situations and circumstances that were related and described with considerable consensus, indicating shared perceptions, in order to uncover a universally applicable causal link I sought the lowest common factor that explained the basis of people's attitudinal responses to what they reported as having experienced. The link I identified is the basis of the predictions of what I call 'proximity theory', explained below.

Two decades after first mooting it, I am prompted by its applicability to the *Leading professors* research findings, to dust off proximity theory and (re-)propose it here.

Proximity theory

In my earlier work on schoolteachers' and academics' job-related attitudes (Evans, 1998; Evans & Abbott, 1998), I explain the fundamental determinant of job-related attitudes as the individual's perceived *current* proximity to what s/he *currently* identifies as her/his 'ideal' job situation, or, expressed another way, job-related ideals. This – the individual's conception of her/his 'ideal' job situation – comprises and reflects, *inter alia*, values, needs, interests and desires: all of those specific psychologically, sociologically, socio-culturally and affectively oriented properties of individuals that occupational psychologists have variously identified as influential on one or more job-related attitudes. The emphasis on currency reflects incorporation of the consideration that individuals' conceptions of their ideals are susceptible to fluctuation resulting from shifting or continually evolving priorities, just as the stability of their *actual* work situations are equally precarious; nothing remains static and immutable – today's actual or ideal job situation may degenerate in the blink of an eye, or gradually and imperceptibly, into being tomorrow's job situation from hell.

Much of this conceptualisation and evaluation is likely to occur unconsciously. Whilst some people may indeed consciously hold conceptions of their 'ideal' job situations, which determine clear goals that may guide their ambitions, many are likely to be unaware of their job-related ideals unless specifically asked to identify them, and even then may not easily recognise them. Yet ideals become apparent through the preferences that people hold and the choices they are able to make. They are also apparent – as with the *Leading professors* data and findings – in people's articulations of what they like and dislike about their job situations, and in what they approve and disapprove of (the (*e*)*valuative* dimension of their professionalism, as I conceptualise it in Chapter 2). By 'job situation' – whether actual or ideal – I mean what may best be explained as the whole, vast 'package' that defines one's working life, including: the physical and geographical workplace location; the nature of the work, including the minute detail of the day-to-day tasks that it involves; one's level of seniority and status; the conditions of service and working conditions – again, including minutiae such as whether one has one's own or a shared workspace, and what facilities one has access to; the quality of internal décor and buildings maintenance, etc.; the level of convenience or inconvenience caused by the work (e.g. whether it involves a long daily commute or is close to home; whether the working hours suit one's personal circumstances and family responsibilities); and the people one comes into contact with. All of these – and many, many more – are the kinds of features whose perceived nature and quality, and how these impact upon an individual, collectively define the landscape of her or his job 'situation'.

Proximity theory posits that job-related attitudes and affect are determined by the proximity of what is subjectively perceived as one's current *actual* to one's current *ideal* job situation. Being a theory in what I call the 'elitist' sense – that is, it 'provides explanations of things; it is interpretive; it has generalisability; it has logical consistency; it incorporates structure; it facilitates prediction' (Evans, 2002, p. 183) – it cuts across contextually-determined variability and heterogeneity to offer a universally applicable explanation for the bases of job-related attitudes and affect. It satisfies the criteria for theory outlined so eloquently by Sutton and Staw (1995, p. 378):

> Theory is the answer to queries of why. Theory is about the connections among phenomena, a story about why acts, events, structure, and thoughts occur. Theory emphasizes the nature of causal relationships, identifying what comes first as well as the timing of such events. Strong theory, in our view, delves into underlying processes so as to understand the systematic reasons for a particular occurrence or nonoccurrence. It often burrows deeply into microprocesses, laterally into neighboring concepts, or in an upward direction, tying itself to broader social phenomena. It usually is laced with a set of convincing and logically interconnected arguments. It can have implications that we have not seen with our naked (or theoretically unassisted) eye. It may have implications that run counter to our common sense. As Weick (1995) put it succinctly, a good theory explains, predicts, and delights.

Jasso (1988, p. 2) identifies two classes of 'distinctive tasks of theoretical analysis': *speculative thinking* and *formal reasoning*. My development of proximity theory represents at least the first of these, which aligns with Jasso's observation (1988, p. 2): '"discursive" theorists tend to the first class and "mathematical" theorists tend to the second class'. Proximity theory stems from the *axiom of comparison*, 'which formalizes the long-held view that a wide class of phenomena, including happiness, self-esteem, and the sense of distributive justice, may be understood as the product of a comparison process' (Jasso, 1988, p. 11). The comparison element in proximity theory is the comparison between the 'actual' and the 'ideal' current job situation, as subjectively perceived. Proximity theory posits that the closer one perceives one's 'actual' job situation to how one would, ideally, like it, the more positive one's job-related attitudes are; conversely, the further from one's ideal job situation one perceives one's 'actual' job situation, the more negative one's job-related attitudes are – typically manifested by, *inter alia*, dissatisfaction and low morale. Encompassing each of the examples of phenomena listed in the quote from Jasso, above, the *underlying* phenomenon in question, underpinning the phenomenon of one's total job situation, is the conception of oneself-at-work or of one's professional or work-related self – which reflects, in turn, a broader, all-encompassing conception of self, for work-related ideals will always be located within a more expansive, holistic, conception of an ideal self that encompasses all aspects and components of one's life: personal as well as professional. (This notion of an ideal self probably equates to the notion of subjective well-being (SWB) – which Weiss (2002, p. 180) explains: 'Numerous SWB researchers now take the position that SWB is an umbrella concept that encompasses three distinct constructs: an overall evaluation or global judgment of life satisfaction, a component that taps into affective experiences, and a belief component' – or as what Rode (2004) and Veenhoven (1991, p. 10) call 'life satisfaction' and which Veenhoven explains as 'the degree to which an individual judges the overall quality of his life-as-a-whole favourably. In other words: how well he likes the life he leads' (p. 10): a judgement that he (Veenhoven) contends is made on the bases of affective and cognitive considerations.)

Consistent with what I call proximity theory, it seems reasonable to argue that work situations are determined and defined by contexts that variously, and to different degrees, facilitate or impede the pursuit of one's ideal self-at-work. I explain these contexts as 'compromising' or 'uncompromising'.

The 'compromising'–'uncompromising' work context continuum

A feature of proximity theory is people's overarching (albeit often unconscious) concern to work within contexts that – almost certainly without applying this term – they perceive as what I call 'uncompromising', in the sense that these contexts do not require them to compromise on the things that they value and approve of, and which reflect, *inter alia*, their values, ideologies and priorities. Defining 'work context' as the situation and circumstances, arising out of a combination and inter-relationship of institutionally- and externally-imposed conditions that constitute the environment and culture within which an individual carries out her/his work or job, I have argued (Evans, 2001) that job-related attitudes are fundamentally influenced (albeit often unconsciously) by perceptions of the extent to which work contexts are 'compromising' or 'uncompromising' in this respect; that is, the extent to which they essentially require an individual to compromise on the conception of her/his ideal self-at-work.

The more 'compromising' work contexts are (that is, the more they require the individual to compromise), the more negatively they impact upon job-related attitudes; the more 'uncompromising' they are (that is, the less they require the individual to compromise), the more positive the work-related attitudes that they foster. The 'uncompromising' work context is thus a principal constituent of the 'ideal' work situation. Conveying the notion of subtle gradations of 'compromisingness', 'compromising' and 'uncompromising' represent the two ends of a work context continuum.

Whilst recognising that any aspects of their work situations have the capacity to influence the extent to which people's work contexts are 'compromising', I have identified (Evans, 2001) specific generic categories of the range of issues upon which the participants in my research into schoolteachers' and academics' working lives based their assessments of their work contexts. Adapting these categories – on the basis not only of my own reconsideration of them, well over a decade after they were first published, but also of their relevance to twenty-first-century academic work contexts – I present them here as applicable to this chapter's analysis. In revised form the five key issues are: *fairness, equity and justice; interpersonal relations; collegiality; administrative and organisational effectiveness;* and *work carried out*.

Just as these, in their original form, were what my earlier research revealed to matter most to people in their work contexts, so too, using the revised descriptors, do I present them as the issues that evidently mattered to the *Leading professors* interviewees in their work contexts. The *extent* to which each matters – the prominence that it is afforded within people's range or hierarchy of concerns – inevitably varies from person to person, and may also fluctuate over time, as competing priorities win ground from each other within people's shifting and evolving conceptions of their ideal selves-at-work. For one person, being treated fairly may be a paramount concern in the workplace; for another – who perhaps has had no cause to complain of unfair treatment personally, but may nevertheless identify procedural inequities within the organisation – the issue may be on her or his radar but without its being a preoccupation, yet s/he may be very affected by problems stemming from what I identify as another key issue: interpersonal relations. The point is that these issues variously act as filters that colour – and hence influence – assessments of the specific features that define one's work situation. For the *Leading professors* interviewees, one such feature that they assessed was professorial academic leadership.

Proximity theory as a basis of assessments of 'leading' professorship

Subjectively, ideal job situations are those in which everything is exactly as one would wish it. Incorporating consideration of what my research has revealed to be the key issues that matter to people, listed above, the ideal work situation may – depending on personal preferences and priorities – be perceived as one in which everyone is perceived as being treated fairly (fairness, equity and justice), where everyone gets on well together (interpersonal relations), where colleagues interact and cooperate amicably and productively on work-related tasks, without undue or unwelcome pressure to perform (collegiality); where the place is well managed in ways that incorporate consideration of staff well-being, and the administrative processes and procedures result in unproblematic efficiency (administrative and organisational effectiveness); and where specific organisational purpose-related functions are performed satisfactorily – by oneself or others (work carried out); for academics these functions are likely to be one or more of what have been identified by the Diamond Report of 2015 (Universities UK, 2015, p. 7) as universities' 'core activities of teaching, research, and knowledge exchange' (or impact activities).

In a university setting, where academics seldom – if ever – work completely in isolation, the ideal job situation must incorporate consideration of other people and how they impact upon one's working life. For the *Leading professors* research participants, one of several constituencies of colleagues with the potential to impact upon their working lives was the professoriate – including professors who were external to their own institutions. Professors therefore featured with varying degrees of prominence and abundance on the landscapes of non-professorial academics' work contexts. As such, they inevitably influenced – as did the countless other people with whom these academics networked and rubbed shoulders in the course of their work – the nature of their (the non-professorial academics') work situations, including the proximity of these work situations to those work situations they may have perceived as ideal.

My analysis of the *Leading professors* data leads me to propose that professors' influence on the extent of this proximity was filtered through one or more of the five categories of issues identified above as those that, to varying degrees, matter to people in the contexts of their work. So, for example, dissatisfaction with professors who were perceived as not pulling their weight or as trying to off-load undesirable tasks and responsibilities onto junior colleagues, may, depending on the circumstances, be analysed as representing one or more of: a fairness, equity and justice-related issue or a collegiality-related issue – or even as an administrative and organisational effectiveness-related issue, or as a work carried out-related issue (insofar as the professors in question may be deemed to have performed badly or inadequately work related to the organisation's core purpose(s) which they may reasonably be expected to have performed satisfactorily – such as educating undergraduates, or sitting on doctoral students' upgrade panels).

Bradley et al. (2017, p. 100) argue that '[u]niversities have a clear expectation that academics will take on greater responsibilities throughout their tenure'. Such expectations are likely to be shared by junior academics, and so professorship perceived as falling short in this respect will have represented a blot on the landscape of their *actual* work situations of those interviewees who complained of it, increasing their distance from their ideal work situations. Consistent with proximity theory, I suggest that the negativity reflected in such complaints fundamentally represents the compromising of their conceptions of their ideal-selves-at-work held by those making them. Yet these conceptions may be quite varied and disparate in nature and focus, reflecting individual differences. For one such academic the conception of her ideal-self-at-work may be one in which, simply as a matter of principle, she is satisfied that she has been given a fair workload; for another, it may be one in which she is allowed time to focus on developing her research profile, and in order for her to do so senior colleagues take on tasks that might otherwise land on her desk; for yet another, the ideal-self-at-work may reflect a more generally Utopian conception of himself as a contented and satisfied member of a happy, collegial department in which all colleagues may be relied upon to pull their weight willingly. The implications of such disparity are that, whilst multiple individuals may be united in their dissatisfaction with or disapproval of a situation that affects them all in common, the *bases* of their responses to it may vary.

Proximity theory may similarly be applied to explanation of the bases of approbation of professors who demonstrated themselves *willing* to take on heavier or more problematic workloads and responsibilities than their junior colleagues. The reasoning here would be that, by pulling their weight in this way, professors contributed towards creating work contexts that, for one reason or another, took their junior colleagues' current perceived work situations a step nearer to matching their ideal work situations. Such a contribution was implicitly identified in associate professor Eleanor's narrative, in which she spoke of the enriching experiences afforded her by involvement in learned society work, through bringing her into contact with professors who were prepared to take on rather time-consuming but sometimes thankless tasks – what Morley (2013, p. 118) calls the morality-focused perception of leadership as 'turn-taking' and 'sacrifice'. For Eleanor, this enrichment involved her feeling welcomed and respected as a valuable member of a disciplinary network in which she found herself watching and learning from distinguished senior academics from outside her own institution, and whom she described as willing to roll up their sleeves and do what was needed to foster and perpetuate cultures of supportive collegiality, for the advancement of their field. This interviewee's interpretation of 'leading' professorship – outlined in her remarks below – incorporated consideration of this kind of service-related dimension that is expressed through a readiness to playing one's part in ensuring that the minutiae and the drudgery of academic life in its widest sense are neither overlooked nor off-loaded onto junior colleagues:

> For me, leadership is something more than simply doing your job; it's about, kind of, showing people a way forward, and, kind of, being an example. ... I do think it's important to maintain a contact with your colleagues and to demonstrate how things are done, actually, and part of that is supporting younger colleagues and students within your own department as well as being a leading researcher outside your department and outside your institution. ... Leadership, for me, is not necessarily about ... just being out there as the pioneer, leading the way, it's also about doing things which demonstrate your commitment to something – which aren't necessarily very impressive – but that you nonetheless take on. (*Eleanor, associate professor, modern foreign languages, pre-1992 university*)

Proximity theory under scrutiny

'Theory is crafted around the data', observe Sutton and Staw (1995, p. 381). But causal logic is absent from not only the quote from Eleanor, but also the reported summary of selected parts of her interview narrative above. The evidence trail that leads from the *Leading professors* data to proximity theory is undoubtedly difficult to discern, not least because data collection was principally focused not on the research participants' job-related attitudes – these emerged incidentally as what appeared a peripheral issue, whose potentially greater significance then became evident at the data analysis stage, as I began to seek answers to the 'why?' questions – but on the participants' perceptions and assessments of professors as academic leaders. Data with the potential to evidence proximity theory are therefore few and far between; in contrast to the two studies that were focused on professors' perspectives (presented in Part Three of this book), *Leading professors* participants were seldom asked to discuss their ideal job situations and the extent to which their current jobs matched their ideals. The problem of evidence occurs not in relation to what proximity theory posits – that an individual's job-related attitudes are determined by her/his current perception of her/his actual work situation's proximity to her/his current perception of her/his ideal work situation – for such evidence is presented both in the published findings of my earlier research, and in Chapter 10 of this book. Rather, the evidence scarcity here is associated with my proposing as plausible a link between what proximity theory posits and individuals' assessments of the quality and nature of a specific feature of their current perceived work situations: professorial academic leadership.

Yet, irrespective of considerations of a focus-determined data scarcity, as links in a chain of correlation or causality that evidences proximity theory, the contributions – however slight – that 'leading' professorship is perceived to make to the enhancement of other people's work situations may in any case be imperceptible and untraceable. Such contributions may be indirect and circuitous, so that their effects may only be surmised or conjectured. It may be, for example, that, by shouldering responsibilities that might otherwise land on junior colleagues' desks, professors not only serve as exemplars and role models, but also indirectly allow their junior colleagues to devote more time to career-building activities, facilitating their advancement, which, in turn, may have the effect of enhancing their conceptions of themselves-at-work, taking them nearer to their current ideals. But such a link represents, at best, reasonable deduction and at worst conjecture.

What I identify above both as what proximity theory posits and as the causal extension to this may in fact be untestable, but this untestability should not preclude my proposing proximity theory as a plausible explanation for my research findings. Indeed, as Teddlie (2005, p. 214) observes, causality is a contentious issue: many qualitative researchers 'have serious issues regarding the possibility of making causal explanations' and, generally, 'postmodern theorists do not think causal explanations are possible owing to contentious epistemological issues', whilst pragmatists tend to sit on the fence in deciding whether causality is or should be provable or not. I am moreover encouraged and reassured by Sutton and Staw's (1995) observations and recommendations relating to how the academic community receives and evaluates authors' proposed theories. They point out that:

> Quotes from informants or detailed observations may get a bit closer to the underlying causal forces than, say, mean job satisfaction scores or organizational size, but qualitative evidence, by itself, cannot convey causal arguments that are abstract and simple enough to be applied to other settings. Just like theorists who use quantitative data, those who use qualitative data must develop causal arguments to explain why persistent findings have been observed if they wish to write papers that contain theory. (pp. 374–5)

I believe I have presented (above) causal arguments to support proximity theory as a plausible explanation for the bases of my research participants' assessments of their professorial colleagues. But particularly encouraging (bearing in mind the date of its publication) are Sutton and Staw's rallying cry – in their capacity as academic journal editors – for a change of attitude on the part of those who are quick to pick holes in new theoretical propositions:

> if a theory is particularly interesting, the standards used to evaluate how well it is tested or grounded need to be relaxed, not strengthened. We need to recognize that major contributions can be made when data are more illustrative than definitive. ... Authors should be rewarded rather than punished for developing strong conceptual arguments that dig deeper and extend more broadly than the data will justify. (p. 382)

In proposing proximity theory here I have achieved, through what Sutton and Staw refer to as 'strong conceptual argument', my purpose of digging deeply; whether this represents digging deeper and more extensively than my data justify is debatable – though I do accept that my data are 'more illustrative than definitive'.

'Leading' professor prototypes: The bases of expectations of professorial distinction and relationality

We must now, finally, return to consideration of where people's prototypes of professors as academic leaders, or 'leading' professors come from. As Chapters 5 and 6 show, the expectations that non-professorial academics hold of professors relate to two broad features that underpin the criteria for 'leading' professorship ascription: professors' *distinction* and *relationality*. These features influence the 'leading' professor prototypes against which people match their perceptions of professors, on the basis of their (professors') enacted professionalism. Essentially, then, the prototypical 'leading' professor – which is the comparative baseline for what I propose above should be termed implicit professorship or professorial leadership 'theories' – manifests scholarly distinction and well-developed relationality that is conveyed through characteristics such as: approachability, empathy, good-naturedness, affability, generosity, and altruistic collegiality. Such a professor is unconsciously valued because, whether an institutional colleague or a member of their external networks, s/he is a key component of what, to most non-professorial academics, represents an ideal work situation. The combination of distinction (which denotes knowledgeableness) and well-developed relationality (which denotes accessibility to such knowledgeableness), makes such a professor an invaluable resource that few academics would shun. Whilst no research participant explicitly used the word 'resource' in alluding to professorial roles or purpose, it seems that 'leading' professors were effectively perceived as such, however unconsciously.

But how do 'leading' professor prototypes form and plant themselves – consciously or unconsciously – within academics' schemas?

The origins of 'leading' professor prototypes

It is easy to see how 'leading' professor prototypes are retained and sustained: once junior academics experience the benefits of interacting with a professor who contributes towards enhancing their work situations, they then measure all other professors whom they subsequently encounter against the work situation-enhancer. Those who measure up earn 'leading' professor ascription – and some of them may even unwittingly usurp the original prototype – while those who fall short may be fully or partially denied 'leading' professor ascription.

For most *Leading professors* interviewees, it seemed that one or more professors had made pivotal and enduring favourable impressions on them at some stage in their careers. Often this impression was made in the early career stage, and, consistent with Bolden et al.'s (2012a) findings, several interviewees acknowledged doctoral supervisors and mentors as model professors – implicitly, as prototypes. Another frequently identified source of prototype was the external professor – one who had never been an institutional colleague, but may have been encountered at a conference or through learned society activities, or even as an external doctoral examiner – and who had evidently demonstrated that admirable mix of distinction and relationality that non-professorial academics seem to find so appealing. The frequency with which external professors – rather than departmental professorial colleagues – were lionised as exemplars or role models is quite easy to understand: these professors were encountered in off-campus mode, often during what Mullainathan and Shafir (2014, p. 74) call their 'slack' time:

We all have experienced slack in time. On a not-too-busy week we leave holes in our schedule. You leave a fifteen minute window between meetings, where in busier times you would have squeezed in a quick phone call. The time is just there, like loose change lying around the house. You feel no compulsion to use it.

In any context, collegial interaction that creates 'slack' opens up opportunities for a 'context' of accessibility and congeniality which is conducive to the forging of what Uhl-Bien (2006) calls the 'relational bonds' that underpins effective academic leadership. Such interaction may occur at conferences, which are recognised as fora for atypical collegial exchanges, such as evoked by Garud's (2008) recollection of a conference whose highlight, for him, was the accessibility of people who would otherwise have remained off his relational radar. The semi-social nature and the external spatiality of such arenas and fora potentially alters people's mind-sets and priorities, promoting a form of spatially-determined empowerment whereby junior academics may capitalise on their senior colleagues' greater (than normal) accessibility and inclination to focus more unwaveringly and with fewer distractions on them (junior academics). Thus perspectives, attitudes and inclinations are encouraged that may be less likely to surface in other, more mundane and familiar, contexts (and physical spaces), under different circumstances. It is, after all, easy to sustain a good impression of a senior academic who is not an institutional colleague and with whom one interacts sporadically or infrequently, in relatively congenial off-campus unpressured environments, where s/he is on her/his best behaviour, with her/his foibles and frustrations under wraps.

But what is it that makes such professors such a hit with the junior colleagues they find time for, thereby identifying themselves as 'leading' professor prototypes? Drilling down to consider the *bases* of people's appreciation of the combination of professors' distinction and relationality that manifested itself as professorial knowledge-repository-and-sharing-capacity, and junior academics' reliance on professors as a resource, a plausible line of reasoning leads us to their (non-professorial academics') professional related self-esteem, and how it may be enhanced. Status in academe is generally associated with success, which, for the most part, is derived from competence and the capacity to do a good job – whether through research or teaching or administrative roles. Such capacity is dependent upon successful socialisation and acculturation within one or more academic communities, which, in turn, involves accruing knowledge – of all kinds. Senior academics who demonstrably have accrued such knowledge and are willing to pass it on to others therefore represent an invaluable resource, for as Parker and Welch (2013, p. 336) observe '[v]isibility and reputational returns are … attained by individuals aligning themselves with other people that have valuable information and resources'. Burt (2000, p. 348) points out that '[b]etter connected people enjoy higher returns', and many junior academics evidently equate networking with professors as a connection-enhancement mechanism that may result in the crumbs of such 'higher returns' being scattered their way. White et al. (2016, p. 283) moreover link the kind of influence that constitutes leadership with social support. Underpinned by consideration of social exchange theory, they suggest that:

> the person one might go to for social support may help in shaping one's status in a group in relation to leadership. Here, individuals support one another, and help to create an environment where other members are valued and appreciated. By actively providing support, individuals are more likely to be recognized in relation to leadership status.

Fundamentally, the value of professors as a status-enhancing resource that junior academics may tap into or draw upon is that, in serving as a compass that indicates the 'right' direction to follow, facilitating academics' status-related acculturation, it has the potential, indirectly, by enhancing these academics' career development, to enhance their self-esteem: their capacity to feel good about themselves and their achievements. Consistent with social exchange theory, then, non-professorial academics ascribe academic leadership status to those whose interaction or relationship with them affords them (the non-professorial academics) some advantage.

Supporting Middlehurst's (1993, p. 193) point that 'leadership touches the emotions, values, self-image and perceptions of individuals and groups', and Bolden et al.'s (2012b, p. 12) finding that '[a]cademic leaders were described as being people who made one feel a valued member of the team, the department, and/or the university', the importance of self-esteem-enhancement is implicit in the comments of chemistry reader Alan, who, in speaking of the first professor with whom he had worked as an academic, and who had mentored him, pinpointed the basis of academics' appreciation of professorial colleagues' interest in and finding time for them:

> He had time for me, and that was clear. And he *did* have time, and he would always take the time to discuss whatever it was, so that's *probably* the most important thing … just … er … availability … clear responsibility – that he had that role and he was my mentor. … He gave me advice in terms of managing research groups; how to … y'know … how to deal with difficult situations in the

lab ... y'know, people ... people fighting ... and friendship ... social ... y'know. We'd go out for lunch reasonably often, get invited to his house for dinner ... . Those things sound trivial, but they're not, are they? ... So perhaps the most important thing was ... I felt that *he* felt I was important ... and that I was an important part of his ... working life.

From the perspective of 'the led', then, professors' relationality is highly rated on account of its generative and facilitative capacity: its link to professorial knowledge and skills that junior colleagues may emulate or learn from. As some of the comments and narratives presented in Chapter 5 imply, being noticed, being taken seriously, being befriended or mentored by a colleague who, by virtue of his or her professorial status, is manifestly a high achiever who enjoys the distinction of being located at the pinnacle of the academic staff hierarchy, is gratifying on account of the boost to self-image that it carries with it. The potency of 'leading' professorship is that, through their relationality, coupled with the credibility derived from their distinct knowledge and achievements, 'leading' professors have the capacity to fuel feelings of self-efficacy in others. The prototypical 'leading' professor, against which other professors are then measured, has that capacity.

Fundamentally, then, for each academic, the prototype is a professor who pushes the buttons that contribute towards enhancing the junior colleague's self-esteem. This does not mean that professors who fail (partially or entirely) to contribute towards boosting someone's self-esteem preclude themselves from 'leading' professorship ascription; many *Leading professors* research participants assessed specific professors positively on the basis of their distinction, and somewhat or slightly more negatively on the basis of their relationality (or vice versa). This compromising of standards represents a form of assessment and ascription that is explained by adaptive resonance theory, outlined above as a dimension of implicit leadership theories. But the point is that such professors are unlikely to serve as 'leading' professor *prototypes*, since they fall short of manifesting the *ideal* combination of distinction and relationality.

'Leading' professorship represents professionalism that is demanded of professors by their junior colleagues, and whose expectations of the professoriate are shaped by the examples of prototypical 'leading' professors, influencing the perspectives of 'the led' that have been the focus of this part – Part Two – of this book. But, from the perspective of professors themselves, what does the notion of 'leading' professorship mean – and how keen are they to embrace, and even practise, it? These issues are addressed in the chapters that follow, in Part Three of the book.

Notes

1 Implicit followership theories.

2 Where micro-level leadership is examined as a process, leader(ship) ascription tends to be carried out by observers analysing the process, since fleeting and rapidly recurring 'episodes' identifying leaders and 'led' may be too subtle to be noticed and identified, at the time of engagement, by those engaged in them.

3 Rather than adhere to the scholarly tradition of defining a theory narrowly and precisely as a universally applicable explanation for why, how, or under what circumstances, something occurs – what I call (Evans, 2002) the 'elitist' interpretation of or perspective on theory – 'theories' as the word is used in the term 'implicit leadership theories' seems to denote the categories that people (unconsciously) create in their heads and that inform their ideas about what something, such as role incumbency, should 'look like': that is, 'theory' as the word is often used in the vernacular.

4 In the field of work or occupational psychology, morale and job satisfaction are traditionally categorised as attitudes.

Part Three

The Professoriate's Perspectives

8

Negotiating a Passage: Becoming a Professor in the UK Academy

'[T]he chair is conventionally, and for the majority, the highest object of vocational ambition', wrote Halsey in 1992. It is unclear whether this statement represents assumption on Halsey's part, or whether it is informed by his landmark study of UK-based academics, carried out in the 1970s and 1980s, but, either way, it seems still to hold water in the twenty-first century, with several commentators (e.g. Douglas, 2013; Macfarlane, 2012a; Özkanli & White, 2008; Rayner et al., 2010; Tight, 2002) recognising professorship as 'a position marking the pinnacle of an academic career' (Rayner et al., 2010, p. 617), while Jürgen Enders observes '[i]n the United Kingdom it seems ... that the expectations of middle rank staff are growing, and that non-promotion tends to be regarded as a failure' (Enders, 2000, p. 22).

Is professorship then a goal that all academics set their sights on? Not necessarily, contends Sutherland (2017, p. 743): 'many academics themselves have no aspirations to a full professorship or chair. What constitutes success for one academic may be low on another's list of priorities' – a view that was borne out by the *Leading professors* study, which revealed less than a third (32.7 per cent) of questionnaire respondents to indicate a 'definite' ambition to become a professor, and over a quarter to declare that they had no such aspirations.[1] Yet whilst it evidently is not for everyone, roughly one-tenth of academics in the UK currently do take a path that leads to professorship. What prompts them to do so, and how easy (or hard) is their transition? To quote Halsey (1992, p. 200) once more 'What enables men and women to negotiate successful passage to this high point of an academic career?' Addressing these questions, this chapter uncovers something of the process of becoming a professor.

Privilege, performance and personalities:
The ingredients of professorship?

John Fisher's appointment in 1502 to the first Lady Margaret professorship of divinity at Cambridge may have had something to do with his being confessor to the chair's foundress. These were the days when one's promotion (in society) depended on whom one knew; it was a process of patronage that inevitably perpetuated privilege – as Brockliss (2016, p. 49) remarks: 'Before the nineteenth century (and even then), it was hard to be upwardly mobile without the right patron.' Yet, if he was typical of a medieval cleric – albeit an exalted one – Fisher's episcopal duties, on account of the income and privileges that he derived from the bishopric of Rochester, would have been of far greater importance to him than his Cambridge chair. In medieval England, an academic career was often a sideline to a much more lucrative and status-ridden senior post in the church.

Nevertheless, even the pin money that academic sidelines brought to Tudor clerics could not be procured without that form of privilege that patronage represents. In a different guise professorship and privilege continued to go hand-in-hand until well into the twentieth century, remaining discernibly linked even in the twenty-first-century academy, for, while Hoskins (2012) identifies eight of the twenty female professors in her twenty-first-century study as having working-class origins, Halsey's earlier study revealed promotion to professorship to be closely aligned with middle-class up-bringing:

> A member of the professoriate is significantly more likely to have sprung from the middle classes. Or to put it the other way round, a manual-class origin is less likely to lead to a professorial position, the odds ratio on this formulation being 0.73. (Halsey, 1992, p. 204)

Both Halsey (1992) and Ward (2001) moreover link elite higher education experience – specifically, at Oxbridge – with professorship; interestingly, whilst it was focused on Scottish universities, Ward's study revealed 'a significantly positive effect of holding a PhD from Oxbridge' on academics' promotion prospects (p. 292). Yet, having identified the dimensions of privilege that featured in 1970s and 1980s professorship, Halsey then presents data that underscore the much greater influence on promotion prospects of research achievement than of 'upbringing, education, and training of entrants to the academic professions' (pp. 206–7):

> We found that research attitudes and performance are strongly associated with entering the professoriate. Professors are more than twice as likely (odds ratio 2.19) as the non-professorial academics to give priority to research. They

are also almost twice as likely (1.94) to value teaching and research equally as distinct from being oriented towards teaching compared with the other ranks. Publication records tell a similar story. A person who has published over twenty articles is eight times more likely (8.36) to be found among the professors than a person who has published less than ten articles. Between ten and twenty articles gives twice the chance of becoming a professor as publishing less than ten. Each book increases the odds on being a professor by 0.43 (1.43); thus three books more than doubles the odds. (Halsey, 1992, p. 207)

A quarter of a century after Halsey's findings were published, it is easy to imagine that little has changed, insofar as research achievement seems to remain the key indicator of professorship potential, and the key promotion criterion – '[b]y definition, becoming a professor is usually achieved through successful research activity', writes Douglas (2013, p. 379), and Macfarlane (2012a, p. 91) contends that 'personal excellence in research still remains the principal reason for … appointment as a professor'. Yet the picture is rather more nuanced than these quotes suggest, for, as Knight and Trowler (2001, p. 119) observe, 'research can take a variety of forms', and the range of activities that count as what he calls 'the research dimension' has widened quite considerably since Halsey collected his data. In contrast to his narrow equation of it with publications, research achievement that is valued in the twenty-first-century academy includes funding capture and research impact – Bradley et al. (2017, p. 97) describe the latter as 'the relatively recent innovation and commercialisation zeitgeist – whereby research value is defined in terms of its more immediate "real-world" outcomes'. Indeed, Ward's study revealed academic promotion prospects to be weighted in favour of 'those with good publication records, *grant winners*, Oxbridge PhD graduates and those paid on the clinical scale' (Ward, 2001, p. 300, emphasis added).

A key distinction between professorship as seen by Halsey and as it appears in the twenty-first century is that – probably dating from the intensive period of higher education reforms that occurred around the turn of the millennium – its nature has evolved to incorporate a wider and more varied remit and disparate range of responsibilities, provoking Laurie Taylor's satirical commentary, presented in Chapter 1. More recently, another new category of professor has emerged as a feature of several UK universities' responses to the government-imposed research impact agenda: the professor of public engagement.[2] The ultimate impact-savvy academic, s/he is generally expected to prioritise (and often has a track record, pre-appointment, of) taking gown to town through television appearance and other media engagement, making the esoteric accessible, and stimulating the general population's interest and intellectual curiosity.

But, whatever 'genre' or 'category' of professor s/he ends up representing, how does an academic arrive at professorship?

Getting started

Reflecting the professoriate's multi-faceted heterogeneity, how academics become professors, and what equips them to do so, varies greatly – as is implied by Hoskins's summary of the transitional experiences of her study's twenty female participants:

> When they applied for a chair, the women no doubt considered their chance of success. For some, even considering applying was a psychological leap. Others in the sample, particularly those who claimed to have planned their careers, viewed it as a taken for granted realisation of their career aims and objectives. *The respondents' starting points and progression routes differed markedly.* (Hoskins, 2012, p. 88, emphasis added)

In revealing the detail of academics' paths to the professoriate, there emerged from my *Professorial leadership preparation and development* study a continuum of attitudes and approaches to career progression, exposing wide variability across the participants. At one end of the continuum lay attitudes that suggest high levels of self-confidence, manifested by professors who implied that they had doubted neither their capacity nor their worthiness to be promoted. Located at the opposite end, sentiments such as those expressed by an anonymous questionnaire respondent in a post-1992 university – 'I was fairly clueless about what professors did until the run-up to becoming one. They were awesome figures. I looked at them from a distance, but never expected to join their numbers' – reflected attitudes that, as they were related or described, suggested rather more self-doubt, or perhaps simply general modesty. Spanning these two extremes was a subtly nuanced spectrum of evident attitudinal variation.

Representing the 'self-confident' or 'self-assured' end of the continuum was STEMM professor Will, who briefly discussed his promotion:

> *LE: Can you remember how you felt when you learned you'd got the job, that they were offering you the post? Were you absolutely elated, or did you just take it in your stride? ... Did you expect to get it?*
> Will: Yes. [slight laugh] ... I took it in my stride, really; yeah. ... So, when I was appointed a professor here I was ... what was I? ... 36. And there were people 20 or 30 years older than me who haven't made that grade, and that's a slightly strange situation.

LE: *Did you find that difficult?*
Will: No, not really [slight laugh]. I'm quite self-confident. (*Will, pre-1992 university*)

Accompanied by apparent conviction of their competence and readiness to take on professorship, such self-assuredness was evident in all of the *Professorial leadership preparation and development* participants who fell into the 'thirty-something' professor category.[3] Three interviewees – all men employed in pre-1992 universities – identified themselves as such, while a fourth appeared to be in his thirties but did not disclose his age.[4] Of these four, two represented STEMM disciplines and the other two were arts and humanities professors. Two of them held named chairs. Of those with whom I broached the thorny question of whether they considered themselves to have been promoted prematurely, each good-naturedly rejected the idea.[5] Asked if he felt he deserved his chair, STEMM professor Harry, for example, responded:

> I think I did. I mean, I think that, judging against the people who were there on the day, I did think I deserved it, because I was able to ... I was able to demonstrate that I've operated well above expectations ... I think I *do* deserve it, and I think there's a lot that they [the university] gained from having me in that position. And whether it was a year or so earlier than expected ... I think, you know, yeah, I think I got it fair and square. And I do have that, sort of, degree of enough self-belief to think that I did deserve it, but I don't think it was by any means, you know, an absolute given. I think there are very few ... people, I think, arrogant enough to think that.

Arts and humanities professor Seamus similarly represented himself as having entirely merited his promotion, on the basis of the quality of his work, and he justified his promotion at what might be considered a young age by arguing that, in a competitive climate, performativity and proven achievement carry more weight than do age-related considerations:

> It's a very competitive field. I mean, that's the simple truth of it, and you've got very talented and intelligent and political people in the field, and that brings enormous, sort of, benefits to the field. But there are certain difficulties that come with that ... and, of course, sometimes you're promoted ahead of people who ... might have been better placed to be promoted instead etc. You have to live with that, really. ... [Professorship] in one sense ... it's simply a title; it's simply a matter of status – and I think it *is* that for a lot of people. But that doesn't interest *me* at all, and it certainly wasn't the motivation for trying to became a professor. I guess, in that sense, I figured that ... my work ... merited me becoming a professor. So, in that sense, it was a, kind of ... a matter of just seeing it as the

next step, I guess, and thinking: okay, I can … I *ought* to be there, so I'm gonna go for that. (*Seamus, arts and humanities professor, pre-1992 university*)

Illustrative of the other end of the continuum was business and management professor Joanne's account of having first been 'knocked back' in a readership promotion application at her current pre-1992 university – a knock-back that she reflected upon with evident equanimity: 'I didn't have any great expectations of getting it, and I was happy, you know, with my feedback. I wasn't *terribly* disappointed; I felt, you know, it was good feedback … very encouraging' – before then successfully applying for internal promotion to a chair. She attributed her eventual success to her record of institutional citizenship through a heavy duty departmental administrative role:

> I'd been in that [role] for two years, and we thought about reapplying [for a readership], and at that stage it was clear … clear*er*, anyway, that I should go the chair route rather than the readership route, because of the experience I'd got through that. Again, no great expectations of getting something – I was *absolutely* dumbfounded, but delighted as well, when I was successful! [slight laugh]. (*Joanne, business and management professor, pre-1992 university*)

It would be easy to make the simplistic assumption, based on these illustrations of contrasting attitudes to being promoted, that women professors are less self-confident or less self-assured than their male counterparts. Yet my research revealed not only no clear evidence of such gender-related attitudinal disparity, but also evidence that undermines such assumption, insofar as, whilst the interview-generated data included several examples of comments that conveyed varying degrees of self-effacement, insecurity, or even (context-specific) relatively low self-confidence, these came from both men and women.

Biological sciences professor Brian, for example, admitted having expected his promotion application to have been unsuccessful – 'I was actually surprised they gave it to me … my expectation was that I wasn't going … to get it … I had no expectation of it succeeding; I was just hoping, actually, for feedback' – whereas linguistics professor Catherine had evidently been rather more confident of success, but not excessively so:

> Well, they very strongly – at least, in this school – encourage people not to apply until they think they'll get it. So there were several people who had sat on that particular promotions committee and they had a reasonably good idea that I would get it. And although I wasn't confident that I'd *get it*, I was confident that I wasn't wasting my time. (*Catherine, linguistics professor, pre-1992 university*)

And, by his own account, mathematics professor Anthony seems to have adopted a slightly hesitant approach to his internal promotion bid – an approach that, whilst incorporating a degree of resolve and mild assertiveness, nevertheless avoided presenting himself as presumptuous, over-confident or arrogant:

> Well, actually, maths is very good at putting people forward. So, certainly, there've been times in the past where, I think, basically, the head of department's just said, 'We're going to put you forward for promotion.' And I guess, to some extent, as you get older, you also think: well, actually, isn't *now* about the time? And then you start to push a bit more. So ... I mean, a couple of years before I was put in for promotion I, kind of, thought it *might* be possible, but I thought it was slightly cheeky to ask about it ... but I did [ask about it] ... because I know the head of department quite well. Er ... the next year, I, kind of, felt ... it almost felt like I *wasn't* being [cheeky], and I, kind of, feel if it ... if I *hadn't* been put in for promotion for much longer it would've felt like I was being *actively* not put in, and I would've started to be really quite worried. (*Anthony, mathematics professor, pre-1992 university*)

Catherine's and Anthony's accounts illustrate how, within the business of going for professorial promotion in the UK, not only is the applicant's own agency key to the nature and outcome of the process, but agency in the form of institutional procedures is also important, with some institutions allowing (only) self-determination of readiness to kick-start the applicant-initiated process, while others apply procedures that rely predominantly on departmental nomination and sponsorship. With all their variability across the sector, institutional procedures add layers of complexity to academics' paths to promotion, for while one academic may think nothing of submitting what risks being received as an audaciously premature application, or of brashly knocking on the departmental head's door to canvass for support, another may shy away from such self-promotion. Moreover, other dimensions of academics' lives contribute yet different layers of complexity to the business of getting promoted. As they were related by interviewees, paths to professorship seem rarely to have been linear, and seldom to have been approached – much less trodden – in isolation; they invariably involved the 'accompaniment' of others, through some form of direct or indirect human agency, that may have manifested itself as moral support, encouragement or sponsorship, or of a set of circumstances or a situation that happened to point the academic in a certain direction. No two paths were the same, and those that shared broad similarities inevitably varied in the detail.

Several interviewees – including modern foreign languages professor Diane, and education studies professor Alison – described their paths as having led them into what business and management professor Joanne called 'the murky world of retention', and which involved their having secured professorial job offers in other universities before their own universities were then prompted to promote them hastily. In some cases, these forays into retention territory were described as having been entirely unplanned and undertaken without guile – with the academic's having fully intended and expected to take up the external professorship offered, until a counter offer had unexpectedly come from the current employer; as Alison explained: 'I wasn't doing it deliberately to play them off because I don't understand how to do that ... I constantly felt like I was in a strange *man's* world having these strange, kind of, truncated conversations that I didn't quite know what the rules were.' In other cases retention-related tactics were described as strategic bluff-calling on the part of academics who presented themselves as knowing how to 'play the system' – as physics professor Tom described it:

> It's useful for your employers to think that: (a) you're doing a very good job and that you're more or less indispensable, and (b) that there are other people out there who are interested in employing you and might steal you. And if your employer thinks that, then that's a lever that you can use to climb up the promotion ladder and get recognition, or get a higher salary. And so there are strategic methods of doing that. I'm not actually actively looking for another job, but ... occasionally, I get enquiries, or I get approached for particular jobs elsewhere, and I make sure the head of department knows that, and indirectly I make sure the university knows that. (*Tom, physics professor, pre-1992 university*)

More general strategic agency also seems to have directed some interviewees' paths – often manifesting itself as single-minded determination and resolve to achieve one's ambitions, in ways that reflect what Sternberg (1999, 2008) calls 'successful intelligence'. Arts and humanities professor Elizabeth, for example, had for over twenty years focused unwaveringly on securing a specific named chair in an ancient Scottish university that she considered perfectly aligned with her research interests and expertise. Reflecting Sternberg's observation (1999, p. 298) 'intelligence involves not only modifying oneself to suit the environment (adaptation) but also modifying the environment to suit oneself (shaping) and, sometimes, finding a new environment that is a better match to one's skills, values, or desires (selection)', she recalled the moment when, as an early career researcher, over two decades earlier, on hearing that a new incumbent had been appointed to the chair, she had firmly resolved to secure it eventually for herself: 'I said, "*I* want that job". And since 19**[6] that's been my career goal.' Her tactical preparation for this specific professorship involved developing her career – including through management and leadership responsibilities that she took on whilst holding a personal chair at a different university – to ensure that she would be a serious contender for it. Her strategy paid off; at the time of her research interview she had held for some five years the very named chair that had for so long been the focal point of her career ambitions.

Other interviewees' paths to professorship seemed to have been trodden less resolutely and strategically, and in some cases to have been circuitous and meandering – even to have been stumbled upon almost by chance, like an unplanned off-piste excursion that somehow manages to come good in the end. Such seems to have been the path that education studies professor Eric found himself following:

> It *happened* that I became a senior lecturer. It *happened* that I became a reader ... almost – and then: 'Oh, I really should apply for a-' – and I *did* apply for chairs elsewhere but, for a variety of reasons, they didn't happen. ... I think if somebody had taken me under their wing a lot earlier, and had sat me down and said, 'Right, you're an SL,[7] Eric; let's look at the criteria for readership, and a chair', then ... [shrugs]. (*Eric, educational studies professor, pre-1992 university*)

Law professor Angie's interest in promotion seems to have developed gradually and incrementally – and to have been intensified by the example of a female role model. Asked if she had always aspired to be a professor, she responded:

> No ... when I first started doing my law degree ... I wanted to qualify ... and I think that lasted about two terms. ... But I was interested in doing research – which is why I did a research degree, and I just found that I loved teaching ... and I never intended to go into teaching ... but I really ... really enjoy teaching. And I enjoy doing the research ... and I think it was those two things combined that started me on the road of thinking maybe I could get a full-time job teaching. And then the idea of carrying on doing the research started, and then the books came ... and...y'know ... things like that started me thinking: well, actually, it'd be nice to be a professor. ... And there was a female professor ... I think she was mid-30s ... late 30s when she was made a professor – and I really aspired to ... I really wanted to do that. ... I suppose, if you're an academic ... I saw being a professor as, sort of, being the highest thing I could achieve. (*Angie, law professor, post-1992 university*)

Whilst, in Angie's case, it was prompted in part by the example of a role model with whom she could identify, awakening to the possibility that professorship may be a viable career option is sometimes dependent upon the kind of validation that comes from another person's intervention – as was related by several interviewees, including education studies professor Alison, who recalled: 'a friend outside the university said, "there's plenty of people with less than you – go for it!"'. Amounting to a form of sponsorship, suggestion that someone has professorial potential, or that her or his promotion is long overdue, can serve as a gentle awakener, or even a sharp prod, that, illustrating what I refer to in Chapter 7 as the shifting nature of most people's job-related ideals, encourages re-contemplation of a future self. It may also kick-start or represent the early stages of a snowballing process of 'collective endorsement' (DeRue & Ashford, 2010; Humphreys et al., 2015): that is, consensual support of a person's membership within a specific social group (such as the professoriate) – which, in turn, may reinforce his or her identity as such a member. Representing a form of agency that complements or works in tandem with promotion applicants' own agency, such collegial encouragement or sponsorship may occur within (formal and informal) institutional procedures that are linked to promotion policy. Chemistry reader Alan, who participated in the *Leading professors* study, identified such procedures as a potential hurdle that loomed on the horizon of his path to professorship:

> If I want to be promoted to a professor then I'm *entirely* dependent on the professors. ... [A]t this university you can make your own case for promotion, but that's not normal, I don't think. Otherwise, there's a panel of professors, who decide whether you should go forwards ... and so you would, naturally, turn to them for guidance on how to make a strong case. (*Alan, reader in chemistry, pre-1992 university*)

Yet, as a spur to pro-activity, suggestive encouragement is not the preserve of work colleagues; it may come from any source recognised by the recipient as trustworthy, credible, and based on authoritative knowledge of the relevant context and prevailing standards. Social sciences professor Greg acknowledged that, in planting in his mind an idea of what *might* or *could* be, and nurturing this with a sense of his self-efficacy that she fostered in him, his wife had given him the push to continue his promotion-bound journey from readership to professorship:

> When my wife and I met, I'd been a reader for a couple of years, and she works ... at ... a Russell Group university ... . She actually works with lots of professors ... and she'd often say to me, y'know, 'You *will* get a professorship one day because you're that good.' Now, y'know, we all tell the people we love how good we are, so I'd say it was a nice thing for her to say, but I didn't necessarily believe it, y'know. ... But, actually, I thought ... wouldn't it be interesting to see

whether the ... *quality* of work that I'm doing is seen to be commensurate with the award of professor? And I had a chat with people here about it, and I got a lot of support. People would say 'Oh yes, another couple of years, another couple of years!' And some others would say, 'Oh, that's three or four years' time!', y'know. And the more people said, 'Another couple of years', the more I thought: actually, it doesn't have to be a couple of years, does it? Let's give it a go and see what happens, and, y'know, what's the worst that happens? – you stay where you are. So it was a, kind of, gradual thing; it was never an ambition, y'know.

... And somebody then said, 'Well, you've got level 1 [professorship]; you should go for level 2. But if I were you, y'know, I mean, that's a hell of jump, y'know; you're going to leave that for a few years.' So I thought: okay, I'll ignore you completely, and we'll try it *far* too soon, as an experiment to see how we might learn from the application process. Sadly, I didn't learn anything from it, because I just got it! (*Greg, social sciences professor, post-1992 university*)

Highlighting the complexity with which different agentic influences intertwine, Greg's account illustrates how 'encouragement' may come in many forms, including advice to hang fire. Manifesting a quiet self-confidence – or, at least, disregard for potential failure – he seems to have been nudged into a perversely defiant response, fuelled by his wife's fostering his self-belief, to what he interpreted as over-cautionary advice.

Greg's full interview narrative illustrates attitudinal change in action, and how his gradually changing perception of his own efficacy and potential influenced his approach to developing his career in a concrete way – through promotion. As his comments above imply, for him the path to professorship did not end with his first promotion to a chair; he continued to develop his mode of doing professorship to the extent that he was promoted yet again: to a higher tier of his institution's professoriate. Though it did not in every case bring such material rewards, post-promotion change was acknowledged by most interviewees as a feature of professorship: a recognition that, having taken them so far, the developmental path that they thought might end abruptly actually continued on.

Crossing the threshold: Achieving professorship

The notion of professorship as a distinct role is evident even amongst those who are not (yet) themselves professors. One of the *Leading professors* interviewees identified what she saw as a feature of 'leading' professorship: recognition that the promotion brings new responsibilities and role reconfiguration:

Some people I know who become professors, actually, see that as … a different kind of job, actually; it's not the same job that you've been doing up to that point. And those tend to be people who do their job better. (*Eleanor, associate professor, pre-1992 university*)

Eleanor's observation aligns with Bruce Macfarlane's (2012b, p. 182) perception that: 'becoming a professor is about more than just promotion to a higher career grade. Most perceive it as a new role that carries important inter-generational responsibilities', and indeed, in outlining what crossing this significant academic career threshold meant for them, several of the professorial contributors to a *THE* piece about what, if anything, changes on becoming a professor acknowledged that it does not imply arrival at a terminus. Durham University geography professor Harriet Bulkeley, for example, remarked, 'I came to see being a professor not so much as a badge of honour or a fixed destination but as a journey', while professor of structural biology Stephen Curry confessed that, having anticipated little or no change, he then found: 'The job does change, and it changes you. Becoming a professor altered my self-image and how I thought about how others saw me' (Contributors, 2016).

A small minority of my research interviewees played down the notion of any such transition, implying that neither their roles nor their attitudes had changed, post-promotion. Asked if she felt professorship involved a different role, linguistics professor Catherine, for example, admitted that she perceived promotion to professorship as simply a means of recognising her achievements:

[T]o be honest, until I filled out your questionnaire I hadn't thought about that. I don't think we were led to believe that there was a specific role for professors, and, in all honesty, it never entered my head. It entered my head more that it was [laughs] – it's gonna sound a bit awful – a, kind of, reward for getting as far as you'd got.

Other members of this minority included an interviewee who represented Oxford University's relatively recently introduced (in the 1990s) cadre of titular professors. Distinct from Oxford's much more prestigious statutory professorships – which are named chairs – titular professorship evidently brings no salary increase nor any expectation of change of role or duties. The interviewee explained: 'I was given the title of distinction of professor, so I'm not *technically* a professor, but I have the *title* of professor – which is one of Oxford's oddities.' Three anonymous questionnaire respondents elucidated the distinct nature of this professorship that makes it an anomaly within the UK's professoriate insofar as it has no distinct salary scale and implies no change or transition, no threshold-crossing, and no implication of academic leadership other than what was practised before the title was bestowed:

My institution (Oxford University) should arguably be excluded from your survey, since its structure actively marginalises professors and their role here is quite unlike the role they play in most other UK universities (I base this on having been a professor in two others).

I currently hold a titular professorship at Oxford, the responsibilities of which are the same as those of 'ordinary' college fellowships. That said, because I have held a statutory chair before, and because I am at a slightly more advanced career stage than many of my colleagues, I do try and take on some of the responsibilities of statutory professors in my current position.

At my institution (Oxford), being a professor is in most cases purely titular/honorific – there's no pay rise or change of duties from lecturer. This is atypical. I am feeling very tempted to take a job elsewhere so I can be a 'proper' professor.

Yet most interviewees acknowledged that, for them, professorship had brought change. In some cases this was described as gradual and persistent change – a kind of continued evolution within what they recognised as a key transitional phase of academic working life: becoming, and growing into, professorship. Education studies professor Eric, for example, recalled a conversation he had had on the day of his promotion:

I remember asking [names a senior professorial colleague], on the day that I got the news, and I said, 'What is it to be a professor?' And he said, 'You won't *really* understand for a couple of years' – and 'it's how you change yourself'. And now ... I mean, for the last four or five years ... six, seven ... I've *undoubtedly* felt a professor, in the sense that I know I'm a leading academic.

In other cases change was described as what seems to have been a dawning realisation that, by moving up a level in the academic career hierarchy, a threshold had been crossed, and that this necessitated and heralded change to one's mode of being as an academic. In some cases such realisation seems to have been abrupt and sudden, occurring at the point of, or very soon after, promotion. Several interviewees recalled mild panic or fear that prompted a plan of action for how to be a professor. Law professor Katy – whose meteoric rise up the academic career hierarchy had propelled her from a lectureship directly to a chair – recalled her initial response to having been offered a professorship:

[I was] absolutely terrified ... and I asked if I could think about it, and I spoke to ... [a colleague outside her institution], and she said, 'Oh, take it. Of course you should take it; don't be ridiculous!'

She related how her initial trepidation had, on her accepting the chair, then given way to concern about her image as a professor, and to the on-set of self-imposed pressure to present and conduct herself in a new way, which she addressed by modelling herself on experienced professors:

> I smartened myself up a bit – well, things have regressed a bit since then! ... I smartened myself up, and I did ask a few people at first what they thought. And then I thought: well, actually, I'll think of role models; I'll think of people I'd like to be like, and people I *don't* want to be like. (*Katy, law professor, pre-1992 university*)

In common with Katy, most of the *Professorial leadership preparation and development* study interviewees recalled having been and felt unprepared for (their first) professorship. Biological sciences professor Brian went so far as to imply that he regretted his promotion, having been so unprepared for the increased workload and changes to the nature of his work that professorship had brought. While his case is presented in more detail in Chapter 10, his comments below outline his general reaction to and outline of the changes that he recalled having accompanied his crossing the threshold to professorship:

> Two or three years ago I looked back and thought: why did I *do* that? – because it was such a *stupid* thing to do! – why did I apply for something I probably wasn't ready for? We get no training, support, guidance. There's no pack the day you get ... you know, the day you get this promotion to the top of the tree ... I mean, it's just the next day at work ... and, of course, what happens is that once you get to a certain level, you become a chair, and then ... the university has extra expectations of you ... of what they want out of *you* in return. ... So, you're *more* committed, you do *more* admin ... blah, blah, blah. (*Brian, biological sciences professor, pre-1992 university*)

Arts and humanities professor Duncan had no regrets about his promotion, but, like Brian, he alluded to his recognition that others had expectations of him. Before outlining the impact that such expectations had on his attitude to and ways of approaching what he clearly saw as a different role from his pre-promotion one, he recalled his initial – and related his enduring – response to what he considered the privilege of having secured the incumbency and associated custodianship of a historic named chair:

> Oh, [I was] like one of these Olympic medal winners! [parody] 'I can't believe it! I can't believe it!' [laugh]. And, you know, you think of all the great names who've held that chair in the past; you know, you do have a sense of history, and 'If they could only see me now!' as it were [laugh] – you know, a sense of having

made it. It wasn't a particular ambition of mine, actually, and I didn't even intend to apply for it until two or three years beforehand; I was very happy as a [junior academic]. … So, yeah, a bit of being daunted, and also feeling, you know, those first seminars I was giving in the chair, you know you're being measured up, as it were, by colleagues as well – in the nicest possible way – and I felt nervous for those. I don't normally feel nervous before giving papers, but I certainly did then! (*Duncan, arts and humanities professor, pre-1992 university*)

A common thread is discernible in the accounts of those academics – the majority of, but by no means all, interviewees – who, to varying degrees, acknowledged that crossing the threshold to professorship brought changes to the ways in which they carried out their work and to how they perceived themselves, their places and positions within the workplace-related contexts in which they found themselves. Though it was articulated more explicitly and eloquently in some cases than in others, their shared recognition that something needed to change, or simply had changed or was changing, reflected their perception that professorship is not simply a job grade with associated salary increments that are earned in recognition for prior achievement, but that it involves a distinct role. The various ways in which they perceived and enacted that role are the focus of the next chapter.

Notes

1 In response to the question: 'Do you aspire to be a professor?' 32.7 per cent of the item's respondents selected 'definitely', 17.8 per cent selected 'probably', 20.9 per cent selected 'possibly', 28.5 per cent selected 'no'.

2 The University of Lincoln, for example, appointed Carenza Lewis as Professor for the Public Understanding of Research in 2015, following the leads of the University of Birmingham's appointment of Alice Roberts as Professor of Public Engagement in Science and the University of Manchester's appointment of Michael Wood as Professor of Public History.

3 I include in this category those who were first promoted to professorship in their thirties. At the time of the research interviews only one of these remained in his thirties, and one was considerably older.

4 Whilst every interview began with an invitation to the interviewee to summarise briefly her or his career history, the ages at which promotions were achieved were often not specified, and such information was occasionally, but not routinely or systematically, sought, and tended to emerge incidentally. It is therefore possible that more of the study's interviewees fell into the 'thirty-something' category than are so-identified here.

5   Whilst Finkenstaedt (2011) identifies disciplinary field as an important variable that should be incorporated into consideration of age- and experience-related readiness for professorship – 'mathematicians and musicians may be ready for a professorship much earlier than junior staff in an experimental science or in history' (p. 165) – he also notes that the promotion of 'too many young professors' (p. 167) in some European countries in the expansion period of the 1960s has led to a generally aged academic staff composition in many universities that has created succession problems.

6   The precise date is omitted in the interests of preserving the interviewee's anonymity.

7   Senior lecturer (see Appendix for clarification of UK academic grade hierarchy).

9

'Enacted' Professorial Professionalism: Doing Professorship in the Twenty-First-Century Academy

The well-documented context within which academics in the developed world must now carry out their work – a context that is most often portrayed as having changed significantly since the last decade of the twentieth century, and as continuing to change – represents in one sense 'demanded' academic professionalism insofar as a competitive, highly focused and fluid climate imposes demands in the form of specific approaches to practice. This professionalism is effectively government-'demanded', since it is governmental policies – specifically, the representation of neoliberal ideologies through new public management – that have influenced the climate and culture that define the developed global academy as it currently is. 'Demanding' or 'requesting' a particular professionalism, however, is not the exclusive prerogative of employers and paymasters; it may also emanate from other stakeholders, such as clients, customers, or colleagues, and Part Two of this book gives voice to one such constituency – the 'led' – that has a stake in the quality and nature of professorial academic leadership.

Yet, as I point out in Chapter 2, 'demanded' professionalism may, in the end, come to nothing. No matter who is its architect, or how thorough and detailed its design, it may end up as a blueprint for a structure that remains half-built; for professionalism is only 'reified' when it is enacted. Of the four perspectival versions of professionalism that I identify in that chapter – 'demanded', 'prescribed', 'deduced' and 'enacted' – only the last is 'real' insofar as it denotes what practitioners actually do. Doing professorship, then – the focus of this chapter – is about 'enacted' professorial professionalism. Incorporating analysis of research participants' accounts and narratives of what, as professors, they do in the course of their work, and how and why they do it, the chapter opens a window on professorship in the UK academy of the twenty-first century.

From 'demanded' to 'enacted' professionalism: Bridges, barriers and by-passes

How closely enacted professionalism matches other versions of professionalism is very much in the hands of those doing the enacting. Yet whilst 'demanded' (or 'requested') professionalism *may* remain an unfulfilled vision, it seldom does so entirely, for expectations that others hold of one's performance may, depending on the circumstances – and, certainly, mediated by individual agency – act as a powerful spur to live up to them, with the result that what is demanded or requested ends up becoming enacted to some degree. So it seems to be with professorship. Tight (2002, p. 28) notes that one of his small sample of professors expressed 'a strong sense of expectation to live up to' – a sentiment that is evident, too, in the recollection of my interviewee Duncan, presented in the penultimate paragraph of Chapter 8, of the pressure he felt to demonstrate himself worthy of his appointment to a historic named chair. A key finding to emerge from my research was that the professoriate, representing academe's highest achievers, who pride themselves on their performance, generally wants to meet people's expectations. Arts and humanities professor Fergal, for example, remarked:

> I think there *are* a set of expectations; I don't think it's just to do with promotion from sergeant to major to colonel. I think the promotion brings with it a certain set of: there are things I need to do. … But, certainly, the title and the role create expectations of you in different people. And I don't think one can be too generic, but they create different expectations, and, you know, as a fairly normal human being, I try to respond to expectations.

Evidently Fergal was not alone in holding such perspectives; particularly interesting are the responses, shown in Table 9.1, to an item within the online questionnaire that served both the *Professorial academic leadership in turbulent times* and the *Professorial leadership preparation and development* studies. Almost one-third (31.3 per cent) of respondents to the question 'Since becoming a professor, have you ever felt the need to change any aspect of your practice to meet other people's expectations?' selected strongly affirmative responses ('very much so' or 'quite significantly so/in most respects'), and another third (35.6 per cent) indicated that they had tried to meet other people's expectations 'to some extent/in many respects'. Yet with almost a third of respondents indicating little or no appetite for adapting their practice to meet expectations, it is evident that professors' attitudes to this issue varied, reflecting varied perspectives on the nature of professorship.

Table 9.1 Questionnaire responses to the item: 'Since becoming a professor, have you ever felt the need to change any aspect of your practice to meet other people's expectations?' (*n* = 1,282)

Response option		Frequency	%	Valid %	Cumulative %
Valid	Very much so	117	9.1	9.4	9.4
	Quite significantly so/ in most respects	271	21.1	21.9	31.3
	To some extent/in many respects	442	34.5	35.6	66.9
	A little/in some respects	253	19.7	20.4	87.3
	No	157	12.2	12.7	100.0
	Total	1,240	96.7	100.0	
Missing	Not sure/difficult to answer	34	2.7		
	System	8	0.6		
	Total	42	3.3		
Total		1,282	100.0		

Perspectives on professorship

Attitudes relating to the purpose and nature of professorship were evidently quite wide-ranging. To a small minority of research participants professorship was considered not as something requiring enactment, but as simply an academic grade attained in recognition of prior performance and achievement. Consistent with such a perspective are the data shown in Table 9.2, revealing 2.7 per cent of questionnaire respondents to consider professors to have no distinctive purpose. Implying that it requires no new or different ways of working, post-promotion, professorship seems to have been so-perceived by a minority of questionnaire respondents, whose comments included:

> I don't think that becoming a professor is a big jump. ... I was made a professor because I was already doing this – rather than an expectation that I will take these roles after becoming a professor! (*questionnaire respondent, pre-1992 university*)

Table 9.2 Questionnaire responses indicating agreement and disagreement with the statement: 'Professors have no distinctive purpose'

		Frequency	%	Valid %	Cumulative %
Valid	No	1,247	97.3	97.3	97.3
	Yes	35	2.7	2.7	100.0
	Total	1,282	100.0	100.0	

I think you should only be promoted to professor if you're already showing evidence of fulfilling the requirements for the job. It shouldn't be a step-change, but more a recognition of what you already do. (*questionnaire respondent, pre-1992 university*)

If I had had to change significantly what I was already doing in order to conform to the role of 'professor' I would have taken that as a sign that I wasn't actually ready to be promoted. The point of the promotion is to reward a set of behaviours and achievements that already exist, in my view, rather than to force an individual into a mould for which they are unprepared. (*questionnaire respondent, pre-1992 university*)

In many respects being a professor is a continuation of one's existing responsibilities, so there is little significant change. (*questionnaire respondent, pre-1992 university*)

A STEMM professor[1] – who, at the time of his participation as an interviewee in the *Professorial leadership preparation and development* study was in his third year as an internally promoted professor – seemed to veer towards this minority perception of professorship as simply as a grade within universities' academic grading and salary structures, denoting no distinct function or purpose. In open-ended questionnaire items he had commented: 'Being promoted to a professor … has made little difference to my working life. I have just as much autonomy as ever, and perhaps a little more status, but nothing particularly significant', and: 'To be honest I think a "professorship" is primarily designed as a career goal, and a reward. … In the end being promoted to professor is a "final promotion".'[2] In his follow-up interview his elaboration on these perspectives highlighted the particular significance of workplace context, as influenced by the combination of institutional and departmental prestige and epistemic cultures. His was an internationally renowned department that frequently attracted global research stars to its professoriate, which comprised over half of the department's academics; he made the point: 'you could argue: well, we're full of great people, and that's why we've got lots of professors'.

Compared with most university departments, in which professors constitute a minority of academic staff, professorship is less rarefied in top-heavy departments that are recognised pockets of excellence, typically resulting in a flatter seniority- and status-related hierarchy. By piecing together the information conveyed in this professor's interview narrative, the following inter-related implications of this rather distinct culture emerge from consideration of those of its features that he identified:

- The standard of scholarship throughout the department tends to be invariably excellent – so, oxymoronically, 'distinction' represents the norm, and is much less associated uniquely with professorship than it is recognised as the whole department's 'kitemark' of quality and prestige.
- Almost all academics have therefore demonstrated themselves to be intellectually distinct within the field's international research community – or potentially so.
- Almost all academics therefore require minimal, or no, academic leadership from their professorial colleagues.
- Almost all academics are very 'driven' high-achievers and expect to be promoted to chairs: professorship as the natural career culmination is the norm rather than the exception.

Reflecting assimilation with the culture of this rather atypical context, this interviewee responded to being asked if he had made professorship an explicit career goal:

Wanting to become a professor … it's just what you *do*. I'm not sure there's anything subtle about it: it's status, it's money … so … why not? … Pretty much everybody will expect to end up as a professor … certainly in *this* department, I would say, almost everybody will expect – certainly from *my* generation, they'll expect to end up as a professor. (*STEMM professor, pre-1992 university*)

He repeated the sentiments expressed in his questionnaire responses, implying that, for him, doing professorship was very much like doing academic work on any grade, yet unencumbered with extra baggage in the form of expectations that he might otherwise have felt obliged or pressured to meet. This professor's job situation – as I define the term in Chapter 7 – was shaped by the rather distinct work context that is probably unique to top-heavy, highly prestigious university departments. Most significantly in the context of this book, this context influenced his perspective on and attitude to academic leadership, and his role as an academic leader – which, he remarked, should be directed at his students, rather than at his colleagues:

I don't really feel my colleagues need any kind of academic leadership, because they're leading themselves. And, I mean, I'd say we're a strong department and everybody's good and, you know, there aren't really people that somehow *need* a … a leg-up.

In highlighting the centrality of people's job situations – including the work contexts that help define them – in shaping the professionalism that they choose to enact, this case serves as a reminder that the role- and function-related expectations that shape 'demanded' professionalism may need to be tempered and qualified by consideration of the nuanced variation of relevant circumstances. More specifically, in relation to professors, this case suggests that, without knowing and understanding, in the context of their job situations, first, how they perceive professorship; second, how they interpret academic leadership; and, third, the bases of and rationales for such perceptions and interpretations, it is over-simplistic to automatically or inflexibly expect them to incorporate academic leadership – at least, of a preconceived form – into their enactment of professorship.

Academic leadership, I point out in Chapter 3, is ill-defined and differentially interpreted within the scant academic literature that incorporates a focus on it. It is therefore unsurprising that it emerged from my research as somewhat variably interpreted within, and enacted by, the UK's professoriate.

Perspectives on academic leadership

For those who adhere to the notion of a distinct professorial role, the consensual default perception is that such a role is, or should be, that of academic leader. Yet, as I argue in Chapter 3, and elsewhere (Evans, 2017b), with no clearly articulated consensual view on what academic leadership means, and what it involves – and hence how professors should demonstrate or 'enact' it – it is little wonder that several interviewees conveyed uncertainty about what it meant to them, sometimes falling back into equating it to formal designated role incumbency. Such was STEMM professor Roger's initial response to being asked to define it:

> Yes … well … the … this is difficult … I'm attending a whole course on it … and I'm not sure I still know the answer yet … . But … it can happen through a defined role – like the heads of department and the directors of teaching or research.

Yet, as Table 9.3 shows, in a questionnaire item that sought views on how academic leadership is interpreted, only half of the item's professorial respondents included administrative role incumbency amongst their selections of its features; descriptors denoting the two generic features of professorship that had been most highly rated by the *Leading professors* research participants: relationality and distinction – particularly developmental-focused relationality – were selected much more frequently.

Table 9.3 Questionnaire responses to the question: '*What do you understand by the term "academic leadership"?*' presented in descending order of popularity, expressed as percentages of the item's respondents who selected the response option (*Professorial academic leadership in turbulent times* study)

Response option (Respondents were permitted to select multiple options)	Respondent selections (%)
Mentoring/advising others	96.7
Demonstrating exemplary scholarship and/or research expertise	93.4
Contributing towards setting the research agenda within the field	92.7
Having an impact on the development of the field internationally	87.4
Practising academic citizenship within the institution	80.4
Being a role model	78.8
Pushing back the frontiers of knowledge in the field	76.1
Holding an important role within the wider discipline	75.7
Manifesting teaching excellence	63.7
Holding a substantial administrative role within the institution	50.2
Having a high public profile	29.4
Making ground-breaking advances in the pedagogy of your discipline	24.4

Social sciences professor Clive also articulated a perspective on academic leadership that was quite distinct from the broadly consensual perspective shared by most professorial interviewees. Overlapping with the narrow interpretation implicit in Roger's first comment, presented above, Clive's conception seems to incorporate a strong service or citizenship dimension, where service is interpreted as performed through recognised formal roles, both within the employing university and in wider disciplinary and academic communities. Service of this nature is often enacted centre stage, in the limelight, and it therefore goes hand-in-hand with a specific kind of distinction that reflects recognition on the basis of a high profile in activities associated with safeguarding quality and standards within, and the reputation of, the subject on a national level: effectively, it represents respected elder statesmanship. Asked in his interview how he interpreted academic leadership, Clive's initial response – 'Well, do you know my record? Have you looked me up?' – is consistent with a perspective that associates academic leadership with high visibility and with activity that leaves a recognition trail. He then illustrated the nature of his enactment, throughout his long career, of such leadership:

> I'm the chairperson of my subject association – of my professorial association … I was on the RAE panel twice, and I was its vice-chair in [date]. I was the chairperson of the group that wrote the QAA benchmarks for my subject. I've

organised national conferences, I edit a journal, blah, blah, blah. And that probably reflects, actually, how I see leadership – and I've been dean of faculty.[3] (*Clive, social sciences professor, pre-1992 university*)

Clive's conception of academic leadership seems to have reflected a perspective on academic acculturation, preparation and professionalism that resonates with some of the views expressed by principal lecturer Ken, presented in Chapter 5. Essentially, this perspective holds that those choosing to embark upon careers as academics must take responsibility themselves for ensuring that they know what is required of them, and they must have the potential and capacity to deliver it. As Clive pointed out in continuing his articulation of what it meant to him, academic leadership whose conception is built upon such a perspective does not encompass mentoring roles or responsibilities:

> That form of citizenship is how I understood leadership to be. In other words, being a professor wasn't about leading in your own institution – or, at least, not leading the *discipline* – but it was the feeling that if you appointed somebody they were qualified to make their own academic judgements ... so, a *degree* of leadership, but certainly not *management* ... certainly not *mentoring* people ... certainly not reading the papers of the junior staff ... all those sorts of things – I did have a glance at the comments of junior faculty about professors.[4] Mentoring is a modern university role, which, if you were to go to the good universities in the States, they would say, 'These people aren't babies; they either cut it or they don't.' If people need encouragement they need colleagues to talk to them.

Lapierre et al. (2012, p. 766) suggest that 'a leader's propensity to mentor' is likely to be explained by her or his self-concept or self-identity, which 'reflects how we define ourselves, and has profound effects on the way we feel, think, and behave'. By these authors' reasoning, as a professor who declared himself unwilling to mentor, Clive may be considered to have weakly relational identity. Yet, whilst this may be so, the basis of his objection to expectations that professors should act as mentors was presented not as introspectively focused – as something that he, personally, had no appetite for – but, rather, as the juxtaposition of such expectations alongside the contradictory wish for professional autonomy:

> There are plenty of people in academic life who want things very well defined, because they're not happy with ambiguity: 'What do I have to do to get promotion, and can you write it down? – preferably in 3 lines precisely, because I don't want to wade through a lot of other things.' And then they say, 'But, I should be autonomous.' No! If you wish for all that detail, you're actually saying, 'I accept that I am to be managed and to be told precisely what to do, and I've

lost my right to be an autonomous academic.' (*Clive, social sciences professor, pre-1992 university*)

Clive's perspective seems to have marked him as somewhat deviant within the *Professorial academic leadership in turbulent times* and the *Professorial leadership preparation and development* interviewee samples. Certainly, some of the features of academic leadership as he conceived it aligned with those included in the interpretations of some of the other research participants; linguistics professor Catherine, for example, was one of a small number of interviewees who echoed Clive's association of academic leadership with service to the wider disciplinary community and with institutional citizenship:

> I think [academic leadership] should involve some kind of service to the general academic community in which you work – so, y'know, for instance, you might expect to be called upon to be president of [a learned society]. ... One of the things that I do, I'm on the council of the [learned society]. That's the kind of thing I'm expected to do, and so that's, kind of, within the wider community. Within the university, it's professors that are going to be the head of the school, and it's typically the professors who are going to be head of the subject 'cos we've got various subjects within our school. It's professors that are going to expect to serve on, you know, things like executive committee, and stuff like that. (*Catherine, linguistics professor, pre-1992 university*)

Research leadership, too, featured in Catherine's conception of academic leadership – 'I guess you should be demonstrating that your research is, if not at the very cutting edge, that it's highly significant in your field' – along with, almost as an afterthought, a nod to the importance of a mentoring-type role: 'I think it should also involve helping people coming up behind you as well who – you know, you should try to be a role model, I think, for people who are not yet professors, to some degree.' But what set Clive's 'take' on academic leadership apart from those of other interviewees were his well-formulated anti-mentoring views, presented above, and which contrasted moreover with what Table 9.3 indicates to have been the more consensual perception: that academic leadership involves a heavy dose of relationality directed towards junior colleagues.

Precisely what form of relationality was implicit or prescribed within interviewees' interpretations varied. Clinical professor Iain highlighted the importance not only of strategic leadership, but also of 'connecting' with people, in order to develop them:

> I think having the ability to work at a strategic level, to say, look, if we're gonna develop and grow research in an institution, or unit, or wherever, then, having,

kind of, strategic and planning ability at that level is key. You've got to have that, but I think also leadership requires, I think ... well, I think you have to connect with the people you're trying to develop, who undoubtedly will be at a lower level. So, there's ability to connect there, and I think there's also the ability to do all of this in a collegiate way. (*Iain, clinical professor, post-1992 university*)

And arts and humanities professor Seamus spoke of research development-focused relationality:

I would've thought that, you know, professors who are there to provide leadership of some sort would be engaged in some sense with the ... with the research of younger members of staff – not necessarily *doing* research with them or ... or *telling* them what to do, but showing a, sort of, active interest in ... in how the younger members of staff are setting about doing research, and trying to encourage them to be a little bit more tactical and strategic. (*Seamus, arts and humanities professor, pre-1992 university*)

As Chapters 5 and 6 show, non-professorial academics greatly appreciate professors' supportive collegiality and can be highly critical of professors who seem reluctant to provide it. But if the *Professorial academic leadership in turbulent times* and *Professorial leadership preparation and development* research participants are representative of the wider UK-based professoriate,[5] such criticism seems rather unjustified, for, as Table 9.4 shows, of those professors who responded to an item that sought the extent of their agreement with the statement, 'A professor should advise non-professorial colleagues and help them develop professionally', over 90 per cent selected the two most affirmative response options: 'definitely/in all cases' or 'probably/in most cases'.

Table 9.4 Questionnaire responses to the item asking respondents to indicate the extent of their agreement or disagreement with the statement: 'A professor should advise non-professorial colleagues and help them develop professionally'

	Response options	**Frequency**	**%**	**Valid %**	**Cumulative %**
Valid	Definitely/in all cases	721	56.2	56.8	56.8
	Probably/in most cases	431	33.6	34.0	90.8
	In some cases	89	6.9	7.0	97.8
	Not necessarily	23	1.8	1.8	99.6
	No	4	0.3	0.3	99.9
	Unsure/difficult to answer	1	0.1	0.1	100.0
	Total	1,269	99.0	100.0	
Missing	System	13	1.0		
Total		1,282	100.0		

These questionnaire data seemed to be borne out by the interviewee sample's interpretations of academic leadership, many of which included reference to direct, face-to-face, developmental-focused or facilitative relationality, in which mentoring and advising junior colleagues featured prominently. Such was arts and humanities professor Elizabeth's interpretation:

> I've always thought that academic leadership was about ... enabling and ... facilitating the opportunities for people, either for whom you are responsible – so, if you are the head of department that's everybody – but ... it's about enabling and assisting the opportunities of those who are in different positions in the department where I'm working and, increasingly, more widely across the university. I have been approached by other people in other departments and asked if I would give them advice ... talk to them about career development things ... and I'm formally mentoring somebody in the administration, who asked specifically if I would do so. So, it's about ... it's about showing other people who haven't got where I've got about the opportunities that might be open to them and trying to persuade them that my ... my example, or different take on things, might be an opportunity for them to rethink their own trajectories. (*Elizabeth, arts and humanities professor, pre-1992 university*)

Several other interviewees articulated similar, developmental-focused interpretations of academic leadership. Business and management professor Joanne, for example, remarked 'I think it's a lot of ... being able to mentor ... to, sort of, provide direction – but not in a, kind of, very patronising way', while biochemistry professor Mona, despite admitting having privileged her students' developmental needs above those of her colleagues, nevertheless identified examples of her academic leadership that had been focused on colleagues:

> But I've done what I could ... to help the younger people, and the women .... So ... CV-improving things ... when I was in the position to do that ... I did them. ... Inviting a colleague to speak at a meeting ... giving advice as to which grants to go for ... reading grant [applications] ... reading papers ... things like that. (*Mona, biochemistry professor, pre-1992 university*)

And social sciences professor Greg's interpretation also highlighted collegial development:

> Academic leadership ... in the context of this university, means, to me ... actually ... developing colleagues ... across their range of expertise. So, not merely developing ... helping staff develop as researchers, but helping staff develop as, for the want of a better phrase, 'fully rounded professional academics'. (*Greg, social sciences professor, post-1992 university*)

Whilst it was common for STEMM professors who led research teams to make reference, within their delineations of academic leadership, to their responsibility to help post-docs secure permanent, career-building posts, some STEMM interviewees identified developmental-focused collegiality as specifically intellectual in nature, rather than pragmatically career advancement-focused. Engineering professors Liam and Denis, for example, both spoke of wanting to challenge people intellectually, leading them to explore new ways of, and to extend their, thinking:

> To me, academic leadership is getting people interested. Two things: getting them interested in their work, giving them ideas. I suppose the picture I'd use is more like serving them rather than commanding them, but, to stir up their thinking, getting them to look over certain walls that they may have built up around their area, asking them 'What if?' So, almost to be pushing them and stretching them intellectually. (*Liam, engineering professor, pre-1992 university*)

> I think academic leadership is to ... obviously, to be at the forefront of any particular disciplinary or scientific developments and to be able to communicate them. ... I think the other area of academic leadership is really to do with helping people approach problem solving ... approach issues ... to think about things differently. ... So, I think it's ... it's to get and encourage people in a supportive environment to question their own way of looking at things. ... Ultimately, I suppose, you're only going to get the former if you undertake the latter ... so you're only going to push the boundaries forward if you get people to think differently. (*Denis, engineering professor, post-1992 university*)

And several interviewees articulated protracted and detailed conceptions that were remarkably similar to each other in the several dimensions or components of academic leadership that they listed. History professor Vincent distinguished between 'different levels' of academic leadership – 'I probably understand it at different levels ... so, there's *intellectual* leadership, and there's *administrative* leadership, and I'd probably differentiate those two pretty fundamentally with regard to the professors that I know' – and the three 'aspects' of academic leadership identified by STEMM professor Harry were almost identical to the 'four potential parts' that education studies professor Eric described:

> One is ... er ... research leadership – in actually *doing* research and writing about it; that side: you know, people publishing high quality articles and books ... okay? Another – and increasingly so – is the generation of research monies, which *may* be related to the quality of the research, but may not be as well. Another one is administrative leadership, in the sense of running an academic faculty and using your expertise as a researcher and as a person who understands the politics of

research in the national picture to help people to grow and develop their own careers. And the final one – and it's one that most universities pay lip service to, but they don't regard it *that* seriously in most cases – and that is teaching. (*Eric, education studies professor, pre-1992 university*)

The *Professorial academic leadership in turbulent times* and *Professorial leadership preparation and development* studies uncovered an array of perspectives on academic leadership, something of whose diversity is conveyed by the illustrative quotes presented above. A minority of the perspectives – exemplified by Joanne's and Elizabeth's respective references to 'providing direction', and to people's rethinking their career trajectories, and Liam's and Denis's aspirations of getting people to think differently – incorporated explicit reference to influencing others, and some of these perspectives highlighted intellectual leadership. Otherwise, rarely did interpretations of academic leadership incorporate an explicit predominant focus on the nature of the *outcome* of leadership agency; rather, the professors tended to identify the kinds or categories of *actions* or *intentions* that they associated with academic *leaders*. With, at most, we may assume, only a vague passing interest in the scholarship of leadership, their default, pragmatic, perspective on academic leadership understandably meant that they were hard-wired to 'personify' it: to focus on what (they as) academic leaders do or should do. In doing so, some – a minority – veered generally towards identifying the kinds of leader actions and intentions that are implicit in or aligned with Bradley et al.'s (2017) definition of academic leadership, presented in Chapter 3, as enactment of institutional strategic vision, while rather more of them implied that their perspectives were much more aligned with Bolden et al.'s (2012a, p. 6) findings, also outlined in Chapter 3, that academic leadership is not about formal managerial roles, but about engagement that supports 'transition and acculturation into academic life'.

It would be over-simplistic to assume that their articulated *perspectives* on academic leadership signalled and reflected these professors' *way of doing* professorship, not least because some may have hastily cobbled together vaguely coherent (and, in a few cases, incoherent) thoughts on academic leadership that they then articulated – possibly, without conviction. It seemed in fact that some were dredging their memories for text book definitions; a few joked about not having had the foresight to look up notes that they had used to prepare for job interviews, and one referred to having discussed academic leadership on a course he was following and was evidently trying to recall the content of that discussion. We therefore cannot know, first, how closely their articulated interpretations of academic leadership match these professors' 'genuine' unarticulated perspectives, and, second, the degree of match between their *enacted* academic leadership and their *articulated perspectives on* academic leadership (some of which took the form of description and some of prescription).

Uncertainty of this kind is a feature of all data collection within social science research that relies on human subjects' representation or recollection. Essentially, researchers must proceed with a degree of caution in accepting that what people *say* they do or think closely matches what they *genuinely believe* they do or think (and, of course, a core research skill involves collecting and analysing data in ways that minimise mismatch or allow it to be identified). In the case of these professors' articulated interpretations of academic leadership, however, perhaps a soupçon more caution than normal is needed, because heightened considerations of self-image and face-saving may have exerted particular pressure on them to rely upon creative rhetoric when asked for an intelligent perspective on something that, as senior academics, they may reasonably be expected to hold considered views – for, as I observe in the opening pages of this chapter, professors seem keen to meet expectations of them. Some of the specific ways in which they try to do so in their enactment of professorship are examined below.

Meeting expectations

Whilst views on this issue were divided, more research participants acknowledged than denied that professorship had brought change, and such change seems to have been consensually interpreted as a product of their efforts to meet new or different expectations of them. Amongst those who acknowledged post-promotion change there was evident variation in the nature and intensity of the change related – and which inevitably influenced ways of doing professorship and, specifically, academic leadership.

For some professors, the expectations they tried to live up to were described as relatively gradually and incrementally identified, post-promotion – and, as a result, seem to have been accepted with equanimity and to have been *reasonably* comfortably met. Such seems to have been Duncan's experience. In outlining the kinds of responsibilities and roles that he felt were expected of him as the holder of a prestigious named arts and humanities chair, he included those appendages to his chair that he felt had emerged from the changing external academic context, and those that were more of a traditional ambassadorial nature:

What has [promotion] changed? Well, as I say, I've accrued different things. For two years … I was president of the [a national learned society] at a time when it was in a terrific crisis … . That was, really, a very big job … er … for those two years. … Er … I became a delegate of [an academic publishing company] after about two years in this … . That's actually quite a lot of work – *fascinating work* – but that's delegates meeting every two weeks in term time … six or seven book proposals, typically … . That came with the territory a little way into it. Sometimes you're on one … committee; sometimes you're on another, and as I was mentioning, I've been on the professorship promotions committee from time to time. Sometimes I'm director of graduate studies. … So, you know, it's always slightly different … and one's priorities change a bit, if things have been successful. … It was … quite important to feel that there was going to be a national role – and an *inter*national role, indeed, and travelling a fair amount to make sure that [the university] as a whole is [represented favourably]. So, giving lots of papers around the place – I remember an interviewer [on the appointment panel] saying that the two most important things to have are a paper and a suitcase! [laughs]. And that is, to a large extent, true, in fact, so I've done quite a lot of that. (*Duncan, arts and humanities professor, pre-1992 university*)

As some of his comments presented in Chapter 8 also imply, for Duncan, his incumbency of such an established historic chair is seen (by him and by interested onlookers within his own university and disciplinary community) as custodianship. Doing professorship in such circumstances – which helped define Duncan's job situation and the work context that shaped it – involved making valued contributions that, building on those of his predecessors, continued to reshape and delineate the chair's purpose and image within the temporally defined external context that frames its prestige, purpose and usefulness. He thus not only perpetuated traditions that remained relevant and appropriate, but also made enhancements by putting his own stamp on the role in response to what he identified as shifting expectations of this specific professorship:

There would be now much more of an expectation of public presence – of being able to communicate outside the subject … you know, be on television, be on radio, or certainly more of an expectation of doing something with outreach … being involved with schools. I don't think – certainly the person doing my job when I was an undergraduate would ever have dreamed of going into school! Er … a lot more involved with creating a graduate school. … When I started there were no master's degrees … . Now we've got two master's degrees and something of the order of 30 people in [X field] and another 15 in [Y field] doing master's degrees every year. Working out what sort of experience we ought to be giving *them*, and giving it to them – taking a very leading role in that – that's certainly a big thing, and that's what I probably would have regarded as … the main job to be looked at when I was appointed, and I continue to regard that as absolutely essential. (*Duncan, arts and humanities professor, pre-1992 university*)

So-defined, professorship seems to be as much about legacy as it is about currency; inherently altruistically-skewed, it is akin to running with a baton that will be passed on to someone else – but making sure that one's lap performance sets up the next baton-holder for retaining a podium place. As Duncan conveyed it, his enacted professorial professionalism seemed to be about consummately and expertly playing his part, yet with modesty and humility, rather than detached heroic status- and self-aggrandisement-seeking.

Yet, for some professorial research participants – those holders of personal chairs that came with neither a historic legacy nor established traditions that might provide guidance – doing professorship involved working out what was expected of them before then deciding how best to meet expectations. Familiar with the kind of management-speak that peppers institutional and sectoral rhetoric, most had grasped that they were expected to show academic leadership, but, when it came to *enacting* it, the finer details of what such leadership involved seems to have been less apparent. Indeed, as Table 9.5 shows, of those professors who responded to a questionnaire item asking: 'Do you understand what your institution requires of you as a professor (i.e. are its expectations of its professors in general – or of you specifically – clearly articulated)?', one-third selected responses that implied a degree of negativity: 'in some cases'; 'not necessarily' or 'no'.

Table 9.5 Questionnaire responses to the item: 'Do you understand what your institution requires of you as a professor (i.e. are its expectations of its professors in general – or of you specifically – clearly articulated)?'

	Response options	Frequency	%	Valid %	Cumulative %
Valid	Definitely/in all cases	246	19.2	19.7	19.7
	Probably/in most cases	579	45.2	46.3	65.9
	In some cases	197	15.4	15.7	81.7
	Not necessarily	172	13.4	13.7	95.4
	No	57	4.4	4.6	100.0
	Total	1,251	97.6	100.0	
Missing	Unsure/difficult to answer	16	1.2		
	System	15	1.2		
	Total	31	2.4		
Total		1,282	100.0		

The academic leadership that they enacted therefore often ended up being self-defined by these professors, and was inevitably informed by their preconceptions of what professorship ought to involve and represent, and of the professor prototypes that made up their schemas within what, in Chapter 7, I call 'implicit professorship theories'. Such prototypes were fashioned around what many interviewees identified as influential role models or exemplars. Business and management professor Joanne, for example, spoke of having had 'a wonderful mentor … and I admired what she was doing … how she operated', and engineering professor Liam admitted having modelled his brand of professorship on others whose approach he approved of: 'I began to meet other professorial colleagues in the university and, sort of, by osmosis and networking, I gradually picked things up'. Influenced by a variant of role modelling, mathematics professor Anthony seems to have found his own way of doing professorship by focusing at least as much on what *not* to do as following the examples of impressive role models: 'I've got, kind of, very much *anti*-role models … people that you've heard [manifest] certain kinds of behaviours that I just don't want anything to do with: you know, talk to someone for about 30 seconds and you think you should be an author on their paper!'

But 'implicit leadership/professorship theories' and the prototypes that are a constituent element of them offer but one explanation for what shapes the nature of professorial academic leadership (practice); there are countless others, located at various levels within the complex hierarchy of overlapping theoretical perspectives. One is social identity theory, which, applied to professors, would explain their enactment of academic leadership as their attempts to consolidate their professorial identity: 'when a social identity is salient (activated) and attended to … [g]roup members act to match their behavior to the standards relevant to the social identity, so as to confirm and enhance their social identification with the group' (Stets and Burke, 2000, p. 232). Consistent with – and encompassing and extending – social identity theory is the social-constructionist perspective of leadership as 'co-constructed through a process involving a series of claims and grants of leader and follower identities. Through this co-construction, identities of leader or follower are individually internalized, relationally recognized and collectively endorsed within the social context' (Humphreys et al., 2015, p. 1390). Implicitly woven loosely into Chapter 3's conceptual analysis of leadership, this theoretical perspective essentially holds that followers' perceptions of leaders and the interpretive social, and hence relational, process of leadership takes precedence in determining whether or not an individual is ascribed leader status on the basis of the social identity constructed for her/him. The implications of this perspective for professors as academic leaders is that it is not only, or even principally, they themselves who may self-ascribe 'leading professor' status – and certainly not on the basis of psychologically-based traits; rather, such status is co-constructed by and with those with whom professors interact. Meeting colleagues' expectations is therefore a key element of this unconsciously played-out social process.

Essentially, despite being shaped by myriad influences, much of the professorship that was enacted seems to have incorporated a dimension of self-stylisation, through improvisation and adaptation – resonant of Barnett's (2011) image, referred to in Chapter 2, of the modern professional skating on thin ice to avoid its cracking behind her – as professors searched for directional steers in their efforts to meet unclearly articulated expectations of them as academic leaders, or as 'leading professors'. Whilst the resultant enacted professorial professionalism was inevitably diverse in nature, it was delineated by features of professorial practice that were discernible as professors' concerns and priorities in relation to meeting expectations. In some professors' accounts or examples of how they enacted academic leadership their (scholarly) distinction emerges as a dominant concern that shaped their efforts to meet expectations; in other professors' accounts it was their relationality that seemed to be a prime consideration; some accounts seemed to feature both of these concerns relatively equally, and in yet others a concern to be accountable shone through – though, in one sense, since they were demonstrating themselves keen to meet other people's expectations of them, accountability to one or another constituency may be seen as a concern that underpinned all of these professors' approaches to doing professorship.

Enacting academic leadership

In what ways then did professors consider themselves to demonstrate or have demonstrated academic leadership? The range of leadership activities identified corresponds with Bolden et al.'s (2012b, p. 14) findings: 'PhD supervision is included, but less prominent; other factors mentioned include providing the voice of experience, external perspectives and connections, guidance through committees and promotions.' Corroborating Macfarlane's (2012b) observation that professors see it as one of their most important functions, for several of the *Professorial academic leadership in turbulent times* interviewees a key feature of their academic leadership seems to have been mentoring others – most often in an unofficial, informal manner, through dispensing advice and guidance.

Such mentoring was often research-focused, and included reading and advising on draft research grant applications and papers intended for publication. Arts and humanities professor Duncan evidently felt it important to support junior colleagues in this way, and also to make himself generally available as a knowledge resource that junior colleagues could tap into:

> I do regard it as terribly important to be available to any of the new appointments who wants to come and talk to me, and will make a point of making myself particularly available to some who are working in areas close to me, or, as has happened in a few cases, with my own old graduate students, or working in the same faculty, or whatever. It's rather radiating a sort of accessibility, I think, rather than imposing on them. But, I hope – and I think it probably is true – that people do assume I'm accessible and will come to me; I mean, people in areas that I don't work in at all … in the last few years one came to me; she was a bit depressed; she'd had an article turned down: could I have a look at it? And, you know, she felt able to do that. Somebody else came for advice on what his REF submissions should be. Somebody else, again, came – he was finding the [work] load a bit heavy and just wanted to know what he could reasonably say, 'No' to. So, feeling that sort of accessibility is there, I think, is important.

Asked for examples of how he tried to 'radiate accessibility', Duncan related a way of doing professorship that corresponds with Bolden et al.'s (2012b, p. 13) finding that '[a]cademic leaders were seen … to create and maintain an enabling environment for high-quality academic work; and to facilitate the acculturation and development of self-leading academic professionals':

> Well sometimes, a bit of: 'do feel free to…' – particularly if people are new to [the university]. I would send them a congratulatory note: 'if I can be of any help with old reading lists that I've used myself…' – things like that; so, sort of, make a first move. But I think, actually, it's more a question of personality, you know … finding yourself in the same pub at the same time, and being prepared to have that sort of conversation. … Certainly, in the case of the article, I'd *offered* that; I mean, I was sitting next to somebody in the pub and she was clearly a bit low about it [slight laugh], so, quietly, you know: 'Oh, do send it along.' And … er … well … I mean … well, it's just such a basic part of the job. I wouldn't like *not* to be doing it. (*Duncan, arts and humanities professor, pre-1992 university*)

Other professors outlined ways in which they had tried to widen colleagues' experiences, in order both to help them develop and enhance their CVs, often by including them in their own activities. Law professor Katy, for example, spoke of co-authoring with junior colleagues:

> I would have several colleagues in the department who are junior to me who work in the same field, and I would be constantly looking to, not only talk to them about ideas in the field, but to write them into publications. (*Katy, law professor, pre-1992 university*)

In cases such as this, despite the obvious CV- and profile-enhancing benefits to junior colleagues, it is not their inclusion in collaborative writing projects per se that represents academic leadership, as I define it, but the potential for their learning, through being introduced to what they recognise as 'better ways' of going about the core academic business of writing for publication. Business and management professor Joanne identified some of the ways in which she felt she had achieved such influence with junior colleagues outside her own institution:

> In our seminar series, somebody fairly new to academia – a colleague in [another university], who approached myself and a long-term collaborator from the University of X – and said, would the three of us put in an application. And he led it. It was great, because he was PI[6] – which was fantastic for him – but, then, it was us, kind of, mentoring on that. Er … I was involved in a post-doctoral [initiative], so, a colleague … [who] did her PhD in [another university] and I was her post-doc mentor, and that was great. We published a paper together from that, and that was great fun writing that paper. (*Joanne, business and management professor, pre-1992 university*)

Education studies professor Eric related similar efforts to facilitate junior colleagues' development and learning, through passing on to them opportunities for widening their experiences and, by extension, their perspectives, in order to increase their promotion prospects:

> I'm on the university's personal professors and readerships committee, and … we've got a senior lecturer and a reader, who I think are just about right for chairs. So one of the things I'm doing with them is: we're going through the [promotion] criteria, we're looking at how they [the colleagues] match up; we're saying, 'Right, well, what d'you need to do?' This guy needs to be known around the university. I've sat on that committee long enough to know that if you're not known it's very difficult. So one of the committees that isn't that important – that he will see all the important people at – I've stepped down and let him take over … which, actually, is good for me, 'cos it means I've got less work to do! But, I explained it as that, and he immediately saw it as that and not me trying to dump stuff onto him. Again, I think that's another role of a professor; it's really bringing people through. (*Eric, education studies professor, pre-1992 university*)

These accounts of mentoring and other, similar, forms of developmental-focused collegiality indicate relational approaches to doing professorship that were preponderant amongst the interview narratives. Eric was by no means unique in demonstrating sustainability-focused academic leadership aimed at ensuring the progression of the next generation of academics and academic leaders. The shift or deviation on the part of 'the led' that I identify as a key component of (academic) leadership was, in several cases, evidently effected through efforts to influence junior colleagues' employability or promotion prospects. Several professors related having advised colleagues on, and supported them in, preparing internal promotion applications; as law professor Katy expressed it: 'giving them some idea of: I think to be promoted you need to do X, Y and Z. Let's see what we can fix up for you.'

Such practical career development-focused leadership seems to have been accepted as a core responsibility of professors in certain STEMM subjects; indeed, several leaders of inter-generational research teams and/or laboratories implied that their own reputations were in some respects reliant upon their success in facilitating or securing their post-docs' career progression. Scathing in his criticism of a colleague whom he considered to have neglected this aspect of academic leadership – 'as far as I know, [only] *one* of his ex-post-docs has gone on to get a permanent job! And I think, for somebody who's been in the game for 30-odd years, that's terrible' – biological sciences professor Brian outlined the nature of his efforts to set his own post-docs on paths to permanent posts:

> I try and encourage [the post-docs] the best I can to communicate directly with our collaborators, rather than it always coming through me. And I've been spending my time forwarding emails ... and it's a simple thing, but it means that *they're* the point of contact rather than somebody else, which then means they've made contacts outside of ... just this lab. And I've also ensured that almost all the post-docs have been involved in one way, shape or form in some sort of collaborative project with somebody else in [the university]. So, again, if they need a reference ... or, you know- or even just to demonstrate on their CV that they're capable of doing more than two things at once – they have that. When I hear of positions that are coming up, which I think are appropriate for those post-docs, I'll let them know. And sometimes you're telling people it's time for them to go – but only because it's an opportunity that might come around in ... infrequently. And I encourage them to go to as many meetings as they can, and sometimes it's like dragging, y'know, literally a ... a horse to water that doesn't want to go; I mean, two or three of my post-docs haven't been to a meeting

in two years, and I go five or six times a year ... so it's: why *don't* you want to do this? And of course these are the people who struggle to get jobs. (*Brian, biological sciences professor, pre-1992 university*)

STEMM professor Will, too, highlighted the importance of giving junior colleagues a leg up the career ladder through such pro-active directional support:

I look after their interests behind their backs sometimes. But I have a range of contacts and, if, you know, a new job comes up – I'll give you an example: a new job came up in Australia recently – a really nice job opportunity for someone. ... I sounded out the people who might be interested and asked them if they'd be interested, to find out how I should respond, and how I can ... push their case, you know, within reason, so that they get a good shot at getting it: a good job which I think they deserve. So those sorts of things, it's a fairly common and continual thing. (*Will, STEMM professor, pre-1992 university*)

Many professors' academic leadership was described as taking the form of generally modelling ways of working and fulfilling the responsibilities that they felt were expected of them, as professors. For arts and humanities professor Fergal, this involved intellectual leadership that was focused on outreach and public engagement:

One thing I value about my title, and whatever profile I have, is it gives me the opportunity in [this city] to say things in public. I can go to the radio, I can put things in the press ... I can become involved – I was chair of the [X] Theatre for three years. ... Now, my area's [names an academic field], but the fact that I'm working in the university – and this is partly that it's a *good* university, as well; it has a certain reputation, and I really enjoy that as well; it gives me the sense that I can make a contribution to public life as well, and that's a *great* source of satisfaction. ... I don't understand how some academics can be so *blind* as to their ... what their worth means publicly. The whole impact debate that's going on at the moment ... I *like* the idea of impact. I *like* the idea that what we do hits different constituencies in different ways. (*Fergal, arts and humanities professor, pre-1992 university*)

And for biological sciences professor Brian, academic leadership was enacted by his turning up where he was expected, doing what he was expected to do, being the model academic citizen and generally creating an environment – his laboratory – that was conducive to collegiality and developmentalism, whilst being aligned with the university's goals and agendas:

I go and do the good thing, and go to meetings where, actually, it's a bit of a waste of time, but you do the right thing – you not only try and maintain an active research group, to bring, y'know, research council money into the university ... and those overheads, you're also trying to make sure you do your bit to post- and undergraduate teaching. And some of my colleagues do *no* teaching. ... In terms of leadership, you also need to provide mentoring skills to students to get them through – and not only their first degree, but also their PhDs. And you need to provide the same sort of mentoring skills to post-docs, so when they leave they don't end up unemployed. ... You need to be able to demonstrate you're leading in your field in some way, shape or form – and also demonstrate that you're doing things within the university context, to show that you are actually *helping out*. That, to me, is leadership. ... So, I think there are ... there are elements across the board, where people can show leadership. And, y'know, perhaps I'm a mug because I try and do too much, I don't know. But if you don't have people trying to make a difference, for the greater good, then the place becomes a hell-hole. (*Brian, biological sciences professor, pre-1992 university*)

Yet for all that he played the role of the model professor, in common with several interviewees, Brian reported doing so at a price: the diminution of his well-being and job satisfaction. His concern to do the right things did not preclude his vociferous criticism of the institutional and wider political contexts that had resulted in his feeling overworked, over-faced with the multitude of diverse tasks he had to do, and under constant pressure to perform. He was by no means the only interviewee to express such negativity, yet – inevitably amongst such a heterogeneous professoriate – his frustration was balanced by those interviewees who reported very positive attitudes to their work, and by those others whose perspectives locate them at various points on a continuum that spans the whole spectrum of their morale and job satisfaction levels articulated by these professors. Those job-related attitudes and the factors that influenced them are the focus of the next chapter.

Notes

1 Since contextual information is presented that may provide clues to identifying this professor's department and institution, in the interests of preserving his anonymity I refer neither to the pseudonym that denotes him in this book nor to his specific subject.

2 Questionnaire respondents remained anonymous unless they volunteered to be interviewed – in which case they added their names and contact details. In such cases their responses could be traced back to them and were often followed up in the interview conversations.

3   Some factual information included in this quote has been changed to preserve the speaker's anonymity. The changes retain the overarching sense and focus of the message conveyed whilst obscuring or disguising some of its detail.

4   Refers to a journalistic report of the *Leading professors* study (Grove, 2011).

5   In Chapter 4 I identify the research sample's evident pro-professorial academic leadership stance as problematic, insofar as it makes for a somewhat skewed sample.

6   Principal investigator.

10

Chasing the Ideal: Morale and Job Satisfaction in the Professoriate

As Blackmore (2016, p. 12) points out, 'satisfaction surveys of academic staff tend to return relatively negative results in the UK'. A survey carried out in 2007 uncovered widespread malaise within the UK academic workforce, whose work satisfaction scores were the lowest of those of eighteen national academic workforces participating (Fredman & Doughney, 2012) within a multi-national longitudinal project focused on changes to academic working conditions (Teichler et al., 2013). More recently, *THE* reported survey data[1] that found 'barely one in ten' of over 2,000 university (academic and non-academic) staff respondents to be satisfied with the way their institutions are managed, leaving 76.5 per cent dissatisfied, and only 15.9 per cent feeling respected and valued by senior management (Reisz, 2017).

Yet people's attitudes and affective reactions to their jobs – what makes them happy or unhappy at work, and why – are crucial. They may impact upon their well-being, their mental health, and their performance and productivity. In the case of university professors, as a dimension of their professionalism (as I conceptualise it in Chapter 2), their morale, job satisfaction and motivation (what I collectively label the motivational dimension of professionalism) potentially underpin the ways in which and how well they enact their professionalism – not least through their academic leadership. This chapter's focus on the professoriate's morale and job satisfaction is therefore highly relevant to the portrayal built up in the book, but since researchers of them have historically found morale and job satisfaction problematic concepts, it is worth taking a closer look at how I define them here.

Conceptualisation and definition

As long ago as the 1950s, when the field was establishing itself, researchers of morale and of job satisfaction lamented the conceptual problems they believed were undermining their efforts to get to the bottom of what influences these attitudes. In this period, when conceptual clarity and definitional precision were recognised as essential to rigorous research, Guion (1958) referred to the 'definitional limb' on which writers about morale find themselves, whilst Redefer (1959) identified morale as a 'complex and complicated area for investigation' that lacked a succinct definition. Almost thirty years later Williams (1986) complained that 'attempts at defining and measuring morale in the literature seem like a quagmire'. Conceptual analyses of satisfaction presented similar problems, with disagreement centring on its bases. To Schaffer (1953) and Sergiovanni (1968), for example, individuals' needs' fulfilment was the basis of job satisfaction, while Lawler's (1973) focus was on expectations, rather than needs, and Locke (1969) dismissed both needs and expectations in favour of values.

A second, more specific, conceptual problem that I have identified (Evans, 1997, 1998, 2002; Evans & Abbott, 1998) is what I call the 'ambiguity' of satisfaction, for the word may denote either or both of two things: that which is satis*factory* (in the sense of acceptable) and that which is satis*fying* (in the sense of fulfilling). Recognition of this conceptual ambiguity has led me to bifurcate satisfaction into two concepts: *job comfort* and *job fulfilment*. Job comfort denotes the satisfactoriness of one's job. Highlighting the importance, in the English language, of prepositional precision, it is about the extent to which one is satisfied *with*, rather than *by*, one's job, while job fulfilment is about being satisfied *by*, rather than *with*, one's job. The latter relates to what is satis*fying*, rather than merely satis*factory*; it

> reflects, and is derived from, a sense of having made a valuable contribution; a feeling of having achieved something; a mental pat on the back. ... It involves, and is a reciprocation of, some kind of personal effort, activity, or contribution. It is a 'return' on self-evaluated job performance. (Evans & Abbott, 1998, p. 88)

Over twenty years ago I published my definition of job fulfilment, as: 'a state of mind determined by the extent of the sense of personal achievement which the individual attributes to his/her performance of those components of his/her job which s/he values' (Evans, 1997). With recognition of the value of conciseness that comes with age and experience, I would probably tweak the wording if I were to be re-formulating it now, but I retain it here since it still does the job of conveying my understanding of job fulfilment.

Irrespective of its bifurcation into job comfort and job fulfilment, how does the overarching concept of job satisfaction differ from morale? In the vernacular the two are often used interchangeably, but those researchers who focused on such issues in the latter half of the twentieth century were often at pains to distinguish between them. Smith (1976), for example, criticised American studies for confusing morale with satisfaction – or at least, for failing to distinguish between them. His own distinction was that job satisfaction is a static, shallow concept, whereas morale is dynamic and forward-looking. My own definition similarly incorporates a temporal dimension; defining morale as 'a state of mind determined by the individual's *anticipation of* the extent of satisfaction of those needs which s/he perceives as significantly affecting his/ her total [work] situation' (Evans, 1998, p. 40, emphasis added), I argue that satisfaction is focused on the present, while morale is focused on anticipation of the future. So-distinguished, high morale may co-exist with dissatisfaction, for – illustrated by an anonymous questionnaire respondent's comment: 'Am about to leave my current uni. therefore morale high' – even though one's current situation may be dire, the hope or expectation of a brighter and better future may sustain high morale. Similarly, low morale may co-exist with high levels of satisfaction, as one lives in dread of an anticipated darker future.

But conceptual clarity is a means to an end, not an end in itself. If there is value or usefulness in researching work-related attitudes and affect it is to be found not in defining them but in elucidating, first, what influences them, and, second, what they, in turn, influence.

Influential bases and links

The occupational and organisational psychology literature that has proliferated since its earliest appearances (in the 1930s) is replete with theories, theoretical perspectives and studies that address the question of what influences job-related attitudes – many of them differing from each other only subtly or slightly in the detail. Maslow's (1954) theory of human needs identifies a hierarchy of needs whose satisfaction is achieved incrementally, through advancement up the hierarchy – with 'self-actualisation' at its pinnacle. Herzberg's (1968) two-factor, or motivation-hygiene, theory posits that the factors influencing job satisfaction are separate and distinct from those influencing dissatisfaction (of which five of each are specifically identified), and Vroom's (1964) expectancy theory distinguishes between the individual's effort, performance and outcomes to posit that people will seek maximum pleasure and minimum pain. And, of course, to these I have added my own 'proximity theory', outlined in Chapter 7.

Yet, adding my voice to the not insignificant criticism that Herzberg's work has provoked, I have exposed its conceptually based flaws that have led me both to conflate Herzberg's five specific motivation theories into one – a sense of achievement – and to dismiss his 'theory' (which, I maintain, is misguided since it was formulated without recognition of what I have revealed as the conceptually based ambiguity of job satisfaction, outlined above) as a non-theory[2] (Evans, 1998, 2002). I have moreover continued to expose methodological weaknesses in job-related attitudes-focused research that fails to recognise the threats to construct validity that arise from overlooking the ambiguity of job satisfaction (Evans & Abbott, 1998). If research subjects – particularly questionnaire respondents, with whom two-way explicatory conversations are not possible – are simply asked to rate their job satisfaction, the researcher often has no way of knowing whether the term was interpreted as denoting what is satis*factory*, or what is satis*fying*, and my own work (Evans, 1997) found such ambiguous interpretation to occur where the researcher's intended meaning is not clarified. Not only do such threats to construct validity undermine data collection, but confusion may continue through to the dissemination of findings.[3]

As far as my own recent research is concerned, had the key focus of the *Professorial academic leadership in turbulent times* and *Professorial leadership preparation and development* studies been professors' attitudes and affective responses to their work, I would have taken care – as I did in my work on teacher morale, job satisfaction and motivation carried out in the early 1990s – to have maximised construct validity at the data collection stage by clarifying concepts and definitions (mine and research participants'), to avoid communicating at cross-purposes. But since attitudes and affect were one of several relevant but *subsidiary* issues included in the foci of this research, conceptualising or defining them precisely was not prioritised. With attention directed at the challenge of soliciting understandings of the main research focus – academic leadership – to avoid disengaging participants by over-egging the conceptualisation dimension, other concepts that featured peripherally were generally alluded to with relatively large doses of interpretative approximation. The purpose was simply to derive some sense of whether professors were happy or unhappy, contented or discontented with their lots – and why, and with what consequences. To this end, an item on the questionnaire that served both studies asked respondents to indicate their morale level, at that precise moment, on an arbitrary 1–10 scale (and offered a link to my definition of morale). In addition, where there was time and opportunity in the very loosely structured interviews, work-related attitudes and affect were discussed with many interviewees – including, in several cases, issues that were intended to 'test', very loosely, and in an unstructured way, the applicability of what I present in Chapter 7 as an explanation for work-related attitudes and affect: 'proximity theory'.

In terms of what is generally known about what work-related attitudes and affect influence in their turn, the literature presents a hazy picture. Common sense reasoning would have it that negative attitudes and/or affect undermine people's motivation and hence lower their performance and/ or productivity, and vice versa. Yet this represents simplistic reasoning, for other factors also impact upon motivation to perform and to deliver, some of which may, depending on the individual's disposition, outweigh or over-ride attitudes-influenced disinclination to perform. Indeed, as Driver (2017) notes – echoing Leonard et al.'s (1999) observation – decades of research have failed to fully uncover the secret of how to motivate people at work, and the focus and associated discourse has shifted in recent years from an instrumentalist approach to inquiry to one that privileges 'self-based' theories 'and the idea that individuals are motivated to the extent that they feel work allows them to construct a desired identity', that is aligned with their self-perceptions (Driver, 2017, p. 619).

What, then, emerged from the *Professorial academic leadership in turbulent times* and *Professorial leadership preparation and development* studies as factors that influence, and are influenced by, professors' morale and job satisfaction?

Work-related attitudes and affect within the UK professoriate

Professors' morale varied across the sample. As Table 10.1 shows, of those who responded to the morale level-seeking questionnaire item, fewer than 10 per cent (6.8 per cent) indicated the highest possible morale level (10), while just over 10 per cent (10.8 per cent) indicated very low morale levels (1–3), including thirty-four (2.7 per cent of the item's respondents) who, in selecting the lowest figure (1), implied that their morale was at rock-bottom. The largest proportion of respondents – almost a quarter – indicated a morale level of 8, with the next most frequently selected morale level indicators being 9 (selected by 16.9 per cent) and 7 (selected by 15.4 per cent). Well over half of these professors thus indicated relatively high to very high morale levels (7 or higher).

Table 10.1 Responses to the questionnaire item worded: 'Please indicate your current level of work-related morale *at this precise moment* (with 1 indicating very low morale and 10 very high morale). If you're interested, you will find our definition of morale by clicking on "more info"'

Respondent-selected morale level		Frequency	%	Valid %	Cumulative %
Valid	1	34	2.7	2.7	2.7
	2	44	3.4	3.5	6.2
	3	58	4.5	4.6	10.8
	4	68	5.3	5.4	16.3
	5	96	7.5	7.6	23.9
	6	141	11.0	11.2	35.1
	7	198	15.4	15.8	50.9
	8	312	24.3	24.9	75.8
	9	217	16.9	17.3	93.1
	10	87	6.8	6.9	100.0
	Total	1,255	97.9	100.0	
Missing	System	27	2.1		
Total		1,282	100.0		

Predictably, questionnaire respondents' comments implied similarly varied morale levels, ranging from the very positive, such as: 'I enjoy my job. I consider myself very lucky to go to work every day looking forward to the variety of interesting challenges it brings' and 'I'm very fortunate. I work in a great school, with great colleagues, dynamic leadership, and wonderful support. I couldn't want for more', through to the very negative, such as: 'Increasingly, I find myself looking forward to retirement. The pleasures of academic life are now few and far between' and 'I loathe my institution. ... You know that something is very wrong when you're in your 40s and the only thing you can think to say when asked about your future career aspirations is "to retire as soon as possible"!'

The follow-up interviews presented a similar overall – albeit impressionistic, since it is unquantifiable – picture of morale and job satisfaction levels, but one that seems to highlight a little more positivity, proportionally, than is implied by the questionnaire data.[4] Reflecting the variation highlighted throughout this book as an indicator of the UK professoriate's heterogeneity, whilst most interviewees expressed varied degrees of qualified satisfaction with their work situations, a minority of interview narratives implied very high satisfaction and morale levels or, conversely, very low ones. Applying proximity theory as a loose framework, something of what influences these wide-ranging attitudes becomes apparent.

The ideal – or near-ideal – job situation

Several interviewees,[5] after being briefly introduced to the notion of proximity theory, were asked specifically how closely their current job situations matched their current ideals and/or what could make things more 'ideal'. Most of them initially focused somewhat narrowly on their roles and responsibilities and conditions of service, rather than more broadly on their whole working life 'package', as I describe it in Chapter 7. Nevertheless, these conversations, particularly when expanded through interviewer probing, provided useful starting points for gauging proximity theory's capacity for explaining professors' attitudes and affective responses to their work situations – though other interview data, irrespective of what questions generated them, also proved very useful in this respect; indeed, every one of the forty-two interviews conveyed something of the interviewee's job-related attitudes and what underpinned them. Overall, the majority of those specifically asked assessed their current job situations as what ranged from quite or reasonably, to entirely, ideal and their morale levels as high. Extracts from the narratives of two of them – Katy and Eric – illustrate the range of aspects and features of their work situations that evidently influenced these assessments.

Katy

Law professor Katy was adamant that her current job was absolutely ideal. Indicated below by quotes from her interview narrative, a range of factors seemed to underpin this assessment, all of which fall into the category of what I call 'job comfort', rather than 'job fulfilment' factors. Illustrating a facet of what Blackmore (2016) identifies as the 'prestige' that is easier to come by and to sustain in smaller UK countries, where strong relationships between a devolved government and a country's top or flagship universities are easier to forge than in England, Katy first highlighted what she saw as the advantages of working within such an environment. Corroborating Blackmore's (2016) findings that senior university personnel in UK countries other than England often enjoyed 'frequent access to the first minister', and 'felt that the national administration was keen to secure their support' (p. 18), she identified the benefits of such links, and the degree of celebrity academic status that they afforded her within a relatively close-knit national and institutional community:

> Oh yeah, [I'm] quite happy; someone would have to offer me a *very* good deal to persuade me to move – or there'd have to be a complete changing of the deal that

I get here. But I do a bit of media work, I do a bit of, sort of, political blogging. I like living in a place that's got institutions that are close to government and that sort of thing – it's much more exciting working here than it is … in any one of 20 other UK cities. … I do like the whole, sort of, politics thing, I like the whole government thing; I like the fact we've got a [names a government institution] here, and that sort of thing. So, it's just very good fun.

Consistent with Lydon's (2016) emphasising the importance of 'creating a sense of identity and a sense of culture and of family' (p. 4) in making people feel welcome in an organisation, and wanting to work there, was what Katy identified as a second positive feature of her work environment: good collegial relations, both in her own department and in the wider institution, and whose familial nature seemed to give her a sense of belonging:

Everyone is so nice. There's nobody in my department that you wouldn't sit down and have a coffee with; sit down and eat a meal with. … I met someone [recently] who'd been at [my department] and left us for a promotion, and we happened to be on the same train back from London (because he still lives here), and I was talking about the [university] family [here], and he said that now, being somewhere else, he could see what people meant when they talked about the '[names her university] *family*' and being part of the [X] family.

But it was by contrasting her current job situation with a much more unsatisfactory one that she related having endured earlier in her career, that Katy was able to identify an example of what I categorise as a 'positive job comfort factor': the physical proximity of her home to her workplace:

Katy: [Y University] was far from my ideal job, and I think you need to go through something like that to realise what your ideal job is.
LE: What was wrong with [Y]?
Katy: I hate commuting, I'm not a commuter … I would go down probably on a Monday and come back on a Thursday, and I *hated* it. … commuting for work was a nightmare!

Provoking negative attitudes or affective responses, negative job comfort factors – such as irritants or frustrations – are much more identifiable than are positive ones, which, being taken for granted, often go unnoticed. Indeed, illustrating what I call the 'relativity factor' as a key basis for attitudes-formation that arises out of assessment of one's work context (Evans, 1998), without the relative perspective afforded her by her earlier unsatisfactory commuter lifestyle, Katy is unlikely to have identified close home-workplace proximity as a satisfactory feature of her current work context.

Finally, illustrating the potency of the notion of pursuit of the ideal-self-at-work, through what I explain in Chapter 7 as seeking out or trying to engineer 'uncompromising' work contexts, Katy spoke of another unsatisfactory experience – a work situation that had threatened to become a 'compromising' one, and that she consequently left behind:

> I remember saying to someone at [my former university] … 'this guy is bullying me', and his response was, 'Yes, I've known about this for some time.' And I thought, well, if you've known about it, why did you wait for me; why didn't you *do* something about it, if *you* thought it was bullying too? And then there were other people [at that university] who just seemed to offer nothing … they were people who'd spent years just sat in their offices, never spoke to anyone, and were just relentlessly negative about anything anyone suggested. And I just thought: *I don't want to be like that. (Katy, law professor, pre-1992 university)*

Katy's last sentence, above, is indicative of avoidance of a compromising work context on the basis of its undermining what, at the time, was her conception of her 'ideal-self-at-work': one who is not undermined by bullying, is surrounded by pro-active, positive, collegiality, and is therefore able to enact the kind of professionalism that she envisages for herself as a 'leading' professor. Colleagues and her relations with them are clearly important to her, as is the feeling of being in the centre of – and of being able to influence, or have a voice in – policy- and decision-making.

It is, of course, very difficult to ascertain what gives people fulfilment rather than what simply meets with their satisfaction, for we cannot see inside their heads, but I argue (Evans, 1998) that is only where they may attribute their satisfaction to their own efforts, allowing them a sense of (significant) achievement in relation to something that they value, that job fulfilment occurs. The difficulty is that, in shaping the environments and contexts within which people operate, job *comfort* factors are extremely important as the channels or vehicles through which people attain job fulfilment, so they are sometimes misread as sources of fulfilment in themselves. In Katy's case we see the potential for her status within the close-knit community that she finds so enjoyable and supportive – and which, as she implies in the first quote above, affords her a platform from which to be heard, to influence and to be recognised – for providing just such a means of her attaining job fulfilment, yet without it *in itself* offering such fulfilment; only as a vehicle or channel for her agency does it play a part in enhancing her fulfilment.

Eric

Lying just within the 'high morale' group of interviewees (in his interview he assessed his morale/satisfaction level as 'a 7 or an 8'), Eric's narrative illustrates the temporal distinction that I identify between job satisfaction and morale, for he implies having one eye on the future, anticipating changes to the nature of his work and working life that would impoverish them. Despite his expressed intention to resist such change, the prospect of having to address it was evidently lurking in his consciousness:

> I have a very strong feeling that, in two years' time, I'm going to be asked to be head of department – okay? Because – and the picture is very clear – I've made, and I'm making, a real success of this. They don't have another professor … so, clearly, there's this guy who's done it all; well, why not ask him? … And I'm likely to say, 'No', because it's such a horrible job! (*Eric, education studies professor, pre-1992 university*)

Like Katy's, Eric's case illustrates the significance of relative perspective in influencing attitudes to and affective responses to one's work situation, for he too assessed his former work situation much less positively than his current one. In his case, it had been a problematic colleague – another professor – who had made Eric's work situation much less ideal than it currently was, and whose departure had brought Eric's situation much closer to his ideal. Asked to give a quantitative indication of his morale/job satisfaction level, he responded: 'This last year it's consistently been somewhere around a 7 or an 8.' The interview conversation continued:

> *LE: You're saying 'this last year', so are you implying that earlier it would've been higher or lower?*
> *Eric:* Oh, lower; lower, without a doubt. … The difference is that a guy who was … in charge of research in the department very suddenly left, and I was asked, at the drop of a hat, to take over … and found that, not only had he hidden a great deal of stuff from people, but that we were two years behind where we needed to be for the REF! … And my job became increasingly difficult as I saw the things he was doing, and the way he was damaging us with the centre of the university, because he was a deeply unpleasant person a lot of the time. And so we got to the stage where education was simply not figuring in the consciousness of the centre, and the kind of things we needed to be doing, some of the stuff we didn't know because he didn't relay it back … and he, of course, controlled the information. So, I was getting to the stage where … had somebody come along to me last year and asked me if I wanted a job at another university, I'd probably have jumped at the chance!

From Eric's perspective, a more ideal situation at that point in time would have been one in which his department was making good progress in preparing for REF2014, was represented effectively at the centre of the university – which, in its (the centre's) turn, would have held the department in high esteem and therefore incorporated full consideration of its interests and development into its decision- and policy-making. These would have constituted positive job comfort factors, yet their absence created negative job comfort factors: a marginalised department whose influential capacity was impaired, and REF unpreparedness.

With the problematic colleague departed, Eric took over as departmental research director, a role that involved leading REF-related activities: not only drafting statements to be included in the university's REF submission, but also ensuring that all of his colleagues' published output that would be selected for submission reached the university's required threshold standard.[6] This was evidently a mammoth task, whose demands, Eric's narrative implied, presented yet another barrier to his attaining his ideal work situation, for they left him with no time for what was a key source of fulfilment for him: his own research.

> But this moment in time, the *only* thing that stops it being the ideal job ... would be the fact that the REF is *so* all-consuming ... that I have no time for my research. And you can live with that for a while – and you can even use previous stuff and reformulate it, for two or three articles, and then you can't.

For Eric, then, the ideal work situation is evidently one that allows him the kind of fulfilment that he associates with pursuing his own research. In denying him such fulfilment, his REF-related role may appear as a negative job fulfilment factor. Yet it is feasible that it is not (only) the fulfilment derived from the creativity injected into his research that is a feature of Eric's ideal job situation, but (also) the esteem that comes from publishing high-quality research, and/or the association of such activity and esteem with professorial distinction. Encompassing issues that were not discussed in Eric's interview, this reasoning goes beyond the data, but it is consistent with the literature relating to what matters to academics, including the findings of my own research (Evans & Abbott, 1998; Evans & Bertani-Tress, 2009), and with Becher and Trowler's (2001) findings that academics place high value on being recognised, through their publications, as authorities in their fields. Eric may have felt a need to publish in order to strengthen his identity as a professor through external esteem – certainly, as several of his remarks suggest, he had a strong professorial identity: 'I see myself as a university professor; this is what it's about.'

But Eric also seemed to have what Lapierre et al. (2012, p. 766) refer to as a 'strongly relational identity' that allowed him to derive 'a sense of self-worth from engaging in appropriate role behaviour with relational partners' and motivated him 'to act in terms of a specific other's benefit'. In this respect his REF-related role was something of a double-edged sword in Eric's job-related attitudes armoury – a positive, as well as a negative, job fulfilment factor – for he related deriving immense fulfilment from the developmental-focused academic leadership that, as he had shaped it, the role allowed him to practise, and which as a consequence allowed him to feel that he was making a significant contribution not only to enhancing individual colleagues' capacity and self-esteem, but also to raising the fortunes of his department and his university. Eric presented himself as a professor whose academic leadership was heavy on relationality that manifested itself through negotiation of consensus, bringing people on-side, and working collaboratively:

> I think I'm known as a ... as a fairly collegial sort of person. ... I don't tend to have rivalries; I don't tend to have enemies. Er ... if somebody doesn't particularly like me they'll be a colleague, but they won't be an enemy. And most people who do like me will be friends. ... I'm a person who has always believed in the idea that you get a better result by sharing ideas than by keeping them to yourself. ... You've got to *handle* the group; you've got to manage them well, and that's part of being a facilitator and not imposing your ideas on each other, but giving a steer as well. So there are social skills involved in that. But that – I think that's largely the kind of ... I *hope* other people would say that's the kind of leader – it's certainly the kind of leader I *aspire* to be.

As he described it, this relationality was a key feature of Eric's research leadership role. He related, for example, not shying away from or avoiding problematic colleagues, but trying to understand the bases of their obstreperousness and to address them head-on, through appeasement – a manifestation of what Brown (2014, p. 18) calls 'collegial and collective leadership'. In organising the procedures for internally assessing colleagues' potential REF-able output, for example, he did his best to bring on-side a colleague with a reputation for truculence:

> One of the first things I did before I sent out ... er ... a letter to people [explaining the procedure], was to go and talk to the most difficult person in the department – who's criticised everything that the senior management has done since he's been here. ... So I said, 'John, I want to do this. You've been a critic of the previous conversations, so how do you improve them? You tell me, okay; I'm listening.'

Eric spoke of deriving satisfaction not only from winning round 'difficult' colleagues, but also from working consistently with all colleagues, often one-to-one, on their writing, with a view to bringing it up to REF-able standard – 'I know I'm having quite a dramatic effect on a lot of other people's lives in the department.' He categorised this way of working as servant leadership:

> When I filled in your questionnaire, I suppose the thing that I realised was …
> I was much more of a servant leader than I'd ever imagined. … I've always felt
> that one of the things you should be doing is bringing on other members of staff,
> anyway; I think that's part of what you're doing.

Asked if he considered such altruistic collegiality and leadership as manifestations of his selflessness, he responded:

> How can you say I'm selfless when the thing I get most enjoyment out of is helping
> others? …What *greater* reward can you have than being able to help? … Now
> that's [sigh of pleasure] – they *pay* you to do this! At times, it's almost immoral!
> It is almost immoral, you know, that something that's so utterly enjoyable … so,
> no, I *really* don't see it as selfless in any way whatsoever. … I genuinely think this
> is … this is – if I had a bit more time for research – this is just a wonderful job!
> … But, no, I don't think 'selfless' is a word I would use.

Yet, despite his contesting how it was labelled, Eric's altruistic developmental-focused approach to professorship shone through as a key fulfilment-deriving vehicle. Asked what makes a good day at work, his answer revealed the influences on his satisfaction level:

> Er … having a tutorial with a student, and knowing that they've not understood,
> and having to … not lay into them, but … having to pull apart the work, and do
> it in a way that opens *their* eyes to what needs doing, and they accept it and they
> go away and do it. … Getting a student through a viva, you know – and a student
> who never thought that they'd get through when they started off – you know,
> that's probably … that's – you know, the ones who just sail through … who are
> brilliant from the word go, and all you're doing is reading their stuff for pleasure
> … yeah, I get a great deal of pleasure, but I know *I* didn't contribute much to
> that. So, it's where I've put in the work and it's going well.

Consistent with my outline explanation above as what I see as the distinction between job fulfilment and job comfort, by his own account Eric's fulfilment appeared to be dependent upon his attributing his own efforts as a contributor to a favourable or successful situation. But, for some professorial interviewees, such efforts seemed to have met with varied success.

Barriers to the ideal

Whilst Eric and Katy were by no means the only interviewees to describe their job situations as ideal or close to ideal, such assessments represented the minority. A broad spectrum of attitudes and affective responses to their jobs emerged from professors' narratives, uncovering – even within otherwise predominantly positive assessments – a miscellany of negative job comfort, or even negative job fulfilment, factors that indicated distance between actual perceived job situations and what were implicitly or explicitly presented as ideal ones.

Some negative job comfort factors were historic: like those related by Eric and Katy, above, by the time the interview conversations took place they had been eradicated or diluted by circumstances. They nevertheless merit attention not only because knowing something of their nature augments our understanding of academic working life, but also because, in many cases (as with some of the narratives of non-professorial academics included in Chapter 6), their legacies have evidently shaped and may continue to shape how the people affected go about their work. Moreover, the job situations and contexts within which negative job comfort factors feature play an important role in providing the relative perspectives that allow more positive, uncompromising, and near-ideal, situations and contexts to be recognised and appreciated.

It is difficult, for analytical purposes, to categorise and label features – negative or positive – of people's work situations because they seldom stand alone; within the chains of causality and influence that fuel the fluidity of interpersonal agency and evolving circumstances that makes up the landscapes and ecologies of working life, they invariably overlap with or spill over into other factors, as either their bases or their consequences. Nevertheless, two broad factors stand out as particularly prominent influences on the attitudes and affective responses to their work situations conveyed in the narratives of the *Professorial academic leadership in turbulent times* and *Professorial leadership preparation and development* interviewees: interpersonal collegial relations; and workload. In their negative forms – as poor or unsatisfactory collegial relations and as work overload – depending on their perceived severity, these factors were identified by many interviewees either as key features of unsatisfactory work situations that were far from the ideal, or (as in Eric's case, above) as barriers to attaining the ideal within what were otherwise relatively 'uncompromising' work contexts.

Unsatisfactory collegial relations

One particular negative job comfort factor – collegial aggression – is important to include in this chapter because it serves to dispel any misconceptions that professors' seniority and status render them immune to or exempt from the kinds of work context-related problems and anxieties that often dog non-professorial academics' lives. Several professors spoke of incidents or situations that involved varied degrees of what may be categorised as bullying, intimidation or other forms of aggressive or antagonistic behaviour – and all of which had evidently occurred not in interviewees' dim and distant early career past, but since their promotions to professorship.

Assessing his morale level, at the time of his interview, as high – '9, probably 8 or 9, you know; at the minute I'm very content' – like both Katy and Eric, engineering professor Liam was nevertheless able to recall times when, diminished by the kinds of conflict and aggression that emanated from brushes with difficult colleagues, his morale would have been much lower. He described as 'vitriolic' some of the exchanges he had had with professorial colleagues, in the course of trying to change the culture of his department. One incident, he recalled, had had a profound emotional impact upon him, giving him frequent sleepless nights:

> There was a philanthropist who was prepared to put four million [pounds] into each of three areas. The university invited us to put forward a bid on one particular research strand which a couple of these guys [professorial colleagues] were leading, or meant to be leading – one in particular. He refused to put forward a proposal unless he got a pay rise, so the possibility of four million was going begging. So I, as head of department, put [the bid] together. ... And I put it to the department first – just for information – and at the meeting there was the guy who'd refused to do it. He attacked me at the board meeting and called me all sorts of names – said I was stealing his research. He went to the union, he threatened to go to the university visitor. ... Everybody else was silent; I didn't want to reveal, you know, that I knew he'd said he'd only do it for a pay rise, but that was ... that was one that still – even after more than ten years – still sticks in my mind. (*Liam, engineering professor, pre-1992 university*)

Linguistics professor Catherine probably fell into the broad mid-range band of the spectrum of morale and job satisfaction levels, and of proximity to her ideal job situation. Describing her work situation as 'not ideal' and assessing her morale and satisfaction level as 'six or seven, I think, probably', she recalled a recent time (the previous year) when she would have assessed it as 'about two, I think ... I mean, I would've ... like, I probably could've left. ... But, you know, *very* low then – absolutely'. The problem had evidently been the bullying behaviour of a head of department whom Catherine described as having been unreasonably critical of her:

> We've had a head of department for the last few years – thankfully, now changed – who I found it very, very, very difficult to get along with. We were actually promoted to professor at the same time, and then she became head of school ... and then she, kind of, underwent a personality change and became a very unpleasant person indeed and upset a lot of people. ... And she put me in the position of [names a departmental administrative role]. And ... there was no job description; you had to, kind of, make it up as you go along. And at the end of a year she decided that I hadn't been doing anything, so she had me in on her carpet – and I felt like I was seventeen and on the headmaster's carpet in my comprehensive school! [laugh] It wasn't pleasant at all. But, I mean, the gist of it, I think, was, y'know, I should've been more proactive ... . But I'm not exactly sure what I wasn't doing that she thought I *should've* been doing. (*Catherine, linguistics professor, pre-1992 university*)

Asked to elaborate on this incident, and her response to it at the time, Catherine continued:

> I was gobsmacked. [laugh] I tried to defend myself, but, I mean, I didn't see it coming. But, I mean, this was something that happened with this person a lot. She would ... she was ... very, very, very volatile, and will blow up for no apparent reason. But she also had these *planned* blow-ups, where, y'know, she'd drag you in like this. And she did this to ... I mean, I know an awful lot of people in the department that this has happened to. In fact, we didn't realise until we started talking to each other how widespread it was. Bullying, basically. ... We'd been to the bullying team about it.

So-described, the head of department's leadership seems to fit Skorobohacz et al's (2016) category of 'dysfunctional' leadership that, *inter alia*, blames and intimidates others, and to have come close to the kinds of 'toxic' leadership identified by Pelletier (2010), and referred to in Chapter 6. The impact upon Catherine's working life was apparently not insignificant, giving rise to feelings of unease and anxiety that prompted avoidance behaviour and such 'misery' that, as Catherine remarks in one of the quotes above, she had wanted to leave the university:

> I mean, my morale is a lot better since ... we've had a new head of school, because *she* seems to have a different attitude. She's much more humane. There's much less ... I've seen no evidence of any bullying or intimidation. But the

previous head, one of my professorial colleagues described her as 'management by intimidation' – and that was right. I mean, you know, I got to a point, about a year ago, where I dreaded coming in the doors. I'd use different toilets in case I bumped into her. It was horrible, and I was very stressed, along with a lot of other people. It was *misery*, actually. (*Catherine, linguistics professor, pre-1992 university*)

Yet, as Pelletier (2010) points out, toxicity in leadership is perceived and assessed subjectively, and hence differentially. So, too, are interpersonal exchanges or communications, so what one professor may categorise as bullying or aggression, may be perceived differently by another. In this respect, arts and humanities professor Elizabeth seemed to accept with a degree of equanimity the kinds of exchanges that may have intimidated or ground down others. More precisely, it was probably the case that Elizabeth – on her own admission, a consummate strategic thinker – was more battle-ready for the kinds of combative environments and exchanges that, being micro-politically savvy, she had learned to deal with and often to manoeuvre to her advantage. Referring generally to the need for female professors to 'carry … weight against a list of names of big, bruising white males', she seemed to have developed a thick outer skin – which obscured what she described as her 'biggest weakness': her need for affirmation: 'Fundamentally, I want them all to like me [slight laugh], and I'm really bad at handling it when they don't' – that allowed her to appear unintimidated and unperturbed. What some professors may have denounced as unacceptable aggression, Elizabeth seemed to accept as part and parcel of being a professor within her particular institutional environment. Whilst it clearly remained a vivid unpleasant memory, she was able to laugh off, for example, a blatant insult that she recalled:

> These big dinners when old boys come back – a very drunk guy in his 70s got me up against the fireplace and waved his finger in my face and said, 'Lady, you're no [X]!' [X] was a holder of my chair in the 1960s … . He was a celebrated eccentric. He was an absolutely pathetic scholar and published almost nothing! … [laughs] I said I thought that was a matter of pride!

And, as she described it, her intellectual response to an incident in which she recalled male colleagues having conducted themselves aggressively had allowed her to sit back impassively and watch events unfold in the way that she had hoped:

> Because they're all men, they spent my first year pussyfooting round me. They didn't know quite how to handle me, and it was quite clear that they didn't know that if they were horrid to me, whether or not I would cry. I chaired a meeting recently where I think they forgot I was a woman, because they behaved *unspeakably* – they shouted, and they talked across one another, and they talked

across *me*, and there was one moment when I was going to say, 'Do we *have* to behave like this?' and then I thought: No; just let them do it, 'cos they've forgotten I'm a woman! And this is what they'd do if I wasn't here. So, actually, that's a most enormous compliment! And I let them do it. And they slogged out a really big thing across the table, and then I said, 'It seems to me that where you want to go is here.' And I didn't have to do anything! Anthropologically, I thought that was really interesting. (*Elizabeth, arts and humanities professor, pre-1992 university*)

Bearing in mind that we have only the barest outline details of each scenario or situation, as interpreted and presented by the interviewee, it is interesting to contrast, as they were related, Elizabeth's response to an aggressively macho environment – the committee meeting that she refers to above – with his response to what chemistry reader Alan, quoted in Chapter 6, describes as a similar environment, and which he confessed had reduced him to tears on occasions. Such impressionistically based comparisons are necessarily crude and allow us only to register, rather than explore in depth, the kinds of power- and personality-related differentials that underpin two seemingly quite different responses to what appear broadly similar contexts. The key point, however, is that, irrespective of whatever biographical or situational advantages may have allowed her to do so, in brushing off as *relatively* insignificant the kinds of interpersonal exchanges that, for some professors, may have degenerated into negative job comfort factors of such severity – potentially identified as features of an oppressively uncomfortable or unbearably aggressive culture – as to provoke deep dissatisfaction and unhappiness, Elizabeth's strategic resilience allowed her to narrow the gap between what she perceived as her actual and her ideal job situations. Most importantly, her case illustrates the subjectivity with which sources of satisfaction and dissatisfaction – negative and positive job comfort factors – are identified, experienced, and impact upon people's working lives. Whilst chasing the ideal, then, may be facilitated or hindered by the contours defining the undulating terrains across which are forged their career paths, people's capacity for negotiating the peaks and troughs lies with themselves.

Work overload

A recurring prominent theme that emerged from the research data was pressure to perform, resulting in work overload. Indicative of the numerous ones that echoed the same sentiments, the following selected comments – responses to an open-ended item within a section of the questionnaire that was labelled, 'morale' – illustrate something of how this theme manifested itself in professors' attitudes to their working lives:

Very few people outside academia have any idea of the workload pressures that we are under and the hours that we work. No sane person would take this role on. (*post-1992 university professor*)

Below professor level it's already more than a full-time job, but as a professor one is expected to do even more. What is worse, one is always given the feeling that it's not enough, that one needs to get one's act together now that students pay such high fees, research is evaluated in the REF, funded research requires high impact, inter-disciplinarity, etc, and at the same time salaries are eroded and fall back further and further behind comparable jobs (doctors, lawyers). (*pre-1992 university professor*)

Chronically overworked, and under-supported by senior management – who welcome my contribution but take it for granted. (*pre-1992 university professor*)

As a professor I teach 1st, 2nd and 3rd year undergraduates, as well as MSc students and PhD students. I am accorded few special privileges in this regard because of my supposed seniority. Indeed, I am expected to set an example in terms of my alacrity to engage with these tasks. And I have to engage in significant academic citizenship (committee membership, chairing appeals, etc.). I have to be an all singing and all dancing colleague. I would imagine most professors do nowadays. (*post-1992 university professor*)

[My morale is influenced by] general state of the institution, work all weekends and evenings, continually assessed for the REF. Would seek other jobs if there were any! (*pre-1992 university professor*)

Feeling overwhelmed by having taken on too much, internally and externally, and exhausted by the 12-hour working days (and work every weekend) necessary to deliver on this. (*pre-1992 university professor*)

Consistent with the implication – with the words 'having taken on' – in the last of these comments, the interview data revealed many professors, to varying degrees, to have been influential in determining their own heavy workloads, revealing the kind of 'pressured' professionalism that Noordegraaf (2007) identifies as a feature of twenty-first-century working life. In the case of professors, pressured professionalism seems to have manifested itself as a relentless concern to demonstrate academic leadership and/or to get a handle on where lay the parameters that defined what was quantitatively acceptable in demonstrating it. The latter concern seemed to have spawned performance-angst amongst those who implicitly or explicitly related not only feeling obliged to agree to many demands on their time – for fear of being branded 'unfit' or 'unworthy' of the professorial title, and the associated 'academic leader' epithet – but also, in some cases, to creating and imposing on themselves *additional* pressures to perform.

For education studies professor Alison, demonstrating her distinction in relation to scholarly achievement seems to have been a key concern. Despite reporting both 'pretty high' morale and reasonably close proximity to her ideal work situation – 'I love it ... no, I do love it. I don't think it's an *ideal* job. I think I'm really privileged to do it, so I'm very positive, but I don't think it's ideal' – she admitted putting pressure on herself to continually justify her promotion through outperforming her junior colleagues in the academic publishing 'game':

> I always do too much. But, I think ... I think I am always anxious about what, you know, about ... like, have I done enough publications? ... So, you know ... so, I think I just – and I *have* actually done more publications than anybody else – and I think, as a result of that, I do ... over-achieve in the things that I'm supposed to do, but more because I keep thinking: oh that's not enough, that's not enough.

Alison's self-imposed pressure to perform in this way represents her chasing the ideal. She confirmed that her self-imposed and self-acknowledged over-productiveness was motivated by her seeking approbation from senior managers and from the university 'centre'. Her comment above was immediately followed by her remarking:

> So, it's quite ... it's still quite hard for me to see what's there, and our performance development review does help that, to some extent. And I know the last one – because I'm reviewed by a fellow chair and my head of department – and ... in the last one they said, 'Oh you're doing really great.' Oh, yeah – and you still need to hear that! ... I'm constantly trying to push myself in all of this – and you can't do it all. (*Alison, education studies professor, pre-1992 university*)

Computer sciences professor Simon similarly spoke of the importance of meeting his university's expectations in relation to producing research outputs that, in the REF, would be graded at the highest level (which, at the time of writing, is 4*):

> Like any university [it] expects people to have good quality publications ... and you know ... if you're a professor and you've not got, you know, four star publications, I mean, people would be looking at you and saying, well, you know, 'Why is this guy a professor?' So there's a certain element of pressure there – not direct, but, sort of, there's the perception that you obviously have to be doing things like that at a fairly high level. ... In terms of as a professor, there's an element of pressure, I suppose, in that you're expected to deliver perhaps things like, you know, publications at a higher rate – and I don't necessarily mean numerically, but certainly in terms of quality. (*Simon, computer sciences professor, pre-1992 university*)

For several professors the ideal remained very elusive. The narrative of STEMM professor Harry – who, in his thirties, had relatively recently applied for and secured a named chair at his own university – was punctuated by remarks, such as 'you have to run to go backwards' and 'you're almost expected to do three full-time jobs, and I don't feel I'm physically capable of sustaining that for the remaining 30 years of my career', that conveyed constant pressure to perform, and dissatisfaction with a workplace context that imposed such pressures. His current work situation, Harry confirmed, was not his ideal one – which, he suggested, was likely to remain elusive:

> My expectation is that I'll never be able to reduce [my workload] to the level that ... would allow me to deliver fully on what I believe is expected of me on the research side, as well as the sort of, y'know, the sort of more, y'know, grown up expectations as a, sort of, reasonably experienced academic, in terms of actually guiding people, and so on. So I think that's probably really my looking forward in terms of the ideals. I think there's too many things expected of me. I'm expected to lead in too many areas, and as I look around and I look for people who appear exceptionally successful, they only really do one thing. ... We can only really deliver *mediocre* stuff because we simply don't have the capacity to deliver at the levels expected, and I feel the expectations at the very top of this university, where it's stated that professors should research more, teach more, do more administration, are unreasonable ... so it comes away a little bit from your ideal job. (*Harry, STEMM professor, pre-1992 university*)

Finkenstaedt (2011, p. 192) argues that 'University teachers everywhere are quite prepared to work more hours than average civil servants. For full professors fifty hours per week during term time and a few hours less when classes are not in session is a realistic average for Europe.' Yet when long working days are combined with pressure and work overload, they often take their toll on morale and job satisfaction. For biological sciences professor Brian, pressure in the form of work overload seems to have been the defining feature of his professorship. In Chapter 8 he is quoted as reflecting on his promotion with ambivalence, perceiving it as having brought additional pressure in the form of new expectations of him: 'you become a chair, and then ... the university has extra expectations of you ... of what they want out of *you* in return'. He went on to refer to 'the extra burdens' that his promotion had brought, and which had changed the nature of his work significantly, taking him away from research and turning him into an administrator – both of his own laboratory, and in relation to wider university citizenship-type administrative responsibilities. His description of a typical day conveys the nature of his particular 'pressured' professionalism:

I just don't get into the lab. ... I mean, my working week is between fifty and sixty hours, and I don't work at weekends any more because if I'm doing fifty to sixty hours during the week ... I don't see that I need to come in on a Saturday! Of course, with the internet, y'know, you're never free. I've taken to reading my email at quarter to seven in the morning just to clear the stuff that accumulates overnight ... er ... so when I get to work I then have a free hour before stuff starts coming in. And I'm just pulled in every which direction ... er ... and yesterday I spent a fruitless hour-and-a-half in a meeting about how we're going to deal with the UK border agency regulations for overseas students. And then it was straight from that and back to the lab here to host parents at open days, y'know. This afternoon I have *got* to go down to the teaching labs to fix two bits of equipment, which I need for my practical – which I run on Thursdays. But because the practical sessions are timetabled so badly ... in that we only have an afternoon to get the equipment ready, and the day then to run the practical, and that afternoon of the practical to put the equipment away again, everything's -there's just pressure on all sides ... all the time ... for doing things *now*! ... because we don't have time to do it *any other way*, and it's just *madness*! And so, what's happened in the last five years is ... the only time I step foot in there [the lab area] is to go to the loo or to go and get a cup of coffee ... . And, y'know ... even actually finding out exactly what my PhD students are doing ... I'm finding now that I spend less time sat over a ... bench with them looking at [X[7]] – which is what I *used* to do – because I just don't have the time. So, y'know, I end up having to get *them* to write the monthly reports, so I can, sort of, go through what they've done ... and find out that they've not done *this* control and not done *that* control ... and if I'd known about it ... y'know ... a month or a week ago ... or two weeks ago ... we could've just stopped all that.

For Brian, then, a key concern seems to have been trying to stay on top of the multitude of tasks that, with his promotion, had begun to land on his desk, and the numerous responsibilities that he found himself shouldering in his capacity as a STEMM professor who was both expected to run an efficient laboratory – a responsibility that, within his disciplinary culture, also involved developing his team of junior colleagues and ensuring they went on to find academic posts – and undertake institutional citizenship. By his own account – as he is quoted in Chapter 9 as admitting – he was conscientious in both of these elements of his work and in many ways may be considered to have been making a rod for his own back by his reluctance to say, 'No', or to cut down on his citizenship. In this respect, his case illustrates the point I make above, that how people negotiate the undulating terrains across which are forged their career paths, lies with them; in Brian's case his reluctance to skimp on what, as a professor, he feels he should be doing indicates his chasing the ideal by trying to sustain a self-conception – his ideal-self-at-work – that evades being compromised by his failure to meet people's expectations of him. Yet all of this took its toll on his work-related attitudes. Asked what aspects of his job gave him the most fulfilment, he responded: 'That's a very difficult question at the moment. Job satisfaction at this moment in time I'm not getting terribly much of, to be frank.'

Rating his morale level as 'two or three', Brian was by no means the only one of the professorial interviewees to report long working days and excessive workloads; many told how they typically get up very early and work until late into the night and/or at weekends – arts and humanities professor Elizabeth described the start of her day: 'The alarm goes off at 5.30 and I get out of bed as soon as I can. I try to be at my computer by 6.00', and computer sciences professor Simon estimated his working week as longer even than Brian's, at eighty hours. Yet Brian was probably the most dissatisfied and demoralised of all the professors interviewed, and spoke of wanting to change jobs:

> I'm currently keeping my eye open for alternative careers – and not just alternative *employment*; alternative *careers*. So I've recently, just this week, I've found out that I've not been shortlisted for a head of department job elsewhere. So I was a bit disappointed to not get shortlisted; I would've thought my CV would at least get my foot through the door for interview, but that didn't happen. ... So, that's a bit frustrating. And, yes, I'm just getting to the point where I'm thinking: well, what can I do with my life instead of this? I'm only 44, and I've got at least 21 more years before retirement – probably 25, the way things are going – and I can have an entire career in a different field ... or run a wine merchant's or something, y'know. So I find my ... I find my weekends spent increasingly pondering what else I can do with my life. (*Brian, biological sciences professor, pre-1992 university*)

In common with a great many of the research participants – as was evident from both interview narratives and questionnaire responses – Brian identified as a key problematic issue one that Harry, too, quoted above, identified: the need for universities, within the performativity culture that is twenty-first-century academe in the UK, to deploy their professors more sensibly and realistically. How they might do so is a dominant theme in the final part of this book.

Notes

1   Deriding the *THE* report as 'fake news', Cuthbert (2017) is very dismissive of the study whose data it reports, identifying as its weaknesses its 'leading questions' and its 'self-selecting' sample as 'likely to be all those who want to complain about senior management in their institution'.

2   The basis of the 'theory' status of Herzberg's work seems to hang upon his discovery that the factors that motivate or create satisfaction are not the same as those that demotivate or create job dissatisfaction. My uncovering what I call the 'ambiguity' of job satisfaction – that it can relate to two quite different things – undermines Herzberg's 'theory', because 'his theory emphasises what has often been regarded as a revelation; that the opposite of satisfaction is not dissatisfaction, but "no satisfaction", and that the opposite of dissatisfaction is not satisfaction, but "no dissatisfaction". The issue is, I believe, much more simple and straightforward. Since one category relates to factors which are capable only of making things satisfactory, and the other, to factors which are capable of satisfying, then, clearly, they *are* distinct and separate. But realisation of this should not form the basis of a theory; it merely follows on from awareness that there are separate, but related, components of what has tended to be regarded as a single concept' (Evans, 1998, p. 7).

3   See, for example, my criticism (Evans & Abbott, 1998) of Oshagbemi's (1996) research into the job satisfaction of UK academics, on the basis of its being unclear not only how he interprets 'job satisfaction' but also what interpretations of it his research subjects held.

4   Without implying any undermining of the sentiments and perspectives that prompted questionnaire respondents' comments, I suggest that the rather more overall positive picture to emerge from the interviews may be partly methodologically based. Reflecting human nature, people tend to communicate less aggressively and dismissively negative attitudes face-to-face in a one-to-one interview situation with an interviewer who has endeavoured to build up a rapport with them than through an open-ended questionnaire response that allows them to remain anonymous, and where the greater effort required to communicate complex, nuanced attitudes and feelings encourages short, sharp and occasionally shock-provoking sentences. It is also possible that respondents who expressed the greatest negativity may have been more disinclined to volunteer as interviewees than did those who expressed more positive attitudes, skewing the pool of participants from which to select the interview sample.

5   This occurred with around half of the forty-two interviewees.

6   Following the format of earlier research assessment exercises, in REF 2014 published output submitted by each university choosing to participate in the REF was assessed by the REF subject panels of peers and assigned a grade on a 5-point

scale, with 4* being the highest grade, denoting 'world-leading work'. Individual publications' assessments are not published, but the proportion of a university's output submission within each subject panel that was assessed at each of the five points on the scale is published. Since the funding they receive from the government post-REF, via the higher education funding councils of each UK nation, reflects the quality of the institution's submitted outputs, many universities – particularly research-intensive ones – operate sophisticated internal assessment mechanisms for grading, by REF criteria, all publications that its departments propose for inclusion in its submission, and these mechanisms generally involve the imposition of an institutionally determined minimum grade threshold (typically 3* in Russell Group and other research-intensive universities) for sifting out which publications will be included in the final submission.

7   The focus of this activity has been obscured, to protect the interviewee's anonymity.

Part Four

Reshaping Professorial Professionalism

11

Pressured Professionalism: Problematising Professorial Academic Leadership

As I remark in its closing paragraph, Chapter 1 marks out, with a scattering of dots, the broadest of outlines of what professorship in the UK looks like. Joining up those dots, the chapters in Parts Two and Three progressively build up a much sharper image of professors in the twenty-first-century UK academy, conveying something of the 'shape' of their professionalism. But that shape nevertheless remains elusive, for – to borrow Lumby's (2012) evocative metaphor of a kaleidoscope's shifting patterns – it is continually reforming itself: reflecting one professor's perceived enactment of it, it takes on a certain form, then, as another professor with different priorities or competencies enacts it, it refashions itself, only to shift and reshape again to reflect yet another professor's enactment. This chapter examines the bases and nature of this professorial professionalism, and its effects on the professoriate's contribution to higher education in the UK and globally.

Heterogeneity and variability: Influences and implications

The shifting nature and 'shape' of *enacted* professorial professionalism reflects differentiated ways of doing professorship. It is a differentiation that seems predominantly contextually-imposed – paradoxically, a by-product of what is widely perceived as the homogenising nature of the twenty-first-century academy, whose performativity-focused cultures and regimes seem to be eroding the distinctions that, irrespective of national and institutional affiliation, as Ylijoki and Ursin (2015) outline, once denoted different disciplinary academic communities' cultures and traditions:

> The image of the university as a territory inhabited by distinct academic tribes
> – with their own disciplinary cultures, and academics as tribe members with

firm disciplinary identities (Becher, 1989) – has been challenged by increasing, and often conflicting, external pressures on higher education. New managerial practices with audits, performance measurements, rankings, profilings and competition for funding have substantially transformed the academy as a workplace. (Ylijoki & Ursin, 2015, p. 187)

So, with the gradual lifting of the 'postmodern fog' (Scott, 2009, p. 69) that shrouded turn-of-the-millennium academic life, what seems to have emerged is diffusion of focus and of perceived purpose – and hence of enacted professionalism – within and across what were once identified (most notably through Becher's (1989) seminal study) as 'tribes' that each followed familiar, well-trodden paths across their distinct epistemic 'territories'; indeed, Rosemary Deem's (1996) autobiographical account of her early career highlights the parochialism that impeded her border-crossing even between three related social science fields.

Disciplinary tribal territories certainly remain intact and very much in evidence – and, as Blackmore's (2016) research reveals, are widely recognised by heads of UK universities – but there is a sense that they are now rather less discernible than they once were against the landscape of performativity that is encompassing, and, arguably, over-running, them: a landscape that has been redeveloped in the Neoliberal architectural style.[1] The edges that demarcate disciplinary norms, cultures and foci seem to have had something of their sharpness blunted by the commonality imposed by indiscriminately applied pressure on academics across the HE sector to perform in more or less the same ways, in pursuit of more or less the same goals. This is, of course, an over-simplistic picture of the twenty-first-century academy, for it is clear that, as I argue in Chapter 1, the UK higher education sector remains marked by heterogeneity and variability, and as Blackmore (2016) notes, different institutions have different priorities and pursue (sometimes subtly) different goals. It is (subtle) distinctions such as these that add complexity to what, at first glance, may appear a simple case of sectoral melting pot-type assimilation. Closer scrutiny reveals layers of distinction that cannot easily be stripped away – some of them disciplinary, some institutional, some personal. But, above all, reminiscent of a Bruegel masterpiece, the image is one of a cornucopia of busyness – a landscape of field and track, covered with exertion and activity of all kinds: people on the move, frenetically coming and going, leaping through hoops, twisting and curling past obstacles, and many, sharp-elbowed, hurdling ahead of everyone else, while others reserve their stamina and persistence for the marathon. And there are the skaters, too, whom Barnett (2011) depicts speeding deftly across the ice breaking behind them. Very few single-track specialists appear in this detail; most have become reluctant triathletes, heptathletes or decathletes, their skills spread more thinly, their foci diffused. And the most prominent figures in this landscape – those who have either snatched some measure of success from it, or, shadows of their former celebrated selves, sit watching it from the sidelines – are professors.

From diffusion to confusion

Chapter 1 outlines the dual bases of the heterogeneity that defines the UK's professoriate: first, the country's higher education sector is itself differentiated and heterogeneous, and, second, this sectoral heterogeneity both reflects and supports differentiated institutional missions, which often make for differentiated institutional goals, agendas and priorities. And since universities in the UK are at liberty to style professorship as they choose, there is no guaranteed inter-institutional uniformity or consensus regarding professorial standards, performance and purpose – though, as I observe in Chapter 1, the threads of sameness and similarity that have long been woven into the fabric of professorship in the UK often facilitate broad consensus both across and within institutional mission groups about what professorship is all about, and what it should look like.

Despite the odd dissenting voice, there is evidently consensus, too – again, across, as well as within, the UK's institutional mission groups – that professors have a distinct purpose, and therefore an identifiable role. This consensual recognition is tied up both with justification of the professorial title and with professors' *raison d'être*, for if professorship cannot be associated with a purpose and a role its risks redundancy. Role and purpose imply functionality and usefulness, providing leverage for universities to devise ways of getting their money's-worth out of their professors. The finer detail of such professorial purpose is examined below and revisited in Chapter 12, but, broadly, consensus has it that professors' overarching purpose is academic leadership.

Academic leadership: An overarching professorial purpose

For the most part, 'rank and file' academics accept academic leadership as a key professorial purpose; not only does it satisfy their sense of fairness – that those enjoying, as they see it, high status, high salaries and privilege, should work for these benefits – but also, in the notion of leadership, they, as 'the led', see something that may work to their advantage. And for the most part professors themselves accept it because, conscious of perceptions (however erroneous) that they enjoy the enviable trappings of academic life that others have not (yet) secured, they feel a responsibility to offer something in return.

But general agreement that professors should be academic leaders gives way to uncertainty, confusion, and even disagreement, when it comes to considering what academic leadership *looks like*, and – and more importantly in the context of this book's focus – what *effective professorial* academic leadership looks like, for perspectives vary between and even within different constituencies.

Inference and conjecture feature heavily in the process of working out what effective professorial academic leadership looks like to those who call the shots in universities: senior leaders and managers and other influential policy-makers and administrators who constitute universities' centres of administrative power (and who, for simplicity and brevity, I refer to collectively as 'universities'). Asked whether he knew exactly what his university wants of its professors, a *Professorial academic leadership in turbulent times* interviewee responded immediately, 'I don't think the *university* knows!' – a sentiment echoed by other professorial research participants. He continued, 'I think the university only cares about the professors that're doing the managerial jobs ... I don't think they look to us for any sort of leadership outside the managerial.' For my part, I have suggested (Evans, 2015a) that universities' promotion of academic leadership as a key professorial activity represents an attempt to label and 'legitimise' the kind of distributed leadership that they hope to promote amongst their senior staff:

> The proliferation of the use of the term *academic leadership* in the academy may be interpreted as a means of articulating an anticipated or hoped-for distributed leadership dimension into higher education leadership and management, and, by extension, as a change initiative mechanism on the part of universities' senior management. (Evans, 2015a, p. 669)

Within a 'cultural ideology of leaderism [that] suggests that certain subjectivities, values, behaviours, dispositions and characteristics can strategically overcome institutional inertia, outflank resistance and recalcitrance and provide direction for new university futures' (Morley, 2013, p. 117), with a cadre of professors-as-academic-leaders ready and willing to 'distribute' approval for whatever changes and shifts would support their marketisation, globalisation, and expansion or modernisation strategies, universities may well have envisaged neoliberal ideologies cascading down through the academic hierarchies – all the better to be assimilated. Youngs (2017) makes a similar point:

Leadership has grown in popularisation and conceptual development, while higher education has undergone transformation through policies and managerial expectations brought on by NPM.[2] Adding to the growth of the leadership industry as an international phenomenon ... leadership can also be positioned as a political project that incorporates managerialist ideology *through positioning institutional leaders as agents of reform.* (p. 141, emphasis added)

Of course, in their efforts to recruit them for such message-cascading purposes, universities would have anticipated much more scepticism, cynicism and downright opposition than readiness and willingness from professors. But, in the decades fringing the turn of the millennium, the term 'distributed leadership' was fast securing a prominent place for itself in the educational leadership research discourse (albeit much more so in the context of the compulsory than in the university sector, into which it has been much slower to edge its way), and the notion of professorial academic leadership may have struck a chord because it seemed to exemplify distributed leadership.

But, digging down to explore what substance lies below a neat label, we might ask what form of 'distributed' professorial academic leadership universities hope for. Certainly, they want to see professors as designated middle and senior managers, holding strategic-focused roles, such as graduate school director, head of department, faculty dean, and pro-vice-chancellor. But, even if there were an appetite for them – which, as recent research (Blackmore, 2016; Floyd, 2012; Sutherland, 2017) suggests, is not the case – there would be too few such roles to go round most universities' professoriates (certainly, in the pre-1992 sector), so something denoting their distinct purpose needs to be found for professors without portfolios.

But what? What else, other than keeping going the cogs of institutional management by holding designated leadership and management roles, do universities want from their professors? The answer, it seems, is: much.

Dissecting academic leadership: Professorial purpose under the microscope

As I discuss elsewhere (Evans, 2016), we may identify at least four broad, overlapping, professorial purposes that reflect what universities, for the most part, expect or hope their professors will serve: *institutional status-enhancement*; *income-generation*; *developing future generations of academics*; and *public engagement*. A closer look at each reveals some of the – often contentious – issues that stem from different constituencies' perspectives on them.

Professorship for institutional status-enhancement

The University of California, Berkeley famously has free parking spaces for the exclusive use of its Nobel laureates (Farivar, 2009). It may certainly be the case that this facility serves to reward those who have achieved academia's most glittering prize, yet the prominent signage on its campus car park also benefits the university by conveying a subliminal message of institutional world class excellence and distinction. In considering what, other than designated leadership role incumbency, universities want of their professors, institutional reputation- and prestige-enhancement must surely appear high on the list.

Indeed, Blackmore (2016) argues that their prestige – which he defines as: 'widespread respect and admiration felt for someone or something on the basis of a perception of their achievements or quality' (p. 10) – is a central concern for universities. Consistent with Winter's (2017, p. 44) observation that, within managerialist cultures, 'academics capable of attracting external funding are "prized"', Blackmore's research revealed professors – more precisely, research stars (who, by implication, if not yet professors, are certainly professors-in-waiting) – to be acknowledged as important players in the prestige-enhancement game:

> Research prestige came from appointing highly able researchers and nurturing them, being sympathetic to them as individuals, and making them feel that they would not want to leave. Several interviewees[3] noted the difficulty in attracting top-flight academic talent, both in terms of the cost of employing them and equipping them and in convincing them that the institution was sufficiently prestigious to be a base from which to develop one's own prestige. (Blackmore, 2016, p. 29)

In the wake of several of them having phased out readerships, can we envisage universities ever dispensing with the professorial title, perhaps using instead numerical academic grades to denote seniority? It would be a brave institution that unilaterally takes this more extreme step because, by and large, through association, its professors indicate and delineate a university's 'worth' and so define its status. 'Professor' is a title that, in connoting erudition and intellectual distinction, commands respect amongst much of the wider public – even where, as I observe in the Introduction, it is not fully understood. Replacing their status-indicative title with a cardinal number, such as 'grade 10', would be unlikely to endear universities to their most senior academics, and whilst many of my research participants complained of feeling undervalued and unappreciated by their institutions, there are certain categories of professors, as Blackmore (2016) notes, that universities are very keen to keep sweet:

Several interviewees in research-intensive universities spoke of having to deal carefully with academic 'stars', who believed that they had a particularly privileged place in the institution and a right to be influential in all matters. One interviewee reported a concern never to be in a position where there would be significant opposition from such colleagues. (p. 29)

In the right hands, professorship adds class and cachet to a university's image. In a few cases – those of 'star' professors (many of who may be what, cited in Chapter 1, Laurie Taylor calls 'buy-in professors') – reputation- and prestige-enhancement may be achieved passively: simply by professors being who they are and associating or affiliating themselves with an institution; otherwise it may require ambassadorial responsibilities: 'acting as an ambassador on behalf of the university, representing its interests on the national and international stage … [b]eing visible or "out and about"' (Macfarlane, 2012a, p. 98). For their universities, this professorial purpose is one of ornamentation, but it is a form of ornamentation that is expected to be generative, and hence it serves a utilitarian purpose – the proud parading of one's valuables in order to attract admirers and investors: embellishment for further enrichment.

Entrepreneurial professorship for income-generation

Income-generation – particularly research funding capture – has become an increasingly prominent representation of the neoliberal ideologies that, since the 1990s, have pervaded and shaped academic culture through the accountability and performativity policies they have spawned. As Enders et al. (2009) note, bringing in money has shifted from being an optional to an expected core academic activity:

In research, the most dramatic change probably concerns the rise of expectations as regards academics' capacities in fundraising and research management. … Certainly, these activities have been carried out by academics for ages, but they were optional, though instrumental, means to another end, which was academic output and reputation. Today, the means have become the ends. (p. 47)

And, of course, as promotions criteria make clear, universities expect their most senior academics to be at the front of the queues to off-load hard-won funds into the institutional coffers – not only in quantitative terms, through bringing in mega-bucks, but also in qualitative terms, through grants from the most prestigious funders.

Yet academics themselves seem, at best, ambivalent about income-generation. On the one hand they recognise it as, in most disciplines, an indicator of individual success *as interpreted by universities*, and therefore as a promotion prospects-enhancer and an activity that, if they are ambitious or wish to show that they are 'on-message', they must embrace. On the other hand, there is much cynical disdain for the prominence that universities afford research income capture, and, as comments offered by anonymous, non-professorial, questionnaire respondents in the *Leading professors* study suggest, it tends not to be seen as an academic esteem-indicator:

> Whilst success in winning research funds is likely to be a major component of their [professors'] experience, [it] should not be regarded as more important than research expertise/excellence and international reputation. Far too much time in academic life already is occupied with research grant applications.

> Professorships should not be available depending only on how much money they have brought into the department.

> Professors should not be appointed solely on the basis of having been successful in getting grant awards but on the discernible academic record which demonstrates outcomes that contribute to the field.

Similarly, Bruce Macfarlane's (2012a) professorial sample afforded income-generation the lowest place in their ranking of professorial roles that they valued – but second highest in their estimate of universities' lists of role priorities for professors, topped only by 'leadership in research'.

The *Professorial academic leadership in turbulent times* study revealed a rather more nuanced perspective, insofar as, whilst several social sciences and arts and humanities professors implied that grant capture did not feature prominently in their skills' repertoires and that other of their activities and achievements were accepted by their universities as compensating for this CV 'shortfall', it was evident that for some STEMM professors, applying for research funding is not an optional pursuit; it is essential to their survival. Without funding they cannot maintain and manage their laboratories and research teams, and without such facilities they cannot remain research-active, and if they are not research-active they will have no findings to publish, and without publications in high ranking journals they will not win research funding.[4]

Nevertheless, when it comes to income-generation, what universities want and what professors want are often difficult to reconcile. Essentially, professors want to do research that interests them, that they consider valuable, and that they can do well – and for which, in some disciplines, lack of external funding is no real impediment. Such activity reinforces professors' self-images as high-achieving, internationally acclaimed senior academics, and acts as a conduit for job satisfaction and high morale by taking them (professors) nearer to their ideal job situations. Universities, in contrast, seem fixated (certainly in the pre-1992 sector) on accruing as much research funding as possible – preferably from prestigious funders – not only to keep their bank accounts looking healthy, but also, through the high quality research that such funding pays for, to enhance their prestige and raise their status within whatever hierarchies matter most to them. These two perspectives and sets of priorities could – and do, in some cases – find common ground where each party's interests are served, such as when academics, however cynically they regard grant-chasing, nevertheless play the game and win, thus enhancing their sense of achievement not only in having met people's expectations, but also of having excelled in highly competitive environments by pulling off a feat considered well-nigh impossible. Yet more often there remains an uneasy tension between the two perspectives, often provoking dissatisfaction amongst the professoriate, which was articulated by many research participants. The following comments from anonymous questionnaire respondents – all professors employed in pre-1992 universities – are illustrative of such negativity:

> [My] morale is lower than usual at present due to lack of funding, feeling undervalued and an increased perception of not feeling as secure in the academic world.

> Total chasm between level of appreciation/respect/status within international research field, and utterly crass treatment within department, entirely driven by research income 'bean-counting'. No assessment of [my] excellent performance in research outputs (i.e. 4* publications, as externally assessed), teaching (at all levels), pastoral care of students, or mentoring of younger staff.

> There are great pressures on clinical professors – the NHS wants forever more work, whereas the university wants more grants income.

> The lack of research funding opportunities is having an effect on [my] morale.

> It is so hard to get funding and even harder to get funding for anything that is not short-term research that this is an all-absorbing challenge.

The last of these comments in particular highlights what is often perceived by academics as not only the demoralising effect of feeling pressured to undertake an activity that both statistical calculation and their personal experience reveals to be a largely futile pursuit, but also of the ridiculousness of expending disproportionately large fractions of their working lives on such futility (Matthews, 2015, 2016). I revisit this issue in Chapter 12 in evaluating the quality of institutional leadership and management that not only exposes its employees to, but also perpetuates, what, for so many of them (employees), must clearly be 'compromising' work situations, in which their efforts and hard work repeatedly meet with failure. Deferring my own commentary to the final chapter in this book, here I allow another author the last eloquent word on this matter. In *Stress in academic life*, Shirley Fisher (1994, p. 64) calls up the work of distinguished Harvard psychology professor Burrhus Frederic Skinner to make a point about persistence in the face of probable or almost certain failure:

> Skinner once noted that whilst it was easy enough to explain reinforced (or rewarded) behaviour, it was always more difficult to explain unreinforced behaviour. The human propensity to persist with behaviour that has a low chance of reward defies simple analysis, yet is an implicit aspect of academic staff survival.

To appreciate the potency of Fisher's next point, it is important to bear in mind that the corrosiveness of the academic work environment that she highlights is surely considerably more evident today, at the end of the second decade of the twenty-first century, than in the latter decades of the twentieth century, when she felt compelled to denounce it. Referring to low success rates in, and dismissive rejections of, research funding applications, Fisher's remarks are as relevant today as when they were first penned:

> It would seem to be a poor managerial strategy to create such unrewarding work conditions. Work demand is high and control over outcome very low. A crude analogy to what happened to the universities in this period would be that of a group of athletes attempting to win a race over an obstacle course while wearing leg fetters. (Fisher, 1994, p. 64)

Developmental-focused professorship

Ever with an eye to the future, universities need to be confident not merely of *maintaining* their positions in the institutional pecking order, but of progressing up the hierarchy by *augmenting* their prestige and enhancing their reputations – ideally, for enrichment. Even in universities whose prestige and reputations are relatively low there is a need to ensure sustainability, through a continuing supply of appropriately skilled and 'trained' workforce. And who better than the professoriate to 'train' and prepare the next generation of academics – to acculturate them into the ways of achieving academic success that benefit the university?

To universities, then, developing the next generation of academics by passing on their (professors') extensive knowledge is a key professorial purpose: one of knowledge repository-cum-capacity-builder. And as the research findings presented in preceding chapters show, such developmental-focused collegiality

– most often manifesting itself as *ad hoc* advice and guidance that are labelled unofficial mentoring – tends to be perceived by professors and non-professorial academics too as a key professorial purpose: one that, for most of them, counts as academic leadership.

It is impossible to gauge how many of those professors who, either in their questionnaire responses or their interview conversations, represented themselves as willing mentors and colleague-developers would in fact shirk such developmental-focused responsibilities if they felt they could get away with doing so. Is developing others a professorial purpose and legitimate role that universities began in relatively recent years to promote, explicitly and implicitly, as part of their overarching distributed professorial academic leadership 'plan' or 'drive', and that professors have, for the most part, and with varied willingness, gone along with in order to justify their salaries and status – not least because, unlike research funding capture, most of them consider it an activity that they may undertake with at least a degree of success? Or – as many of them implied – are these *apparently* willing mentors and developers *genuinely* willing? Their skewed, predominantly pro-professorial academic leadership, samples (referred to in Chapter 4) undermine the capacity of the *Professorial academic leadership in turbulent times* and the *Professorial leadership preparation and development* data to address this question, but in the form of a throwaway remark or an odd shoulder-shrug picked up in a research interview, these data nonetheless uncover a grain of possibility that, *in some cases*, developmental-focused collegiality has been thrust upon professors rather against their will, but that, ever keen to meet expectations of them – not least from their 'junior' colleagues – they have rolled up their sleeves and begun to incorporate it into their enacted professionalism. Such, as I observe in Chapter 9, is how roles evolve and professionalisms reshape themselves.

Professorship for public engagement

Fuelled by the impact agenda that most UK universities have had to incorporate into their strategies in recent years, to maximise overall REF success,[5] professorial purpose has expanded to include public engagement that indicates the relevance and usefulness of their research and their knowledge. Macfarlane's (2012a, p. 80) comment that '[f]ew modern professors see their role as … extending beyond [their] immediate specialism into areas of public policy and debate' as 'public intellectual[s]' is undermined somewhat by the increasing focus on public engagement that, as I observe in Chapter 8, universities have had to start taking seriously. It is certainly quite feasible that the focus of professors' impactful dissemination-oriented engagement with user communities may remain narrowly focused on their research specialisms, so that, as Macfarlane argues, they avoid overstepping their specialist mark – indeed, Finkenstaedt (2011) argues that specialisation emerged as an inevitable consequence of the exponential growth in knowledge and the internationalisation of science: 'Specialization has thus become a "must", at least in the natural sciences' (p. 167). But REF2014 opened the impact floodgates, and so we are also seeing, increasingly, expectations that, as the informed, analytical 'voice' of expertise that resounds beyond the parameters of academe and into the wider public domain, professors will venture beyond their cloisters and campuses. Of course, this in itself is not new; as a remark made by a *Leading professors* interviewee implies, knowledgeable academics – particularly professors – have always been in demand as experts:

> I do think the most important thing about being a professor is that you know your stuff. You look at what goes on in the media – you know, the professors that are wheeled out on *Newsnight*, they're not there because they're a nice guy and can help people, are they? They're there 'cos they can give you an expert point of view on something.

But what is discernible is a subtle shift from perceptions within the academy that such public engagement, first, is directed predominantly at the educated middle class, and, second, is an extra-curricular academic activity, to perceptions that public engagement should be more inclusive than exclusive and niche, and should be part and parcel of the job of being a 'leading' professor: an academic leader.

This consultative or advisory professorial purpose meets (as it always has done) with universities' approval, for, in combining with the role of institutional ambassador, it allows each university to bask in the reflected glory purchased by the range and uniqueness of its professorial expertise, and the frequency with which it is called upon. As such, it is an extension or variation of professors' institutional status-enhancement purpose. It is the role of public informant: taking gown to town by informing – and, in some cases, initiating – debate and discourse; making research-informed or reasoned analytical input in order to influence or to educate.

Amongst the professoriate there seems to be an ambivalence, that may be gradually giving way to acceptance, towards their public engagement role – which is inevitably linked to the UK government's impact agenda. When first aired, as Chubb (2017) observes, the impact agenda prompted sighs and groans – mainly, it seems, from the ivory tower-closeted 'Professor[s]-of-Clever-Things, locked in a study or laboratory' identified, with levity, by Durham professor Harriet Bulkeley (quoted in Chapter 1). Whilst these professors were likely daunted at the prospect of having to cast their esoteric pearls before the public 'swines' who might respond with biblical predictability, it is evident (Chubb, 2017) that where there is no danger of underfoot trampling into mud, or of being torn to pieces,[6] disseminating their work to appreciative audiences of any constituency is a source of satisfaction for many professors – including, most notably amongst my research interviewees, arts and humanities professor Fergal (whose comments on impact are presented in Chapter 9). For the most part professors appreciate the self-affirming, self-esteem-raising potential of this role, for with many of them seeing 'professing' as their key purpose, the acclaim and recognition that public engagement can bring is likely to take them closer to their ideal selves-at-work, within their ideal work situations.[7]

The source of confusion: The academic leadership 'box'

How many, and what aspects, of these four broad professorial roles sit under the umbrella purpose, with its catch-all label, *academic leadership*, that represents universities' default perspective on professors and why they should be employed? There seems little doubt that, as it is interpreted in the UK, academic leadership, as Bolden et al. (2012a, 2012b) found, is generally considered to include developmental-focused collegiality, such as mentoring. But, as we see in some of my research findings, not everyone counts mentoring as academic leadership; social sciences professor Clive (featured in Chapter 9) was a vociferous gainsayer, and other, smaller, voices questioned the mentoring-academic leadership association.

There will inevitably be disagreement over what we might call, with a little authorial licence, the 'terms of reference' of an idea or notion that is not well defined, and which, as a concept, is unclear – as is academic leadership. But when it is associated with professorial purpose and function, academic leadership's lack of conceptual clarity underpins confusion about where its parameters lie: what counts as it, and what doesn't. For all that universities in the UK seem to have appropriated the term to denote the overarching purpose of the professoriate, they have provided little elucidation on precisely what such leadership entails, and what it might look like; conveyed through vaguely expressed ideas and general hints, these are implicit, rather than explicit. Working out what – and, most importantly, *how much* – universities want from professors as academic leaders involves interpretive imagination and guesswork. Although it is explicitly directed at early career academics' situations, Sutherland's (2017) observation below is in many respects transferable to being applicable to professors, from whom are obscured the calibrations on the yardstick of acceptability against which their enactment of academic leadership is likely to be measured:

> Expectations … are laid out in promotions documents and handbooks, but, as my findings show, are *lacking in specificity, and open to broad and differentiated interpretation* depending on, for example, one's discipline, department, colleagues, and years of experience. Promotions documents and handbooks … are clear on the areas required to do well, *but not clear about how much, how often, for whom, and when.* (Sutherland, 2017, p. 756, emphases added)

It may be that, lacking the imagination to think outside the managerialist-shaped box that gives every formal leadership role a designation and accompanying job or role description, universities simply cannot cope with the vagaries and imprecision that reflect *ad hoc*, opportunistic, and often boundary-less support and guidance that one person may offer another – which is what research reveals to be generally considered, in UK academic contexts, the essence of academic leadership (Bolden et al., 2012a, 2012b) – or, even more obscure, the myriad ways in which one person, often imperceptibly, may influence another's academic activity (which is how I define academic leadership in Chapter 3).

The highly visible and easily identifiable – and quantifiable – elements of professors' performance, such as research income capture and publications, are easy to list as institutional expectations or requirements; the more nebulous output that represents what I call professors' relationality, along with their direct or indirect influence on others, is much more susceptible to lurking under the radar of accountability, and so – unsure how best to deal with it, while yet recognising it as something to be valued and encouraged – universities seem to have thrown it all carelessly into a box, fastened down the lid tightly, and stuck a label on it that reads 'academic leadership'. But because this box remains, for the most part, out of sight, undisturbed and unopened, few are willing or able to have a go at listing – much less describing – its contents. And for their part, professors – as much in the dark as anyone about the box – overestimate its capacity and imagine it filled to the brim with an incalculable miscellany of every conceivable academic activity.

The result of this confusion and uncertainty is that performance angst is rife amongst the professoriate. Rather than risk tarnishing their reputations and denting their self-esteem, professors – a constituency that, representing academia's highest achievers, prides itself on its performance and, as we see in Chapter 9, is keen to meet people's expectations – often take on ever more demanding workloads and expansive arrays of tasks, evidently hoping that this constitutes satisfactory discharging of their academic leadership duties.

Herein lies another key source of the heterogeneity that defines UK-based professorship: the diffuseness of the activities that many of them are finding themselves taking on – the expansion of their repertoires – as they try to prove themselves, to all interested constituencies, effective academic leaders. Unsure about what they may legitimately say 'no' to, and what they ought to agree to, and finding themselves chasing unachievable targets and struggling to cope with a job whose boundaries are no longer clearly delineated, many professors seem to be trying to be all things to all people – or, as some of the comments and narratives presented in Chapter 10 show, collapsing under the pressure to do so. 'Profs have to be all-singing, all-dancing' wrote a questionnaire respondent. Another complained, 'I am less and less involved in doing things I'm good at and more and more tied up in admin work/bureaucracy, petty politics and HR activity', and another wrote 'the job demands a level of multitasking that I can't do any more. I have no intention of being a passenger, and so I've applied for the soonest possible retirement.'

And, of course, the greater the number and the wider the array of activities and tasks that are perceived to lie within their remits, the more varied will be professors' enactment of them. Whilst neither varied approaches to doing professorship nor a heterogeneous professionalism are undesirable or problematic per se – indeed, I argue in Chapter 12 for redesigning professorship along lines that celebrate and capitalise on such variation and diversity – they *become* both undesirable and problematic if they are allowed to impoverish the quality of working lives by undermining workers' well-being.

'All-singing, all-dancing' professors: A continuous variety performance takes its toll

The effects on the professoriate of what a great many – if not most – of them see as the increasing demands that they feel obliged to meet is important to consider, for it underpins the discussion in Chapter 12 about how the professorial role might be redesigned. Chapter 10 touches upon the issue of work overload and highlights an interesting aspect of professorial professionalism: for the most part, irrespective of morale and satisfaction levels, professorship is pressured because professors accept – and, in some cases, take on of their own volition – pressure.

Pressure does not necessarily indicate or create the kind of negativity that prompts people to throw in the towel; it was a minority of interviewees who were so-affected, reporting rock-bottom morale. Nevertheless, a recurring complaint from the professorial research participants became something of a refrain in the research data: the job of being a professor is evidently considered extremely demanding, and in many respects unmanageable. A questionnaire respondent wrote: 'It is an all-encompassing fluid role that has to be flexible. The problem is that it's just too big, and doing any of it requires compromises elsewhere'; another commented: 'I have felt well supported and well prepared, but expectations have grown and I am expected to take on more and more'; and another complained: 'the competing demands across the board create a feeling of inability to cope most of the time'.

There was an overwhelmingly prominent perception amongst professorial interviewees and questionnaire respondents alike – as well as among many non-professorial *Leading professors* research participants – that unclearly defined parameters were diffusing the professorial role, pressurising many professors to spread themselves too thinly, across too many disparate activities, and, as a result, doing none of them as well as they would have liked; a comment from STEMM professor Harry, presented in Chapter 10, sums up the essential problem: 'We can only really deliver *mediocre* stuff because we simply don't have the capacity to deliver at the levels expected.'

If such mediocrity is the product of a model of distributed leadership that labels university professors 'academic leaders' in order to increase universities' effectiveness, measured against the kinds of neoliberal-inspired performativity criteria that inform institutional league tables and rankings, then the model seems seriously flawed. It is surely time for a rethink, for in many respects universities in the UK do not seem to be deploying their professors as effectively as they might – for the good of all parties. Addressing some of the problematic issues raised in this and preceding chapters, the book's final chapter focuses on rethinking professorial academic leadership.

Notes

1   That disciplinary tribes and territories seem less visible than they were once thought to be may, however, have less to do with any policy contextual backdrop that frames them than to initial exaggeration of their differentiality. In fact, Trowler (1998) questions – and presents his own compelling research data that undermine –

epistemological essentialist-informed conclusions about academic professionalism and culture. In his later collaboration with Tony Becher the two authors (Becher & Trowler, 2001) revisit and modify the epistemological essentialist paradigmatic basis of Becher's single-authored analysis (Becher, 1989) on the grounds that it privileged an elitist interpretation of power and influence within disciplinary culture(s) that was not borne out by empirical evidence.

2   New public management.

3   Blackmore's interview sample comprised twenty heads of UK HEIs.

4   The importance of this feature of academic life in some STEMM subjects is discussed in Evans and Homer (2014).

5   REF2014 introduced a significant impact dimension into its assessment mechanisms, principally involving impact case studies, which allow universities to present evidence of the impact of its research on relevant non-academic users.

6   A reference to a biblical quote in Matthew's Gospel, Chapter 7, verse 6, in which Jesus is recorded as having preached, 'Do not give what is holy to the dogs; nor cast your pearls before swine, lest they trample them under their feet, and turn and tear you in pieces.'

7   Yet the impact agenda is perceived as presenting barriers as well as benefits to academics; Chubb's (2017) research, for example, effectively revealed it to be perceived by academics as something of a double-edged sword, and, more specifically, Durand and Stewart (2014) identify it as constraining for some critical researchers – particularly those whose work embraces an anti-capitalist dimension – since it encourages the subordination of 'critical engagement to the needs of a marketized, business facing academia' (p. 1013).

12

From Academic Leaders to Leading Academics: Redesigning Twenty-First-Century Professorship

Professorship was never *designed*. There was no sitting around a table somewhere in medieval Europe devising a new role that would be called professorship; no thrashing out a job description for the men who would be known as professors. Professorship, as we see in Chapter 1, came about gradually, through evolution.

And, of course, it has continued to evolve. For most of its evolution, professors' purpose was teaching. Then there have been periods when, as we see in Chapter 6, judged by their output, professors effectively had *no* purpose; their salaries were often sinecures. Only relatively recently on the evolutionary timescale did research begin to be tagged onto the teaching duties, before emerging as the predominant professorial activity. Whilst it has never, since then, lost its dominance as a feature of professors' work, at least two recent phases in the evolution of professorship in the UK have not so much undermined or lowered, as *qualified*, research's status; it retains its dominance, but no longer in splendid isolation. The first of these phases is the teaching-matters,-so-professors-should-teach-as-well-as-research phase, which raised the status of teaching as a core activity for research-intensive universities – and, by extension, for research-focused professors. This phase then evolved into the second one: the *everything-matters,-so-professors-should-do-everything* phase – otherwise known as the current professors-as-academic-leaders phase. As we see in preceding chapters, to those who have seen its evolution and are living through it, this phase of professorial omnifariousness is not without its problems.

This final chapter considers what may be done to address these problems through redesigning twenty-first-century professorship in ways that work for all parties. And since its redesign must be an amelioration project, it is important first to establish what features of professorship should be retained and what should be modified.

Taking stock: The good, the bad, and the ugly

Professorial proliferation has been a feature of the UK academic workforce since the 1990s, reflecting increased democratisation that has manifested itself through a widening of the pathways to professorial promotion that, a few decades ago, were barred to all but a privileged elite. But, because it meets universities' current needs, this is a skills-based, rather than a social-based, democratisation. Whilst Halsey's (1992) study, as discussed in Chapter 8, identified published research output as the key indicator of an academic's promotion prospects in the latter half of the twentieth century, by the end of the twentieth century academics were being promoted on the basis of alternative or compensatory skills that universities currently value – such as capacity to attract research income, or to think strategically, or to present themselves well and their sound ideas articulately and compellingly, or to inspire and motivate others. Consistent with Finkenstaedt's (2011, p. 194) comment that 'the growth of R & D co-sponsored with industrial partners has already transformed the place and role of professors with the entrepreneurial talents to promote their field of study', discernible in my research data was a sense that the expansiveness expected of professors has diluted the strength of professorial intellectuality and scholarship. This dilution is associated with what are perceived as the erosion of standards within an institutionally-led performativity culture that places cash above cleverness by allowing research funding success to trump intellectual distinction and the pursuit of scholarly excellence; a female professor, for example, argued: 'The currency has been debased over the last twenty years … there are many more professors than there used to be, and what you have to have done in order to get there is manifestly much less than it was.'

Democratisation opens doors that were previously closed, widening access. By and large, the wider the access, the greater number of participants; and the greater number of participants, the more diversity. So far, so good. But diversity is most – and perhaps only – effective if it injects different and more varied perspectives and ways of doing things into an endeavour, by allowing participants to play to their appropriate strengths. Yet, as is particularly evident in Chapters 10 and 11, rather than play to their strengths, in their efforts to be all things to all people – which is how many of them interpret their academic leadership roles – most professors feel pressured to widen their activity repertoires, diffusing the fine focus that they would ideally like to define how they do professorship. Not only does this diffusion seem to be stifling creativity, leaving many feeling stretched beyond their capacity, and, as a consequence, that they are falling short of the standards of intellectual excellence they set for themselves, but the mediocrity that often represents the best that they are able to achieve, also, ironically, undermines their institutions' efforts to excel. The expansiveness and diffusion that define twenty-first-century professorship in the UK therefore seems to undermine everyone's interests.

Yet universities are probably unaware that their own interests are not best served by diffuse professorial activity, for on the surface all may look well to them. Unable to detect the subjective feelings of perpetual under-achievement (in qualitative rather than quantitative terms) to which many professors are resigned – but which they are reluctant to divulge, lest they be thought deviant or incompetent – universities may well be labouring under the misapprehension that, apart from the inevitable odd loose stitch and broken thread, they have got performativity and professorship all sewn up. Satisfied with professoriates that, for the most part, seem to be busting their guts to show that they are going along with institutional game plans, universities may be blissfully unaware that they could potentially do so much better.

There are two significant ironies with the parts played by many academics – but by professors in particular – in perpetuating the performativity and accountability regimes that exemplify universities' buy-in to the marketisation of higher education. The first is that, whilst UK universities invariably embrace the well-being at work agenda and are fully tuned into its discourse, they promote academic performance cultures that, in privileging as a predominant performance indicator the capture of research income whose scarcity reduces its pursuit to what is widely considered (Matthews, 2015, 2016) a lottery or game of chance,[1] they are knowingly and carelessly sanctioning, and even encouraging, their academics' repeated failure. The second irony is that, despite signing up to the impact agenda that highlights the need for research to make a difference in the real world, universities are themselves evidently impervious to the messages emanating from the plethora of studies that could – if they would take note of them – impact upon their own organisation and policies: studies to have been published on, *inter alia*, academic working life, effective educational leadership, and work psychology, many of which reveal neoliberal-inspired managerialist cultures to have deleterious effects on those exposed to them.

Whilst the second of these ironies uncovers their irrationality and hypocrisy, the first casts universities in the mould of what have come to be labelled 'greedy institutions' (Coser, 1974; Sullivan, 2014) – a label that Teresa Sullivan, president of the University of Virginia, believes is warranted:

Academic workers at colleges or universities have a vested interest in asking the question, 'Are universities greedy institutions?' I believe they are, and the trajectories for universities as workplaces are not encouraging. Academe was once considered a haven from the corporate rat race, a refuge for serious scholars and teachers, a place for measured thought and unhurried instruction – the 'life of the mind' concept. Mention of the Ivory Tower conjured up images of devoted scholars bent over their dusty books, scientists experimenting in their laboratories, or professors engaged in Socratic discourse with attentive students. ... But how many professors have time now to sit down ... for a sustained, one-on-one dialogue with a student? They have too many competing demands. Conducting research, advising students, serving on various committees, and staying abreast of the latest research in our fields – these demands can eat up their entire lives, and this means that universities fit the profile of 'greedy institutions'. (Sullivan, 2014, pp. 10–11)

Sullivan's argument reflects her concern that academics' work-life balance is compromised by the pressures imposed by competitive academic cultures and precarity-inducing employment practices in the American academy. This is a fair assessment, and one that resonates across the Atlantic – for as we see in Chapters 9 and 10, a long-hours culture defines professorship in the UK, and is perpetuated by professors who are driven by competitiveness and/or by their concern to meet expectations of them. But the most distasteful dimension of UK universities' 'greed' in pursuing prestige and status through research income capture that, in many disciplines, is about as accessible as the pot of gold at the end of the rainbow, is surely evident in their disregard for the demoralising effects on their employees of the repeated failure to which such futility exposes them. This is a depiction not only of a *greedy*, but also of a *callous, uncaring* institution.

President of Cardiff University, Colin Riordan, articulates the tension between leading a university effectively and efficiently and enacting authentic leadership that engages people:

You're often under a set of pressures that's quite difficult to convey and you can't ignore and sometimes you get driven down a line where people think you're only interested in getting students in because you need to balance the books or we're dropping standards, or whatever else it might be. I think that's the real challenge – how we can live up to the real ideal of a university, which I think people out there absolutely want, and we see that all the time. (Riordan, in Lydon, 2016)

The challenge he refers to is evidently one that many UK universities have been unable to meet. My research revealed varying degrees of dissatisfaction with and implicit contempt for neoliberal-inspired institutional policy and practice that reflects subtle disregard for staff welfare and morale. One of the most vociferous critics was *Professorial academic leadership in turbulent times* interviewee, Fergal, who expressed himself as a discarded partner in a once happy and satisfying long-term relationship with his university that had soured when one party – the institution – began, as he saw it, to change. In speaking of his 'fantasies' of ringing up a rival university to negotiate a job, he used the metaphor of romantic infidelity: 'it's ... an infidelity fantasy: You've actually hurt me so much that I am considering being unfaithful to you!' The basis of his 'injury' and disappointment is explained at length in his own words:

> I don't *care* about the institution. I don't love it with the same love and reverence that I once had for it ... . It's been hijacked by something which I think is a problem in our institutions nationally, generally ... and I don't think it should have happened in universities. But it has, and I think that's a major sense of dissatisfaction in my life ... . So, I suppose my deep-rooted sense of dissatisfaction is that universities are changing around us. And I think we now, as institutions, are not concerned with truths any more ... it's the sense that universities are no longer honest, open places – we have commercialisation strategies now, rather than really caring about our students – and I'm lucky enough to be a dinosaur, and still able to enjoy those workings of the university. But I see other of my colleagues who've become very anxious, and ... they really do have to mould themselves to an expectation that the university has of them ... er ... to bring in all the grants, to bring out two or three articles a year, to meet the demands of the REF or RAE cycle ... to teach lots of classes and stuff. And our university really *does* make demands now, and I am sufficiently long in the tooth, and sufficiently senior, to say, 'You know, I don't think you can touch me!' ... So I'm disengaged ... for better and for worse. ... I don't *care* how we do in the REF! But I care about my *work*. ... I don't *like* that sense of dissociation from my institution; it's something that gives me no pleasure. ... Institutions are changing around us, radically. ... So much of my life has taken place in and around [this university]; [it] has given me so much *corporate* pleasure, that to have lost that now is very significant for me. And I've no doubt other universities are as bad. (*Fergal, arts and humanities professor, pre-1992 university*)

So-perceived – as 'greedy', callous and uncaring – universities undoubtedly represent a disfiguringly ugly blemish on the face of a twenty-first-century academy that might otherwise see much more potential in professors than is implicit in expectations that they will play key roles in perpetuating what an anonymous professorial questionnaire respondent described as 'metrics, the "tick box" culture, and the obsession with grant income [that] have corrupted scholarship'. Other respondents complained that 'senior managers do not seem to understand and care about how their plans for growth (in ... student numbers, research income) affect the quality of everything we do from teaching to research to administration', and that 'there is a split in the Russell Group university between the greed for grant income and the inability to comprehend the demands and hard graft of intellectual work. This schizophrenia is demoralising to someone like me who defines herself as an intellectual.'

Paul Blackmore's research findings suggest that heads of UK HEIs recognise the need to handle staff with care – though the reference to attracting and retaining 'desirable talent' implies that such care may be strategically motivated:

> Interviewees pointed out that careful attention to the 'soft' aspects of people management can make a major difference to recruitment and retention, and can both attract desirable talent to an institution, and ensure that all members of the institution feel they have a share in its achievements. (Blackmore, 2016, p. 7)

Yet, whatever their motivation, such sentiments are likely to be dismissed as hollow rhetoric by those who consider themselves to have witnessed or fallen foul of institutional greed. Middlehurst (1993, p. 196) ends her book, *Leading academics*, with the words: 'Realizing the full potential of our creative institutions requires leadership that is brave enough to stand and be counted, yet wise enough to listen and learn', and interviewee Fergal's eloquent commentary, above, opens a window into a dimension of work psychology that universities would do well to peer into if they genuinely want to understand how to get the best out of their academic staff – particularly those whom they are especially keen to recruit, and upon whom they most depend: professors. But there is a danger that they will not even cast a glance towards that window; that their gaze will remain fixed on the road they have chosen to follow, and disgruntled academics who happen to be trampled underfoot on that institutional journey will be shrugged off as regrettable but inevitable collateral damage. For, however hard it may be for some commentators to swallow, neoliberalism will not be ejected from the academy by railing against it; it will be systemic political or economic shift or evolution, not the whining and whingeing whimpers of its casualties or disgruntled observers, that will eventually send it packing – as Mason (2015, p. xii) notes, 'Over the past two decades, millions of people have resisted neoliberalism but in general the resistance has failed.' It is important to keep this in mind; the marketised university is not about to rebrand itself in a hurry, so in considering professorship redesign there is a need to work around it and with(in) it.

Squeezing into a narrow frame

Any new picture of professorship in the UK must fit into a frame whose dimensions are limited by the pervasive systemic policy context that shapes institutional strategies, goals and priorities. Blackmore's study revealed this context to manifest itself prominently as universities' pursuit of prestige, tempered by concerns to achieve efficiency and effectiveness:

> The views of the leaders interviewed here suggest that institutions may be prestige-seeking or reputation-seeking, and that some institutions may be a mix of the two. ... Prestige-seeking may often sit uncomfortably with conventional endeavours to achieve value for money but it remains a strong explanatory driver in universities, and a significant factor in the actual and likely effects of current and future policies to achieve efficiency savings in the sector. (Blackmore, 2016, pp. 6–7)

In highlighting the neoliberal university's concern for effectiveness and efficiency – what I suggest may serve as its double mantra: be effective, be efficient – Blackmore makes a valid point that is central to this chapter's consideration of how professorship may be redesigned: any revision to the *status quo* must represent effectiveness and efficiency; for, as he notes:

> universities deal in social, cultural and symbolic capital, which have an indirect relationship with economic capital. This points to a need to look again at what motivates groups and individuals in and around universities, so that a financially based drive for greater efficiency and effectiveness can achieve its aims. (Blackmore, 2016, p. 12)

Yet prestige, as Blackmore points out, is pursued not only by institutions, but also by many who work in them – and none more so than professors. There is a recognised theoretical model of academic work attitudes – the *prestige value system* – that 'posits that individuals attempt to maximize their prestige – in part through attachment to distinguished institutions' (Morrison et al., 2011, p. 25), and indeed my own reluctance to relinquish the prestige that comes from affiliation with a Russell Group university is examined elsewhere (Evans, 2015c). So there is a symbiotic dimension to some professors' (those who are preoccupied with their own prestige) affiliation with prestigious universities, as well as an ambivalence in their complaints about the means by which such universities pursue the prestige that they (such professors) appropriate to enhance their own.

Prestige and success go hand-in-hand, and what most professors have in common with their universities is that, *for the most part*, they both seek both, though not necessarily or consistently by the same means, for the neoliberal university defines success differently – more widely – from how most academics define it. Moreover, as Sutherland observes, it is not only within the institution that the criteria for academic success are defined; many academics' reference groups are located in the wider disciplinary community, creating a tension in relation to pursuing success in two (or more) worlds:

> success in academia is constructed by the institutional rules, expectations and policy manuals, and the ability (and willingness) of individual academics to comply with or resist these structures. But success is also constructed outside of and separate from institutional expectations and discourses; individual academics have their own personal goals, ambitions, and focuses, and, for many, success comes from their ability to make these personal goals fit within the institution's expectations, or at least to minimise conflict between the two. (Sutherland, 2017, pp. 745–6)

To have a realistic chance of being taken seriously, any proposal for redesigning professorship in the UK must seek to reconcile the divergent priorities underpinning this tension. One way of doing so may be to modify perspectives on professors' academic leadership role.

From academic leaders to leading academics

Perceiving professors as academic leaders represents what I call the 'personification' of leadership, and which, as discussed in Chapter 3, is identified within critical leadership scholarship as an unfortunate distraction from the focus on the activity of leadership that critical discourse promotes. Ascription of leader status to professors, by referring to them as academic leaders, seems to have predisposed people – including professors themselves – towards such 'personification', and with it have evidently come expectations that those ascribed leader status will or should undertake *all* activities associated with academic leadership. Such expectations, as we see in preceding chapters, have created problems by imposing pressure on professors in the form of expanding task repertoires, role diffusion and work overload. Leader status ascription of this kind, which involves labelling a person or persons as leaders, represents the most simplistic of interpretations of distributed leadership, as *devolved* leadership. In what is perhaps *its* simplest form, this devolved leadership involves a designated, formally recognised leadership hierarchy (where the 'distribution' dimension of it is implicit in the hierarchy's cascading of leadership downwards through different levels, ostensibly from 'singular' to 'plural' leadership), and in a more informal and slightly more subtle form it involves the ascription of leader status to those – such as professorial academic leaders – who, being without portfolios, operate in what I refer to in Chapter 7 as leadership's twilight zone. These forms, *inter alia*, represent what Gronn categorises as 'distributed leadership as numerical action', which he explains:

> If focused leadership means that only one individual is attributed with the status of leader, an additive or numerical view of distributed leadership means the aggregated leadership of an organization is dispersed among some, many, or maybe all of the members. (Gronn, 2002, p. 429)

Whilst this is not the place for an extensive critique of distributed leadership scholarship, it is worth noting that, in promoting professorial academic leadership that is personified in this way, and that represents what Gunter et al. (2013, p. 559) call 'functionalist knowledge production', whose starting point is that 'the job [of leading] is too big for one person', universities seem to be missing the point that distributed leadership may, and often is, interpreted much more broadly than is implied by professors taking on leadership roles and undertaking activities that may be labelled 'leadership'. As a consequence, they seem also to be missing a trick in terms of effectively deploying their professors.

If, instead of implicitly expecting professors to play their part in the cascading of leadership down a pyramidal hierarchy – reflecting what Harris (2013, p. 547) identifies as a prevalent 'misuse of the term [distributed leadership] … as a convenient descriptor for any form of shared, collaborative or extended leadership practice' – universities shifted their focus from 'personified' leadership to leadership-as-practice, there is scope for developing an effective model of professorial academic leadership with the potential to satisfy both universities and the professoriate. Consistent with the thrust of Chapter 3's critical perspectival discussion of leadership, in offering it as 'an alternative ontology that goes beyond some of the limitations inherent in distributed leadership' (p. 146), Youngs (2017) explains leadership-as-practice:

> A central tenet of leadership-as-practice decentralises leadership away from an individual, usually pre-established as the leader, and repositions leadership as an outcome rather than a prerequisite of practice involving more than one person and non-human artefacts. Leadership-as-practice shifts our gaze more to practice as it unfolds, so *the verb leading, rather than the noun leader comes to the forefront of our understanding.* (p. 141, emphasis added)

Adding that 'the leadership construct is not always needed ... or should at least not be positioned as a practice elevated above others' (Youngs, 2017, p. 146), he calls for, *inter alia*, less reliance: 'on the generic term of leader and leadership as pre-existing constructs and use [of] language that more clearly identifies the practices in use' (p. 149).

In the case of professors, what might those 'practices-in-use' comprise? As highlighted in preceding chapters, currently, *as academic leadership*, professorial practices seem to comprise an unwieldy array of diverse activities – herein lies the key problem with the prevalent 'model' of professors as academic leaders that has been socially co-constructed by universities, professors, and non-professorial (academic) staff, and that most professors feel obliged to enact. As *academics* only, however – with their leadership tags removed – professors have to manage a much narrower range of 'practices-in-use', comprising activities that, *for the most part*, reflect their interests, expertise and skills, and that pull them in far fewer disparate directions. But whilst ditching their academic leader tag may meet with some – but not necessarily all, or even most – professors' approval, it would not go down well with the efficiency-conscious neoliberal university that wants to exact their pounds of flesh from its best remunerated academics. Professors-as-academics-only, then, is not an option; to satisfy universities, they (professors) would have to do leadership of some description.

But, revisiting Chapter 3's conceptual analysis, professors' enactment of leadership, as I define it there, identifies their 'practices-in-use' as activity that, in its most singular, basic form: *may reasonably be considered to directly or indirectly prompt or have prompted or facilitate or have facilitated an individual's shift or deviation, without coercion, from one position or direction to what s/he (the individual) perceives as a superior position or direction: a 'better way'.* Switching the focus from professors as academic leaders to professors as academics who lead, through practices that have much scope for influencing others, has the potential to inject quite a different meaning into professorial academic leadership, by identifying professors' day-to-day academic activity, rather than their activity that is tailored specifically for 'leading', as the conduit for influencing. So-interpreted, leadership may be implicit, 'enacted' through a myriad of what may be unconscious, unplanned ways of working that potentially touch and impact upon others – such as exemplification of ways of behaving or going about something, role modelling, advising or acting as consultant, key contributions to shaping a culture, or articulation (orally or on paper) of views and ideas that raise awareness or provoke a reaction, and which may be considered intellectual leadership. Such are academics' – particularly 'successful' senior academics' – practices-in-use. Universities, I argue in Chapter 1, have long called the shots in defining professorial professionalism. Most recently, as I suggest in Chapter 11, they have been instrumental in widening the parameters of what professorship implies, in terms of professorial purpose and roles. With a view to harnessing the skills and talents of their most senior academics – and justifying their salaries and status – they appear to have re-invented professorship to support the fulfilment of their institutional objectives and the enactment of their strategies (as is their prerogative), through branding professors as academic leaders. But in doing so they have not only inevitably defaulted to personifying leadership, but they seem to have also, through widening professorial remits and responsibilities, devalued professors' intellectual distinction.

Moreover, what seems to have been obscured by the prevalent personification of leadership that makes a much bigger deal of leadership than it appears when viewed through a critical, relational-focused, lens, is that, at the micro-level (as I explain it in Chapter 3), leadership is pervasive and reciprocal – meaning that more or less everyone dishes it out and receives it, though not necessarily in even measures – and that, in the context of academe, professors, as the most senior and often most experienced academics, generally have much more experientially based influencing capacity than do junior academics, but predominantly through their simply doing their work as professors: *as leading academics.*

If universities recognised and accepted this – leadership as or through practices-in-use – as a key purpose of professors that is centred upon their (professors) being identified not as *academic leaders*, but as *leading academics*, many of the debilitating side-effects of professors' having swallowed their universities' concoction of the professorial academic leadership pill would be assuaged – particularly if intellectually based specialist knowledge and knowledge generation regained their centrality and their prominence in doing professorship. Liberated from what most of them perceive as the overbearing compulsion to be all things to all people – that requires their being seen to be ladling out their academic leadership liberally, offering different flavours to suit different tastes – professors could be free to supplement their 'natural' implicit leadership as leading academics with whatever 'processed' leadership activities they liked, as often as they liked. Those who have developed a taste for 'explicit', up-front, in-your-face, and clearly signposted leadership *à la personification* could therefore continue to gorge themselves on it, leaving their more abstemious colleagues to enjoy a leaner diet, confident of avoiding complaints that they have trimmed too much fat off their plates.

This practices-in-use approach to imaginative distributed leadership that is centred on recognition of professors as leading academics is likely to be a hit with the professoriate, freeing up professors to focus their efforts – their activities – broadly or narrowly, as and where they see fit. It implicitly identifies the professoriate as a resource that others may access – as indeed it is identified within the current professors-as-academic-leaders model – but the difference is that, whilst *implicitly* transmitted knowledge and guidance would be transmitted unconsciously and without effort, in relation to *explicitly* transmitted knowledge and steers, the onus would shift to being much more on resource-*seekers* to tap into the professorial resource, than it would be on professors to seek out and spoon-feed pearls of wisdom to those who appear to need them. This would represent a shift towards the kinds of perspectives articulated by principal lecturer Ken, in Chapter 5, and social sciences professor Clive, in Chapter 9: that responsibility for learning how to be successful academics lies with junior academics themselves, rather than with the professoriate; being an academic, after all, implies intelligence and capacity to acquire knowledge and to work out what is needed, and these two interviewees evidently felt that those who lacked such capacity were ill-suited to academic life. Moreover, we see in Chapter 5 examples of early and mid-career academics who evidently *have* worked this out, and who, of their own accord, seemed to have recognised 'leading' professorship as exemplifying academic practice worth emulating, and as a yardstick against which to measure their own practice.

So the professors-as-leading-academics approach is analogous to the mobile library's relocating to a central, static site – but one that operates long opening hours and, to quote senior professor Duncan, radiates accessibility; to retain the analogy: through advisors that go the extra mile in answering any query from any intellectually curious reader who crosses its welcoming threshold. With removal of the pressure to ensure that its circuitous vehicular route reaches all those in need of it, the mobile-turned-static library is clearly signposted as a resource that all may easily find and access.

Would the universities accept such a redesign of the professoriate's leadership capacity? The key challenge would be to persuade them to remove their blinkers so that they may then see leadership as influence that may – and does – occur in a myriad of ways, many of which are never identified as leadership agency because they go unnoticed and unrecognised. For universities that like to label everything, so that it may be identified, quantified and costed, and its value to the institution assessed, the flexibility of the leadership as practices-in-use approach may be an intellectual step too far. If they are ever to respond 'why; they are leading academics', rather than, 'they are academic leaders' to the question: 'what purpose do professors serve?', universities need to be convinced that being leading academics is indeed a professorial function worth promoting.

Covering all bases: Utilising the professorial team

The UK professoriate, we have seen, is heterogeneous. This heterogeneity has been amplified by universities' having seen a need or use for a broader skills set amongst the professoriate than was historically prevalent, and having gradually extended the parameters of professors' role(s), refashioning their purpose(s) in line with universities' performativity-focused agendas. So, though it may hazard a good guess, based on knowledge of the employing institution, the academic community in general does not *necessarily* know what someone who enjoys the title 'professor' in the UK should represent, and what scale and nature of performance might be expected of her or him: a successful research grant winner, a lone scholar, a confident and engaging speaker, a research team leader, a knowledgeable specialist of a narrow field, a polymath, a public intellectual, or perhaps a non-researcher who holds an administrative or management role – indeed, expectations that any professor will be most of the above do not seem unwarranted, given the diffusiveness of professors' roles.

The effects of this role expansion and diffusion – the pressures to perform that it imposes on professors – are regretted or resented by many of them. This negativity underpins a significant academic workforce issue that needs addressing: one of professorial well-being and, by extension, effectiveness. Back in 1994 Shirley Fisher warned: 'Academics faced with tasks such as lecturing, research, writing research grant applications and organizing administrative tasks, are potentially in overload situations' (Fisher, 1994, p. 66). In reaching adulthood, the embryonic neoliberal university that she discerned in the early 1990s has exacerbated the effects of such overload – not least in its demands on professors. Moreover, quite apart from the pressure felt by professors to engage in a wide range of activities – for many of which they may consider themselves unqualified or ill-equipped – this width of focus is having the unfortunate effect of diluting professors' intellectual activity, and impoverishing their (and, by extension, their universities') scholarly output. A key issue therefore is whether universities are making the best use of their professors. In the light of Bacon's (2014, p. 23) argument that universities are generally underusing their 'greatest resource': 'their highly educated, intellectually smart, often eloquent staff', it is unsurprising that it seems they are similarly not making best use of their professors. Indicating how they might do so may incline them towards rebranding professors as leading academics, rather than academic leaders.

From mediocrity to magnum opus: Playing to professors' strengths

Two alternative perspectives present two potential ways in which universities might better utilise and deploy professors, through rebranding them as leading academics. The first perspective recognises the purpose of professors as practising exclusively as intellectually outstanding academics whose distinguished, world-leading, research generates ground-breaking knowledge for the intrinsic benefit of the discipline and, by extension, the extrinsic benefit of the university. This purpose would involve a single, unambiguous and uncomplicated role – that of distinguished researcher – and would preclude the incorporation of any additional or supplementary responsibilities that detract from it, making professors essentially one-trick ponies. Since it effectively represents backtracking on their refashioning of professorship, referred to above, done to better suit the needs of their performativity agendas, universities would be most unlikely to entertain any such shift, as long as neoliberalism continues to reign supreme in the academy.

The second perspective acknowledges that, faced with increasing pressure to expand their own remits and purposes and to do so effectively and efficiently, universities must widen their foci and repertoires of activities, while yet maintaining their quality, and must continue to utilise their professors to help them do so. But where this perspective deviates from what has already been set in motion as the professorship-refashioning that universities have already effected, is its being based upon recognition that this utilisation – this refashioning of professors as 'all-singing, all-dancing' performers – must be spread across the professoriate as a whole, which, *as a collective*, may achieve a broader and more expansive purpose than has historically been associated with professors. Reflecting Lydon's (2016, p. 5) concern, as a university vice-chancellor, that universities have 'generated a culture where conformity is the norm', and that there is a need to break through 'groupthink' in order 'to show that difference and to enable that difference to contribute to the team', the sum of the parts would thus succeed in fulfilling the purpose, not of *professors* as individuals, but of the *professoriate* as a (departmental or institution-wide) group. Individual professors, in fact, would sharpen their foci, and in order to expose more of their individuality and utilise their different and unique talents, each would be expected to cover a narrower range of activities than has come to be expected of most of them. This narrowing of activity focus and therefore of role remit was in fact proposed by – once again – Shirley Fisher as a solution to the overload that she identified as a source of academic stress: 'The answer may be to have academic staff who are self-selected for particular balances of teaching and research. *They then operate within their own perceived specialities*' (Fisher, 1994, p. 94, emphasis added); Middlehurst (1993, p. 159) similarly makes the point that 'individuals are likely to develop strengths in different areas and will be more or less effective in their different roles'. It seems blindingly obvious that, in more general terms that go beyond a simple binary split of teaching from research, this 'task-talents matching' that I first mooted around the turn of the millennium for academics generally (Evans & Abbott, 1998, p. 159) is the way in which professorship must evolve *if the quality of the professoriate's intellectual activity and output are to avoid being compromised.*

Indeed, an interviewee in the *Professorial academic leadership in turbulent times* study proposed such a view of the professoriate – as a collective of specialists with complementary strengths and skills:

> It goes back, I think to some extent, to Meredith Belbin's stuff way back in the '60s, where it isn't that you have the most balanced individuals, where *everybody* is a brilliant researcher, brilliant fundraiser, brilliant administrator, and brilliant teacher, but that you have a number of people in the faculty who complement each other's strengths and each other's weaknesses. So you might have a superb writer, who's not particularly good at grant-gaining, but you can have another person doing that. And I think that's part of building a senior leadership team. I'm not sure that I would want to, sort of, describe the professorial role without knowing what was the role that they were fulfilling within the department, and who are the other people there. (*Eric, education studies professor, pre-1992 university*)

How might the notion of such a collective of specialists be received by universities? To justify their having re-invented professorship for performativity, university senior leaders and managers may argue that the days of the mono-focused academic are gone, and that all professors must now endeavour to adapt to the changed and dynamic environment that is the twenty-first-century academy by expanding their repertoires of skills and extending the parameters of their territories or domains, in terms of ground that they feel they should cover. Pressures, they may say, are part and parcel of such a dynamic work environment – indeed, an anonymous professorial contributor to a recent piece in *The Guardian* reports having been berated by his line manager: 'You're supposed to be stressed! Professors here are supposed to be stressed! That's the job' (Anonymous academic, 2014).

Certainly it is difficult to dispute the value of adaptability, and of noting in which direction the winds of change are blowing and then following their course. Most professors – certainly amongst those appointed within the last decade or so – having achieved their promotions by metaphorically jumping through whatever hoops have been placed before them, will be acutely aware of the need for, and will be adept at, compliant performance-indicative practice, however strategic their compliance may be. Accordingly, representing consummate adaptability to the current environment, they are likely to have presented themselves to promotions panels as expansive in focus, interests and expertise.

But whilst the twenty-first-century professor is expected to have considerably more strings to her or his bow than the professor portrayed in Halsey's (1992) study of the UK academy in the last quarter of the twentieth century, this does not necessarily create a better tune. It is worth noting that most of the great thinkers and intellectual giants have been mono-focused, and needed peace and tranquillity – often isolation – to be creative; Isaac Newton, Cropper (2004) tells us, was self-centred and reclusive and, 'at least during his most creative years, was a secret introvert' (p. 21), and James Clerk Maxwell 'decided that he did not need an academic appointment, with all its accompanying duties for which he was not well suited, to continue his researches' (Cropper, 2004, p. 159), and so resigned his post at King's College London to continue his work in the peace and solitude of rural Scotland. Not for them the frenzied, multifarious existence that requires constant refocussing; if this had been their lot, society is likely to have missed out on their scientific legacies.

'The tradition of the lone scholar is largely gone', observes arts and humanities lecturer François in Chapter 7. What seems to be lacking from twenty-first-century academic life in the neoliberal university is widespread recognition that those academics with evident creative potential – those who demonstrate a capacity for profound and original thinking – must be permitted to cocoon themselves in order to generate what may turn out to be knowledge that unhinges paradigms and sets new courses towards revolutionary change. If their time on quiet thinking, repeated experimentation, microscope- or telescope-gazing, or manuscript-perusal is curtailed by their having to be in too many other places, too often, the insight and breakthroughs that turn accepted knowledge on its head may never see the light of day. Teresa Sullivan's (2014) lamenting the erosion of academe's offering a haven of tranquillity for 'the life of the mind', in which serious scholars sought quiet, calm refuge from the distractions that impeded their creativity may herald a simmering backlash against the frenetic omnifarious activity that defines academic life in the neoliberal university. For something must give, and if it turns out to be scholarship we will have sold academe's soul to the devil. Are universities aware that he is already pacing up and down restlessly, anticipating the transaction – or are they totting up how much they should ask him to pay? Surely, with all bases covered, from universities' perspective, the idea of a multi-talented, multi-task-focused professoriate, that combats the dilution of intellectual output quality through the specialist expertise of its individual members, ticks all boxes – and keeps the devil at bay.

Professorial specialism of this kind would aim *broadly* to allow each professor to play to her or his strengths, and in doing so increase her/his job satisfaction. It would allow, say, those who are good at winning research funding to make applying for funding – and helping others apply – their main activity, just as those who are skilled educators and have creative ideas for curriculum and course or pedagogical development could devote the bulk of their time to such work, whilst those who have proved themselves skilled scholars and theorists would be permitted to focus predominantly on pioneering research – rather than, as biological sciences professor Brian complained (see Chapter 10), having been unable to get into the lab for weeks, due to competing demands on his time. And, of course, there would remain a clear pathway for those who feel their strengths lie in institutional management. Specialism would denote and signal the professor's *core* strength, upon which s/he would be permitted to spend a larger proportion of her or his time than is currently the case for most professors. It would in most cases be a *predominant*, rather than an *exclusive*, specialism – though exclusivity would be reserved as an option for those deemed, on the basis of their potential to contribute to knowledge growth by breaking through barriers, to need it. Moreover, as leading academics in their specialist fields, the exemplary manner in which they carry out the work that they do best would inevitably serve as a conduit for the influence that represents academic leadership.

Specialism of this kind, within professoriates that, collectively, cover all the bases that institutions want covering, may require a rethink in relation to professorial titles, generating a widened repertoire of qualifying prefixes or suffixes to describe a range of revised professorial roles, distinguished on the basis of key focus. Without such focus-indicating labels there is a danger of defaulting to misplaced expectations of professors that would encourage multifariousness. The basic idea of professorial specialism has in the past been mooted by others (see, for example, Macfarlane, 2012a; Middlehurst, 2004), and in one sense it has been kick-started by those universities, referred to in Chapter 8, that have appointed professors of public engagement. But it risks promoting hierarchically based stratification, giving rise to the kind of professorial caste system that is implicit in the differential professorial grading policies already adopted by most UK universities. To combat the threat of such negativity, differentiated professorial roles and associated titles ideally would be chosen and delineated with the aim of implying parity of academic status and standing – an almost impossible feat, since perceptions of these are subjectively determined and therefore susceptible to multiple and various interpretation, and the 'purists' who rate intellectual capacity and scholarly distinction above all else are likely to be disdainful of alternative forms of professorship that accommodate different skills sets.

Watching a television documentary on Westminster Abbey some time ago, I learned that its senior canons have such differentiated titles that elucidate their roles: canon theologian; canon steward; and canon treasurer and almoner. According to its website, St Paul's Cathedral similarly boasts a canon treasurer, a canon pastor, and a canon precentor. Applying such a system of specialised categories to university professorship is worth serious consideration. Titles could be employed that each denotes particular expertise and proven skills in – and a continued narrow focus on – one of the following (which I present as nothing more than indicative examples):

- generating theory and theoretical perspectives;
- securing research income and carrying out funded research;
- institutional leadership and management;
- teaching, along with the development of higher education pedagogy;
- impact, and public engagement.

And would a canonical-type system of nomenclature work for professorial roles or foci of expertise – *professor theoretician* (or *professor scholar*); *professor entrepreneur*; *professor administrator*; *professor pedagogue*; and *professor of public engagement*? (Those who may baulk at – or find amusing – the idea of borrowing the church's titular traditions, are reminded that European universities have their origins in the early medieval church, and, as preceding chapters show, the two were for many centuries inextricably linked – though I do not suggest a rapprochement!)

Professorial professionalism for the twenty-first century

It used to be clear and straightforward: professors were considered distinguished intellectuals who, with a few exceptions, represented the pinnacle of scholarly excellence – academia's elite minority. They 'professed' – and, for the most part, people sat up and took notice of their professing, expecting to learn something. Then, gradually – and accompanying the seeping of performativity into academic working life and culture – a new term began to enter the lexicon of promotions policy: academic leadership. It summed up – and still does sum up – what was/is presented by universities as their professors' overarching role and purpose. But, denoting the current shifting shape of 'demanded' professorial professionalism, academic leadership represents an idea in principle that seems to have been sketched out roughly and imprecisely, without its finer details having been afforded the consideration they needed, and then snatched up hastily as a purpose for universities' most senior academics that seemed to tick most boxes. So it has emerged as a somewhat half-baked idea: fine in principle, but, in terms of workability, dubious, because the implications of asking and expecting people to enact something whose nature, parameters and definition are discretionary, variable, and subjectively determined by any stakeholder, seem to have been misjudged. As a model of distributed leadership, setting up and branding professors as academic leaders where such leading ends up being boundless in scope, scale and intensity is a poor example – one, moreover, that represents leadership that, being unproblem*atised* at the conception stage, becomes problem*atic* at the execution stage. It is not a disaster, certainly, but neither does it work as it should; its costs – particularly to well-being and to scholarship – are too high.

So it is time for a rethink. It is time to reshape professorial professionalism, so that the business of doing professorship in the UK is not only manageable, but satisfying and satisfactory, to, respectively, professors themselves and the universities that not only employ and deploy them, but also have a duty of care to them. Mine is not the only articulation of such views – the sub-title of Bruce Macfarlane's (2012a) book, rather tellingly, is: 'renewing the role of the university professor'; a former *THE* editor has highlighted the opacity of the professorial role and the confusion that it engenders (Mroz, 2011); and, of course, Malcom Tight (2002) set the ball rolling over a decade ago by asking what it means to be a professor – implying, with his concluding question ('What sort of professor do you want to be?') that, when it comes to doing professorship, anything goes. But we have moved on from such uncertainty and liberality; professorial professionalism needs a clearly defined shape if it is to be enacted in ways that allow professors to make a real difference to society. The shape of professorial professionalism that I prescribe, above, is one that enables them to do so, as leading academics.

Professorship, we have seen, has evolved since its emergence in medieval Europe as a title that denoted its holders' purpose and the nature of the activity it denoted: professing. But evolution is a responsive transition; it is always prompted by circumstances and context, and it is these that have reshaped professorial professionalism and professors' roles down the centuries. It was the neoliberal model that, over the last two decades, effected the gradual reshaping of professors as academic leaders, to serve the marketised university. But the neoliberal model, Mason (2015) argues, is moribund – and, with a particular focus on the university sector, Scott (2017) seems to agree:

> The ground is shifting. The details of the endgame may still be obscure, but there can now be little doubt that the age of under-regulated markets, the small state, the deliberate erosion of the public sphere, and the cults of 'modernisation' and 'management', is drawing to a close.
>
> The tragedy for universities, as a sector and as organisations, is that they have become so thoroughly used to that world, whatever their initial resistance to its values and practices, that they can imagine no other.
>
> So they are at real risk of ending up on the wrong side of history. They will be seen as accomplices in failing neoliberal markets, against which their students are in revolt, and spurious 'modernisation', which alienates many of their staff. They need to get back on the right side of history – quickly.

Whether the demise of neoliberalism is as imminent as Mason and Scott suggest remains to be seen, but they are certainly right in one respect: its days are numbered; for, as surely as night follows day, every doctrine behind a political or economic model runs its course, and is replaced. The winds of change are undoubtedly blowing, and when neoliberalism does become a thing of the past, quite a different university will emerge from its shadow – indeed, Scott (2017) is already discerning its outline – and the shape of professorial professionalism will shift yet again.

But, for now, pushing against the professors-as-academic-leaders-shaped professorial professionalism are different circumstances and a different context: unmanageable demands on professors, work overload, job unwieldiness, task diffusion, and the dilution of standards. Something must give, and a compromise found. Professorship is ripe for an evolutionary spurt: from professors as academic leaders to professors as leading academics.

Note

1 While there are disciplinary variations, in the UK, research council funding success
   rates are particularly low, with funding from the Economic and Social Sciences
   Research Council (ESRC) being notoriously difficult to secure. Data presented
   in a *Times Higher Education* report (Matthews, 2015) on UK research council
   funding success rates shows that, in 2014–15, the success rate for ESRC funding was
   12 per cent. Success rates with the other five research councils were higher, but only
   one – the Engineering and Physical Sciences Research Council (EPSRC) – reported
   a success rate (38 per cent - explained in the report as 'abnormally high') in excess
   of 25 per cent. It was remarked that 'once success rates drop below 20 per cent, the
   process "becomes more of a lottery" as reviewers are more stretched, and it becomes
   more "demoralising" and even inefficient for researchers to bid for grants … A
   2006 report by the research councils warned that success rates of below 20 per cent
   create "unacceptable inefficiencies" in the process.' A later *THE* report (Matthews,
   2016) found support for the idea of replacing the current peer review process with 'a
   lottery system to prevent academics wasting time on normally fruitless proposals'.

References

Aarrevaara, T., & Pekkola, E. (2010). *Muuttuva akateeminen professio suomessa - Maaraportti (The changing academic profession in Finland, national report)* (Higher Education Finance and Management Series). Tampere: Tampere University Press.

Alvesson, M., & Spicer, A. (2012). Critical leadership studies: The case for critical performativity. *Human Relations, 65*(3), 367–90.

Alvesson, M., Bridgman, T., & Willmott, H. (Eds.) (2009). *Oxford handbook of critical management studies.* Oxford: Oxford University Press.

Anonymous academic (2014). Bullying in academia: 'Professors are supposed to be stressed! That's the job', Higher education network: Academics anonymous, Friday 24 October. Retrieved 30 April 2017 from http://www.theguardian.com/higher-education-network/blog/2014/oct/24/bullying-academia-universities-stress-support#comments

Austin, A. (2002). Preparing the next generation of faculty: Graduate school as socialization to the academic career. *The Journal of Higher Education, 73*(1), 94–122.

Bacon, E. (2014). *Neo-collegiality: Restoring academic engagement in the managerial university.* London: The Leadership Foundation for Higher Education.

Barker, D. (2017). Ninjas, zombies and nervous wrecks? Academics in the neoliberal world of physical education and sport pedagogy. *Sport, Education and Society, 22*(1), 87–104.

Barnard, C. (1997). The nature of leadership. In K. Grint (Ed.) *Leadership: Classical, contemporary and critical approaches* (pp. 89–111). New York: Oxford University Press.

Barnett, R. (2011). Towards an ecological professionalism. In C. Sugrue & T. D. Solbrekke (Eds.) *Professional responsibility: New horizons of praxis* (pp. 29–41). Abingdon: Routledge.

Becher, T. (1989). *Academic tribes and territories: Intellectual enquiry and the cultures of disciplines.* Buckingham: Open University Press/SRHE.

Becher, T., & Trowler, P. R. (2001). *Academic tribes and territories: Intellectual enquiry and the cultures of disciplines,* 2nd edition. Buckingham: Open University Press/SRHE.

Berlingieri, A. (2015). Workplace bullying: Exploring an emerging framework. *Work, Employment and Society, 29*(2), 342–53.

Birnbaum, R. (1992). *How academic leadership works: Understanding success and failure in the college presidency.* San Francisco, CA: Jossey-Bass.

Blackmore, P. (2016). *The role of prestige in UK universities: Vice-chancellors' perspectives: Research report.* London: The Leadership foundation for Higher Education.

Bolden, R. (2007). The shadow side of leadership. *Effective Executive, 9*(2), 42-3.

Bolden, R., Gosling, J., O'Brien, A., Peters, K., Ryan, M., & Haslam, A. (2012a). *Academic leadership: Changing conceptions, identities and experiences in UK higher education, research and development series, full report to the Leadership Foundation for Higher Education.* London: Leadership Foundation for Higher Education.

Bolden, R., Gosling, J., O'Brien, A., Peters, K., Ryan, M., & Haslam, A. (2012b). *Academic leadership: Changing conceptions, identities and experiences in UK higher education, research and development series, summary report to the Leadership Foundation for Higher Education.* London: Leadership Foundation for Higher Education.

Bolman, L., & Gallos, J. V. (2011). *Reframing academic leadership.* San Fransisco, CA: Jossey-Bass.

Bostock, J. (2014). *The meaning of success: Insights from women at Cambridge.* Cambridge: Cambridge University Press.

Bottero, W. (1992). The changing face of the professions? Gender and explanations of women's entry to pharmacy. *Work, Employment and Society, 6*(3), 329–49.

Bradley, A. P., Grice, T., & Paulsen, N. (2017). Promoting leadership in Australian universities. *Australian Universities' Review, 59*(1), 97–105. Retrieved 12 March 2017 from http://www.aur.org.au/article/Promoting-leadership-in-Australian-universities-%28AUR-59-01%29-19357

Brockliss, L. W. B. (2016). *The University of Oxford: A history.* Oxford: Oxford University Press.

Brown, A. (2014). *The myth of the strong leader: Political leadership in the modern age.* London: Bodley Head.

Bryman, A. (2007). Effective leadership in higher education: A literature review. *Studies in Higher Education, 32*(6), 693–710.

Bryson, C., & Barnes, N. (2000). Working in higher education in the United Kingdom. In M. Tight (Ed.) *Academic work and life: What it is to be an academic and how this is changing* (pp. 147–85). New York: Elsevier.

Burt, R. S. (2000). The network structure of social capital. *Research in Organizational Behavior, 22,* 345–423.

Choi, S., & Schnurr, S. (2014). Exploring distributed leadership: Solving disagreements and negotiating consensus in a 'leaderless' team. *Discourse Studies, 16*(1), 3–24.

Chrobot-Mason, D., Gerbasi, A., & Cullen-Lester, K. L. (2016). Predicting leadership relationships: The importance of collective identity. *The Leadership Quarterly, 27*(2), 298–311.

Chubb, J. (2017). Academics fear the value of knowledge for its own sake is diminishing, *The Conversation,* 19 June. Retrieved 24 June 2017 from https://theconversation.com/academics-fear-the-value-of-knowledge-for-its-own-sake-is-diminishing-75341

Clark, J. J. (2010). Social work, psychobiography, and the study of lives. In W. Borden (Ed.) *Reshaping theory in contemporary social work* (pp. 81–113). New York: Columbia University Press.

Coates, H. B., Dobson, I., Edwards, D., Friedman, T., Goedegebuure, L., & Meek, L. V. (2009). *The attractiveness of the Australian academic profession: A comparative analysis.* University of Melbourne: Melbourne.

Collinson D. (2011). Critical leadership studies. In D. Collinson, A. Bryman, K. Grint, B. Jackson, & M. Uhl-Bien (Eds.) *Handbook of leadership studies* (pp.181-94). London: SAGE.

Collinson, P., Rex, R., & Stanton, G. (2003). *Lady Margaret Beaufort and her professors of divinity at Cambridge, 1502 to 1649.* Cambridge: Cambridge University Press.

Combes, P-P., Linnemar, L., & Visser, M. (2008). Publish or peer-rich? The role of skills and networks in hiring economics professors. *Labour Economics, 15*(3), 423–41.

Contributors (2015). Don't shut down Heythrop College, *Times Higher Education,* 6 August.

Contributors (2016). Promoted from doctor to professor: What changes? *Times Higher Education.* Retrieved 10 November 2016 from https://www.timeshighereducation.com/features/promoted-from-doctor-to-professor-what-changes

Coser, L. A. (1974). *Greedy institutions: Patterns of undivided commitment.* New York: Free Press.

Cropper, W. H. (2004). *Great physicists: The life and times of great physicists from Galileo to Hawking.* New York: Oxford University Press.

Croxford, L., & Raffe, D. (2013). *Social and ethnic inequalities and institutional differences in entry to UK higher education (1996–2010),* CES Briefing, Number 61, Edinburgh, Centre for Educational Sociology, University of Edinburgh. Retrieved 11 March 2017 from http://www.nuffieldfoundation.org/sites/default/files/files/Briefing%2061%20-%20colour(1).pdf

Croxford, L., & Raffe, D. (2015). The iron law of hierarchy? Institutional differentiation in UK higher education. *Studies in Higher Education, 40*(9), 1625–40.

Cullen-Lester, K. L., & Yammarino, F. J. (2016). Collective and network approaches to leadership: Special issue introduction. *The Leadership Quarterly, 27*(2), 173–80.

Cunliffe, A. L., & Erikson, M. (2011). Relational leadership. *Human Relations, 64*(11), 1425–49.

Cuthbert, R. (2017). Editorial: What's wrong with management in higher education?, *SRHE News,* 28 April, p. 1.

Debowski, S., & Blake, V. (2004). The developmental needs of higher education academic leaders in encouraging effective teaching and learning. In *Seeking Educational Excellence.* Proceedings of the 13th Annual Teaching Learning Forum, 9–10 February. Perth: Murdoch University.

Deem, R. (1996). Border territories: A journey through sociology, education and women's studies. *British Journal of Sociology of Education, 17*(1), 5–19.

Denis, J-L., Langley, A., & Sergi, V. (2012). Leadership in the plural. *The Academy of Management Annals, 6*(1), 211–83.

Department for Business, Innovation and Skills (2016). *Success as a knowledge economy: Teaching excellence, social mobility and student choice.* London: Department for Business, Innovation & Skills.

DeRue, D. S., & Ashford, S. J. (2010). Who will lead and who will follow? A social process of leadership identity construction in organizations. *Academy of Management Review, 35*(4), 627–47.

Diezmann, C. M., & Grieshaber, S. J. (2010). Gender equity in the professoriate: A cohort study of new women professors in Australia. In M. Devlin, J. Nagy, & A. Lichtenberg (Eds.), *Research and development in higher education: Reshaping higher education*. Paper presented at The 33rd HERDSA Annual International Conference, 6–9 July 2010 (pp. 223–34). Melbourne: Australia.

Dobson, R. (1995). A serious outbreak of professors, *The Independent*, 6 August. Retrieved from http://www.independent.co.uk/news/uk/home-news/a-serious-outbreak-of-professors-1595032.html

Douglas, A. S. (2013). Advice from the professors in a university Social Sciences department on the teaching-research nexus. *Teaching in Higher Education, 18*(4), 377–88.

Driver, M. (2017). Motivation and identity: A psychoanalytic perspective on the turn to identity in motivation research. *Human Relations, 70*(5), 617–37.

Durand, J.-P., & Stewart, P. (2014). The birth of French labour sociology after the war: Some reflections on the nature of the corporate state and intellectual engagement for the sociology of work in the UK today. *Work, Employment and Society, 28*(6), 1003–15.

Elliott, J. H. (1990 – 15th impression [first published 1968]). *Europe divided: 1559–1598*. London: Collins Publishing.

Enders, J. (2000). Academic staff in Europe: Changing employment and working conditions. In M. Tight (Ed.) *Academic work and life: What it is to be an academic and how this is changing* (pp. 7–32). New York: Elsevier.

Enders, J. (Ed.) (2001). *Academic staff in Europe: Changing contexts and conditions*. Westport, CT: Greenwood Press.

Enders, J., & de Weert, E. (Eds.) (2009). *The changing face of academic life: Analytical and comparative perspectives*. Basingstoke: Palgrave Macmillan.

Enders, J., de Boer, H., & Leisyte, L. (2009). New public management and the academic profession: The rationalization of academic work revisited. In J. Enders & E. de Weert (Eds.) *The changing face of academic life: Analytical and comparative perspectives* (pp. 36–57). Basingstoke: Palgrave Macmillan.

Epitropaki, O., Sy, T., Martin, R., Tram-Quon, S., & Topakas, A. (2013). Implicit leadership and followership theories 'in the wild': Taking stock of information-processing approaches to leadership and followership in organizational settings. *The Leadership Quarterly, 24*(6), 858–81.

Eraut, M. (2004). Informal learning in the workplace. *Studies in Continuing Education, 26*(2), 247–73.

Eraut, M. (2007). Learning from other people in the workplace. *Oxford Review of Education, 33*(4), 403–22.

Evans, L. (1997). Addressing problems of conceptualisation and construct validity in researching teachers' job satisfaction. *Educational Research, 39*(3), 319–31.

Evans, L. (1998). *Teacher morale, job satisfaction and motivation.* London: Paul Chapman.

Evans, L. (2001). Delving deeper into morale, job satisfaction and motivation among education professionals: Re-examining the leadership dimension. *Educational Management and Administration, 29*(3), 291–306.

Evans, L. (2002). *Reflective practice in educational research: Developing advanced skills.* London: Continuum.

Evans, L. (2008). Professionalism, professionality and the development of education professionals. *British Journal of Educational Studies, 56*(1), 20–38.

Evans, L. (2011). The 'shape' of teacher professionalism in England: Professional standards, performance management, professional development, and the changes proposed in the 2010 White Paper. *British Educational Research Journal, 37*(5), 851–70.

Evans, L. (2013). The professional status of educational research: Professionalism and developmentalism in 21st century working life. *British Journal of Educational Studies, 61*(4), 471–90.

Evans, L. (2014a). What is effective research leadership? A research-informed perspective. *Higher Education Research and Development, 33*(1), 46–58.

Evans, L. (2014b). Leadership for professional development and learning: Enhancing our understanding of how teachers develop. *Cambridge Journal of Education, 44*(2), 179–98.

Evans, L. (2015a). A changing role for university professors? Professorial academic leadership as it is perceived by 'the led'. *British Educational Research Journal, 41*(4), 666–85.

Evans, L. (2015b). What academics want from their professors: Findings from a study of professorial academic leadership in the UK. In U. Teichler & W. K. Cummings (Eds.) *Forming, recruiting and managing the academic profession* (pp. 51–78). Dordrecht: Springer.

Evans, L. (2015c). Competition, elitism and neoliberal performativity: The formation of a Russell Group academic identity. In L. Evans & J. Nixon (Eds.) *Academic identities in higher education: The changing European landscape* (pp. 149–66). London: Bloomsbury.

Evans, L. (2016). *The purpose of professors: Professionalism, pressures and performance.* London: The Leadership Foundation for Higher Education.

Evans, L. (2017a). The worst of times? A tale of two French institutions: Their merger, and its impact on staff working lives. *Studies in Higher Education, 49(9), 1699-717.*

Evans, L. (2017b). University professors as academic leaders: Professorial leadership development needs and provision. *Educational Management, Administration & Leadership, 45*(1), 123–40.

Evans, L., & Abbott, I. (1998). *Teaching and learning in higher education.* London: Cassell.

Evans, L., & Bertani-Tress, M. (2009). What drives research-focused university academics to want to teach effectively? Examining achievement, self-efficacy and self-esteem. *International Journal for the Scholarship of Teaching and Learning,* 3(2), 1–18.

Evans, L., & Cosnefroy, L. (2013). The dawn of a new academic professionalism in the French academy? Academics facing the challenges of imposed reform. *Studies in Higher Education,* 38(8), 1201–21.

Evans, L., & Homer, M. S. (2014). *Academic journal editors' professionalism: Perceptions of power, proficiency and personal agendas – Final Report.* London: The Society for Research into Higher Education. Retrieved from http://www.srhe.ac.uk/downloads/ EvansHomerReport.pdf.

Evans, L., Homer, M., & Rayner, S. (2013). Professors as academic leaders: The perspectives of 'the led'. *Educational Management, Administration and Leadership,* 41(5), 674–89.

Evans, R. J. (2013). On Her Majesty's scholarly service, *Times Higher Education.* Retrieved 18 April 2016 from https://www.timeshighereducation.com/features/on-her-majestys-scholarly-service/2001293.article

Evetts, J. (2013). Professionalism: Value and ideology. *Current Sociology,* 61(5-6), 778-96.

Farivar, C. (2009). Berkeley's prize for Nobel winners: Free parking, National Public Radio (NPR), 17 October. Retrieved 17 April 2017 from http://www.npr.org/ templates/story/story.php?storyId=113883274

Finkenstaedt, T. (2011). Teachers. In W. Rüegg (Ed.) *A history of the university in Europe,* IV (pp. 162–203). Cambridge: Cambridge University Press.

Fisher, S. (1994). *Stress in academic life.* Buckingham: Open University Press.

Floyd, A. (2012). 'Turning points': The personal and professional circumstances that lead academics to become middle managers. *Educational Management, Administration and Leadership,* 40(2), 272–84.

Foskett, N., Lumby, J., & Fidler, B. (2005). Evolution or extinction? Reflections on the future of research in educational leadership and management. *Educational Management, Administration and Leadership,* 33(2), 245–53.

Fredman, N., & Doughney, J. (2012). Academic dissatisfaction, managerial change and neoliberalism. *Higher Education,* 64, 41–58.

Fulton, O., & Holland, C. (2001). Profession or proletariat? Academic staff in the United Kingdom after two decades of change. In J. Enders (Ed.) *Academic staff in Europe: Changing contexts and conditions* (pp. 301-21). Westport, CT: Greenwood Press.

Gallos, J. V. (2002). The dean's squeeze: Myths and realities of academic leadership in the middle. *Academy of Management Learning and Education,* 1(2), 174–84.

Garud, R. (2008). Conferences as venues for the configuration of emerging organizational fields: The case of cochlear implants. *Journal of Management Studies,* 45(6), 1061–88.

Gemmill, G., & Oakley, J. (1992). Leadership: An alienating social myth. *Human Relations, 45*(2), 113–29.

Gentle, P. (with Forman, D.) (2014). *Engaging leaders: The challenge of inspiring collective commitment in universities.* Abingdon: Routledge.

Gewirtz, S., Mahony, P., Hextall, I., & Cribb, A. (2009). Policy, professionalism and practice: Understanding and enhancing teachers' work. In S. Gewirtz, P. Mahony, I. Hextall, & A. Cribb (Eds.) *Changing teacher professionalism* (pp. 3–16). London: Routledge.

Gibney, E. (2013). Oxford consults on 'associate professor' grade, *Times Higher Education*, 14 February.

Grint, K. (Ed.) (1997). *Leadership: classical, contemporary and critical approaches.* New York: Oxford University Press.

Gronn, P. (1999). Leadership from a distance: Institutionalizing values and forming character at Timbertop, 1951–61. In P. T. Begley & P. E. Leonard (Eds.) *The values of educational administration* (pp. 140–67). London: Falmer Press.

Gronn, P. (2000). Distributed properties: A new architecture for leadership. *Educational Management and Administration, 28*(3), 317–38.

Gronn, P. (2002). Distributed leadership as a unit of analysis. *The Leadership Quarterly, 13*(4), 423–51.

Gronn, P. (2009). Leadership configurations. *Leadership, 5*(2), 381–94.

Grove, J. (2011). 'Prima Donna' professors lambasted for failure to mentor, *Times Higher Education*, 17 November.

Grove, J. (2014). King's College London criticised for closing theology programmes, *Times Higher Education*, 23 August.

Grove, J. (2015). Casual lecturers 'stigmatised' by job titles, *Times Higher Education*, 27 August.

Grove, J. (2017). One in three UK universities going backwards on female professorships, *Times Higher Education*, 25 May. Retrieved 31 May 2017 from https://www.timeshighereducation.com/news/one-in-three-uk-universities-going-backwards-on-female-professorships

Guion, R. M. (1958). Industrial morale: The problem of terminology. *Personnel Psychology, 11*(1), 59–64.

Gunter, H. (2001). *Leaders and leadership in education.* London: Paul Chapman.

Gunter, H. (2016). *An Intellectual history of school leadership practice and research.* London: Bloomsbury.

Gunter, H., Hall, D., & Bragg, J. (2013). Distributed leadership: A study in knowledge production. *Educational Management, Administration and Leadership, 41*(5), 555–80.

Halsey, A. H. (1992). *Decline of donnish dominion: The British academic professions in the twentieth century.* Oxford: Clarendon Press.

Harris, A. (2013). Distributed leadership: Friend or foe? *Educational Management, Administration and Leadership, 41*(5), 545–54.

Hartley, D. (2009). Education policy, distributed leadership and socio-cultural theory. *Educational Review, 61*(2), 139–50.

Hartung, C., Barnes, N., Welch, R., O'Flynn, G., Uptin, J., & McMahon, S. (2017). Beyond the academic precariat: A collective biography of poetic subjectivities in the neoliberal university. *Sport, Education and Society, 22*(1), 40–57.

Hecht, I. W. D., Higgerson, M. L., Gmelch, W. H., & Tucker, A. (1999). *The department chair as academic leader.* Phoenix, AZ: American Council on Education/Oryx Press.

Henkel, M. (2000). *Academic identities and policy change in higher education.* London: Jessica Kingsley.

Herzberg, F. (1968). *Work and the nature of man.* London: Staples Press.

Hibbert, C., & Hibbert, E. (Eds.) (1988). *The encyclopaedia of Oxford.* London: Macmillan.

Higher Education Statistics Agency (HESA) (2017). *Table B – Academic staff (excluding atypical) by source of basic salary, academic employment function, salary range, contract level, terms of employment, mode of employment and sex 2015/16.* London: HESA.

Hill, S. E. K., Bahniuk, M. H., & Dobos, J. (1989). The impact of mentoring and collegial support on faculty success: An analysis of support behaviour, information adequacy, and communication apprehension. *Communication Education, 38*(1), 15–33.

Hollander, E. P. (1992). The essential interdependence of leadership and followership. *Current Directions in Psychological Science, 1*(2), 71–5.

Hoskins, K. (2012). *Women and success: Professors in the UK academy.* Stoke-on-Trent: Trentham Books.

Humphreys, J. H., Novicevic, M. M., Smothers, J., Pane Haden, S. S., Hayek, M., Williams, W. A., Oyler, J. D., & Clayton, R. W. (2015). The collective endorsement of James Meredith: Initiating a leader identity construction process. *Human Relations, 89*(9), 1389–413.

Ismail, M., & Rasdi, R. M. (2008). Leadership in an academic career: Uncovering the experience of women professors. *International Studies in Educational Administration, 36*(3), 87–103.

Jacob, A. K., & Teichler U. (2011). *Der Wandel des Hochschullehrerberufs im internationalen Vergleich: Ergebnisse einer Befragung in den Jahren 2007/08 (Changes to the academic profession: An international comparison – Survey results for the years 2007-08).* Bonn and Berlin: Bundes-ministerium für Bildung und Forschung.

Jasso, G. (1988). Principles of theoretical analysis. *Sociological Theory, 6*(1), 1–20.

Jonasson, O. (1993). Women as leaders in organized surgery and surgical education. *Archives of Surgery, 128*(6), 618–21.

Jones, M. K., & Underwood, M. G. (1992). *The King's Mother: Lady Margaret Beaufort, Countess of Richmond and Derby.* Cambridge: Cambridge University Press.

Juntrasook, A. (2014). 'You do not have to be the boss to be a leader': Contested meanings of leadership in higher education. *Higher Education Research and Development, 33*(1), 19-31.

Juntrasook, A., Nairn, K., Bond, C., & Sproken-Smith, R. (2013). Unpacking the narrative of non-positional leadership in academia: Hero and/or victim? *Higher Education Research and Development, 32*(2), 201–13.

Kauppi, N. (2015). The academic condition: Unstable structures, ambivalent narratives, dislocated identities. In L. Evans & J. Nixon (Eds.) *Academic identities in higher education: The changing European landscape* (pp. 31–46). London: Bloomsbury.

Keller, T. (1999). Images of the familiar: Individual differences and implicit leadership theories. *The Leadership Quarterly, 10*(4), 589–607.

Keller, T. (2003). Parental images as a guide to leadership sensemaking: An attachment perspective on implicit leadership theories. *The Leadership Quarterly, 14*(2), 141–60.

Kelly, S. (2008). Leadership: A categorical mistake? *Human Relations, 61*(6), 763–82.

Kelly, S. (2014). Towards a negative ontology of leadership. *Human Relations, 67*(8), 905–22.

Kets de Vries M., & Balazs, K. (2010). The shadow side of leadership. In F. Bournois, J. Duval-Hamel, S. Roussillon, & J. Scaringella (Eds.) *Handbook of top management teams* (pp. 183–90). Basingstoke: Palgrave Macmillan.

Kivinen, O., & Piiroinen, T. (2006). On the limits of a realist conception of knowledge: A pragmatist critique of Archerian realism. *The Sociological Review, 54*(2), 224–41.

Knight, P. T., & Trowler, P. R. (2001). *Departmental leadership in higher education.* Buckingham: Open University Press.

Kogan, M., Moses, I., & El-Khawas, E. (1994). *Staffing higher education: Meeting new challenges.* London: Jessica Kingsley.

Kolsaker, A. (2008). Academic professionalism in the managerialist era: A study of English universities. *Studies in Higher Education, 33*(5), 513–25.

Krantz, J. (2015). *Leaders or leadership: The century of the system*, Inaugural lecture of the Further Education Trust for Leadership, presented at King's Place, London, 10 March. Retrieved 24 September 2016 from http://www.fetl.org.uk/wp-content/uploads/2015/05/2-Leaders-or-Leadership.pdf

Ladkin, D. (2010). *Rethinking leadership: A new look at old leadership questions.* Cheltenham: Edward Elgar.

Lakomski, G. (1999). Against leadership: A concept without a cause. In P. Begley & P. Leonard (Eds.) *The values of educational administration* (pp. 36–50). London: Falmer.

Lakomski, G., & Evers, C. W. (1999). Values, socially distributed cognition, and organizational practice. In P. Begley (Ed.) *Values and educational leadership* (pp. 165–81). New York: SUNY Press.

Lapierre, L. M., Naidoo, L. J., & Bonaccio, S. (2012). Leaders' relational self-concept and followers' task performance: Implications for mentoring provided to followers. *The Leadership Quarterly, 23*, 766–74.

Lawler, E. E. (1973). *Motivation in work organizations.* Monterey, CA: Brooks/Cole.

Leonard, N. H., Beauvais, L. L., & Scholl, R. W. (1999). Work motivation: The incorporation of self-concept-based processes. *Human Relations, 52*(8), 969–98.

Locke, E. (1969). What is job satisfaction? *Organizational Behavior and Human Performance, 4,* 309–36.

Locke, W., & Teichler, U. (Eds.) (2007). *The changing conditions for academic work and careers in select countries* (Werkstattberichte/International Centre for Higher Education Research Kassel, Vol. 66). Kassel: Jenior.

Lumby, J. (2012). *What do we know about leadership in higher education? The Leadership Foundation for Higher Education's research: Review Paper.* London: LFHE.

Lumby, J. (2015). *In the wings and backstage: Exploring the micropolitics of leadership in higher education.* London: The Leadership Foundation for Higher Education.

Lydon, J. (2016). *Why should anyone work here? – The leadership experiences of a vice-chancellor.* Leadership lecture, October 2016, London: The Leadership Foundation for Higher Education.

Macfarlane, B. (2011). Professors as intellectual leaders: Formation, identity and role. *Studies in Higher Education, 36*(1), 57–73.

Macfarlane, B. (2012a). *Intellectual leadership in higher education: Renewing the role of the university professor.* Abingdon: Routledge.

Macfarlane, B. (2012b). Whisper it softly, professors are really academic developers too. *International Journal for Academic Development, 17*(2), 181–3.

Marini, G. (2014). Italy's new requirements for academic careers: The new habilitation and its worthiness, *Working Paper Cnr-Ceris, No. 03/2014,* Rome, CNR-CERIS National Research Council of Italy, Institute for Economic Research on Firm and Growth.

Marini, G. (2016). New promotion patterns in Italian universities: Less seniority and more productivity? Data from ASN. *Higher Education,* doi:10.1007/s10734-016-0008-x.

Maslow, A. H. (1954). *Motivation and personality.* New York: Harper and Row.

Mason, P. (2015). *Post-capitalism: A guide to our future.* London: Penguin/Random House.

Matthews, D. (2015). Success rates: Surge in applications to 'struggling' research councils, *Times Higher Education,* 29 October. Retrieved 29 April 2017 from https://www.timeshighereducation.com/news/success-rates-surge-applications-struggling-research-councils

Matthews, D. (2016). UK grant success rates prompt worldwide comparisons, *Times Higher Education,* 6 October. Retrieved 29 April 2017 from https://www.timeshighereducation.com/news/uk-grant-success-rates-prompt-worldwide-comparisons

Mayo, M., & Pastor, J. C. (2007). Leadership embedded in social networks: Looking at inter-follower processes. In B. Shamir, R. Pillai, M. C. Bligh, & M. Uhl-Bien (Eds.) *Follower-centered perspectives on leadership: A tribute to the memory of James R. Meindl* (pp. 93–113). Greenwich, CT: Information Age Publishers.

McLachlan, F. (2017). Being critical: An account of an early career academic working within and against neoliberalism. *Sport, Education and Society, 22*(1), 58–72.

Meindl, J. R. (1993). Reinventing leadership: A radical, social psychological approach. In J. K. Murnighan (Ed.) *Social psychology in organizations: Advances in theory and research* (pp. 89–118). Englewood Cliffs, NJ: Prentice Hall.

Menand, L. (2001). *The metaphysical club*. London: HarperCollins.

Meyer, L. (2012). Negotiating academic values, professorial responsibilities and expectations for accountability in today's university. *Higher Education Quarterly*, 66(2), 207–17.

Middlehurst, R. (1993). *Leading academics*. Buckingham: Open University/SRHE.

Middlehurst, R. (2004). Changing internal governance: A discussion of leadership roles and management structures in UK universities. *Higher Education Quarterly*, 58(4), 258–79.

Mixon, F. G., & Treviño, L. J. (2005). Is there gender discrimination in named professorships? An econometric analysis of economics departments in the US South. *Applied Economics*, 37(8), 849–54.

Morley, L. (2013). The rules of the game: Women and the leaderist turn in higher education. *Gender and Education*, 25(1), 116–31.

Morrison, E., Rudd, E., Picciano, J., & Nerad, M. (2011). Are you satisfied? PhD education and faculty taste for prestige: Limits of the prestige value system. *Research in Higher Education*, 52, 24–46.

Mroz, A. (2011). Leader: Absence-minded, ill defined, *Times Higher Education*, 17 November. Retrieved from http://www.timeshighereducation.co.uk/418151.article

Mullainathan, S., & Shafir, E. (2014). *Scarcity: The true cost of not having enough*. London: Penguin.

Mumford, E. (1906). The origins of leadership. *American Journal of Sociology*, 12(2), 216–40.

Noordegraaf, M. (2007). From 'pure' to 'hybrid' professionalism: Present-day professionalism in ambiguous public domains. *Administration and Society*, 39(6), 761–85.

Oc, B., & Bashshur, M. R. (2013). Followership, leadership and social influence. *The Leadership Quarterly*, 24(6), 919–34.

O'Loughlin, D., MacPhail, A., & Msetfi, R. (2015). The rhetoric and reality of research reputation: 'Fur coat and no knickers'. *Studies in Higher Education*, 40(5), 806–20.

Oshagbemi, T. (1996). Job satisfaction of UK academics. *Educational Management and Administration*, 24(4), 389–400.

Oxford English Dictionary (OED) (2007). Third Edition – fully updated (OED Online version March 2016).

Özkanli, Ö., & White, K. (2008). Leadership and strategic choices: Female professors in Australia and Turkey. *Journal of Higher Education Policy and Management*, 30(1), 53–63.

Parker, M., & Welch, E. W. (2013). Professional networks, science ability, and gender determinants of three types of leadership in academic science and engineering. *The Leadership Quarterly*, 24(2), 332–48.

Pelletier, K. L. (2010). Leader toxicity: An empirical investigation of toxic behaviour and rhetoric. *Leadership, 6*(4), 373–89.

Perkin, H. (1969). *Key profession: The history of the association of university teachers.* London: Routledge & Kegan Paul.

Podolny, J. M., Khurana, R., & Hill-Popper, M. (2004). *Revisiting the meaning of leadership* [electronic version]. Retrieved 1 June 2016 from Cornell University, ILR school site. Retrieved from http://digitalcommons.ilr.cornell.edu/articles/918

Pyke, J. (2013). Women, choice and promotion or why women are still a minority in the professoriate. *Journal of Higher Education Policy and Management, 35*(4), 444–54.

Raelin, J. A. (2016). Imagine there are no leaders: Reframing leadership as collaborative agency. *Leadership, 12*(2), 131–58.

Ramsden, P. (1998). Managing the effective university. *Higher Education Research and Development, 17*(3), 347–70.

Rashdall, H. (1895). *The universities of Europe in the middle ages* (Vol. II, Part II). Oxford: Clarendon Press.

Rayner, S., Fuller, M., McEwen, L., & Roberts, H. (2010). Managing leadership in the UK university: A case for researching the missing professoriate? *Studies in Higher Education, 35*(6), 617–31.

Redefer, F. L. (1959). Factors that affect teacher morale. *The Nation's Schools, 63*(2), 59–62.

Reisz, M. (2017). Overpaid and overbearing: UK university staff on management, *Times Higher Education*, 30 March. Retrieved from https://www.timeshighereducation. com/news/overpaid-and-overbearing-uk-university-staff-management

Richardson, H. (2017). University heads asked to justify pay over £150,000. *BBC News Online*, 7 September. Retrieved from: http://www.bbc.co.uk/news/education-41176337

Rode, J. C. (2004). Job satisfaction and life satisfaction revisited: A longitudinal test of an integrated model. *Human Relations, 57*(9), 1205–30.

Rolfe, G. (2007). Nursing scholarship and the asymmetrical professor. *Nurse Education in Practice, 7*(3), 123–7.

Sabatier, M., Musselin, C., & Pigeyre, F. (2015). Devenir professeur des universités: Une comparaison sur trois disciplines (1976–2007). *Revue économique, 66*, 37–63.

Schaffer, R. H. (1953). Job satisfaction as related to need satisfaction in work. *Psychological Monographs: General and Applied, 67*(14), 1–29.

Schilling, J. (2009). From ineffectiveness to destruction: A qualitative study on the meaning of negative leadership. *Leadership, 5*(1), 102–28.

Schostak, J. (2016). Leaders, leadership and democracy – are they compatible? *Management in Education, 30*(1), 4–9.

Scott, G., Coates, H., & Anderson, M. (2008). *Learning leaders in times of change: Academic leadership capabilities for Australian higher education.* Sydney: Australian Learning and Teaching Council.

Scott, P. (2009). Markets and new modes of knowledge production. In J. Enders & E. de Weert (Eds.) *The changing face of academic life: Analytical and comparative perspectives* (pp. 58–77). Basingstoke: Palgrave Macmillan.

Scott, P. (2017). The end of tuition fees is on the horizon – universities must get ready, *The Guardian*, 4 July. Retrieved 4 July 2017 from https://www.theguardian.com/education/2017/jul/04/end-tuition-fees-universities-get-ready

Scott, P., & Callender, C. (2017). United Kingdom: From binary to confusion. In P. G. Altbach, L. Reisberg, & H. de Wit (Eds.) *Responding to massification: Differentiation in postsecondary education worldwide* (pp. 121–30). Hamburg: Hamburg Transnational University Leaders Council and the Körber Foundation.

Scribner, J. P., Sawyer, R. K., Watson, S. T., & Myers, V. L. (2007). Teacher teams and distributed leadership: A study of group discourse and collaboration. *Educational Administration Quarterly*, 43(1), 67–100.

Sergiovanni, T. J. (1968). New evidence on teacher morale: A proposal for staff differentiation. *North Central Association Quarterly*, 42, 259–66.

Shamir, B. (2009). From passive recipients to active co-producers: Followers' roles in the leadership process. In B. Shamir, R. Pillai, M. C. Bligh, & M. Uhl-Bien (Eds.) *Follower-centered perspectives on leadership: A tribute to the memory of James R. Meindl* (pp. ix–xxxix). Greenwich, CT: Information Age Publishers.

Shondrick, S. J., Dinh, J. E., & Lord, R. G. (2010). Developments in implicit leadership theory and cognitive science: Applications to improving measurement and understanding alternatives to hierarchical leadership. *The Leadership Quarterly*, 21(6), 959–78.

Showunmi, V., Atewologun, D., & Bebbington, D. (2016). Ethnic, gender and class intersections in British women's leadership experiences. *Educational Management, Administration and Leadership*, 44(6), 917–35.

Sidek, S., Dora, M. T., Kudus, N., Abu Hassan, M., Arif, S., Mohamed, S., Bidin, N. A., & Idris, M. F. M. (2015). Achieving excellence in academic work practices: The experience of Malaysian distinguished professors. *Asian Social Science*, 11(17), 83–9.

Skorobohacz, C., Billot, J., Murray, S., & Khong, L. (2016). Metaphors as expressions of followers' experiences with academic leadership. *Higher Education Research & Development*, 35(5), 1053–67.

Smith, K. R. (1976). Morale: A refinement of Stogdill's model. *Journal of Education Administration*, 14(1), 87–93.

Spiller, D. (2010). Language and academic leadership: Exploring and evaluating the narratives. *Higher Education Research and Development*, 29(6), 679–92.

Starkey, D. (2003). *Six wives: The queens of Henry VIII*. London: Chatto & Windus.

Sternberg, R. (1999). The theory of successful intelligence. *Review of General Psychology*, 3(4), 292–316.

Sternberg, R. (2008). Applying psychological theories to educational practice. *American Educational Research Journal*, 45(1), 150–65.

Stets, J. E., & Burke, P. J. (2000). Identity theory and social identity. *Social Psychology Quarterly, 63*(3), 224–37.

Sullivan, T. A. (2014). Greedy institutions, overwork and work-life balance. *Sociological Inquiry, 84*(1), 1–15.

Sutherland, K. A. (2017). Constructions of success in academia: An early career perspective. *Studies in Higher Education, 42*(4), 743–59.

Sutton, R. I., & Staw, B. M. (1995). What theory is not. *Administrative Science Quarterly, 40*(3), 371–84.

Taylor, L. (2012). To a professor: Are you a professor? *Times Higher Education*, 2 August.

Taylor, P. G. (1999). *Making sense of academic life.* Buckingham: Open University Press.

Teddlie, C. (2005). Methodological issues related to causal studies of leadership. *Educational Management, Administration & Leadership, 33*(2), 211–27.

Teichler, U., Arimoto, A., & Cummings, W. K. (2013). *The changing academic profession: Major findings of a comparative survey.* Dordrecht: Springer.

Thompson, D. R., & Watson, R. (2006). Editorial: Professors of nursing: What do they profess? *Nurse Education in Practice, 6*(3), 123–6.

Tight, M. (Ed.) (2000). *Academic work and life: What it is to be an academic, and how this is changing.* Amsterdam: Springer.

Tight, M. (2002). What does it mean to be a professor? *Higher Education Review, 34*(2), 15–32.

Tight, M. (2008). Higher education research as tribe, territory and/or community: A co-citation analysis. *Higher Education, 55,* 593–605.

Tight, M. (2010). The golden age of academe: Myth or memory? *British Journal of Educational Studies, 58*(1), 105–16.

Tourish, D. (2015). Some announcements, reaffirming the critical ethos of leadership, and what we look for in submissions. Editorial. *Leadership, 11*(2), 135–41.

Trowler, P. R. (1998). *Academics responding to change: New higher education frameworks and academic cultures.* Buckingham: Open University Press.

Tysome, T. (2007a). Number of chairs up 63% in decade, *Times Higher Education*, 27 April. Retrieved from http://www.timeshighereducation.co.uk/208694.article

Tysome, T. (2007b). Competition swells ranks of professors, *The Times Higher Education*, 27 April. Retrieved from http://www.timeshighereducation.co.uk/208719.article

Uhl-Bien, M. (2006). Relational leadership theory: Exploring the social processes of leadership and organizing. *Leadership Quarterly, 17*(6), 654–76.

Uhl-Bien, M. (2009). Series Editor's note. In R. Pillai, M. C. Bligh, & M. Uhl-Bien (Eds.) *Follower-centered perspectives on leadership: A tribute to the memory of James R. Meindl* (pp. vii–viii). Greenwich, CT: Information Age Publishing.

Uhl-Bien, M., Riggio, R. E., Lowe, K. B., & Carsten, M. K. (2014). Followership theory: A review and research agenda. *The Leadership Quarterly, 25*(1), 83–104.

UK government (2013). Cabinet Office news item. Retrieved 19 April 2016 from
   https://www.gov.uk/government/news/the-queen-awards-prestigious-regius-
   professorships-to-twelve-universities

UK government (2015a). Regius Professorships: Entry guidelines. Retrieved 19 April
   2016 from https://www.gov.uk/government/uploads/system/uploads/attachment_
   data/file/473008/Regius_professorships_Entry_guidelines.pdf

UK government (2015b). Regius professorships: Questions and answers. Retrieved
   23 April 2016 from https://www.gov.uk/government/uploads/system/uploads/
   attachment_data/file/473009/Regius_professorships_QA_.pdf

Universities UK Efficiency and Modernisation Task Group (2015). *Efficiency,
   effectiveness and value for money* (the Diamond Report), London, Universities UK.
   Retrieved 20 April 2017 from http://www.universitiesuk.ac.uk/policy-and-analysis/
   reports/Documents/2015/efficiency-effectiveness-value-for-money.pdf

van Knippenberg, D., van Knippenberg, B., & Giessner, S. R. (2007). Extending the
   follower-centered perspective: Leadership as an outcome of shared social identity.
   In B. Shamir, R. Pillai, M. C., Bligh, & M. Uhl-Bien (Eds.) *Follower-centered
   perspectives on leadership: A tribute to the memory of James R. Meindl* (pp. 51–70).
   Greenwich, CT: Information Age Publishers.

Veenhoven, R. (1991). Questions on happiness: Classic topics, modern answers, blind
   spots. In F. Strach, M. Argyle, & N. Schwarz (Eds.) *Subjective well being* (pp. 7–26).
   Oxford: Pergamon.

Verger, J. (1992). Teachers. In H. De Ridder-Symoens (Ed.) *A history of the university in
   Europe*, I (pp. 144–68). Cambridge: Cambridge University Press.

Vroom, V. H. (1964). *Work and motivation*. New York: John Wiley and Sons.

Ward, M. E. (2001). Gender and promotion in the academic profession. *Scottish Journal
   of Political Economy, 48*(3), 283–302.

Watson, S. T., & Scribner, J. P. (2005). Emergent reciprocal influence: Toward a
   framework for understanding the distribution of leadership within collaborative
   school activity. In *Conference proceedings for the 2005 Convention of the University
   Council for Educational Administration: 'Democracy in Educational Justice: The
   Unfinished Journey Toward Justice'*. Retrieved 19 September 2016 from http://
   static1.1.sqspcdn.com/static/f/275549/9729846/1291751461597/WatsonUCEA2005.
   pdf?token=m56x0jisXbsUqHltdyh8I4meQTs%3D

Weir, A. (2001). *Henry VIII: King and court*. London: Pimlico.

Weiss, H. M. (2002). Deconstructing job satisfaction: Separating evaluations, beliefs and
   affective experiences. *Human Resource Management Review, 12*(2), 173–94.

White, K. (2001). Women in the professoriate in Australia. *International Journal of
   Organisational Behaviour, 3*(2), 64–76.

White, L., Currie, G., & Lockett, A. (2016). Pluralized leadership in complex
   organizations: Exploring the cross network effects between formal and informal
   leadership relations. *The Leadership Quarterly, 27*(2), 280–97.

Williams, G. (1986). *Improving school morale.* Sheffield: Sheffield City Polytechnic, PAVIC Publications.

Winter, R. P. (2017). *Managing academics: A question of perspective.* Cheltenham: Edward Elgar.

Wisker, G. (1996). *Empowering women in higher education.* London: Kogan Page.

Wood, M. (2005). The fallacy of misplaced leadership. *Journal of Management Studies, 42*(6), 1101–21.

Ylijoki, O-H., & Ursin, J. (2015). High-flyers and underdogs: The polarisation of Finnish academic identities. In L. Evans & J. Nixon (Eds.) *Academic identities in higher education: The changing European landscape* (pp. 187–202). London: Bloomsbury.

Youngs, H. (2009). (Un)Critical times? Situating distributed leadership in the field. *Journal of Educational Administration and History, 41*(4), 377–89.

Youngs, H. (2017). A critical exploration of collaborative and distributed leadership in higher education: Developing an alternative ontology through leadership-as-practice. *Journal of Higher Education Policy and Management, 39*(2), 140–54.

Appendix: UK Academic Grade Hierarchy

Main academic grades in the UK, shown alongside the North American equivalents:

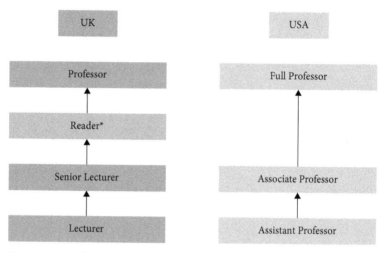

*Some universities do not use the reader grade.

This diagram represents the *core* academic grading system, excluding research fellows, used in most UK universities. Some UK universities have adopted North American nomenclature, but in such contexts the title 'professor' remains reserved, for the most part, to denoting only the most senior grade; associate and assistant professors tend not to be referred to or addressed as professors.

Academic grading systems used in the UK's post-1992 university sector may include additional grades, such as principal lecturer.

Index